The Comedy of Dave

The Comedy
of Dave Chappelle
Critical Essays

Edited by
K.A. WISNIEWSKI

McFarland & Company, Inc., Publishers
Jefferson, North Carolina, and London

LIBRARY OF CONGRESS CATALOGUING-IN-PUBLICATION DATA

The comedy of Dave Chappelle : critical essays /
edited by K.A. Wisniewski.
    p.   cm.
Includes bibliographical references and index.

ISBN 978-0-7864-4188-4
softcover : 50# alkaline paper

1. Chappelle, Dave — Criticism and interpretation.
2. Chappelle show (Television program) 3. Comedy —
Social aspects — United States. 4. Comedy — Political
aspects — United States. I. Wisniewski, K. A., 1981–
PN2287.C517C66 2009
792.702'8092 — dc22   2009016878

British Library cataloguing data are available

On the cover: Dave Chappelle in a publicity shot for the second
season of *Chappelle's Show*, 2004 (Comedy Central/Photofest)

Manufactured in the United States of America

McFarland & Company, Inc., Publishers
Box 611, Jefferson, North Carolina 28640
www.mcfarlandpub.com

Ambiguity ... is a fundamental attribute of power.
— Georges Baladier

There can never be enough said of the virtues,
dangers, the power of a shared laugh.
— Françoise Sagan

Acknowledgments

So many introductions thank friends and family for providing the necessary distractions while completing a manuscript, but this book was, in fact, the distraction. This project began while I was already juggling two full-time jobs: professor at Cecil College and graduate student at the University of Pennsylvania. Although it seemed ridiculous to attempt anything else, a project on comedy and mass media kept calling out to me. I urged friends and colleagues, "Someone should do this." Somehow classroom viewings and discussions turned into an essay co-written with colleague Andrea Cumbo. In the following months, my follow-up, a much more critical essay, lost focus; it kept expanding, evolving into something else. At one point, feeling overwhelmed and looking for advice, friend and teacher, Arthur J. Magida wrote me that sometimes the work is what keeps us from the breakdown. This was such a project.

This collection presented here is truly the product of a team effort. The contributors here are a diverse group of emerging scholars, like Chappelle, willing to take chances and push forward into new, sometimes difficult, terrain. We learned much from each other from the long series of correspondences and conversations, and I wish to thank them for their hard work, collective efficiency, and overall good humor. While the proposal was being passed around, Bambi Haggins published *Laughing Mad: The Black Comic Persona in Post-Soul America*. Her chapter on Dave Chappelle improved the overall scope and delivery of this collection.

In addition, I appreciate Cecil College and especially the English department for the teaching opportunity, for their friendship, and for allowing me to quietly slip in and out of the occasional meeting, and I thank my students for their honest observations of various clips.

Additional thanks go to my friends from Lancaster University who are still key advocates, to Kathleen Brown for her long time backing, to Eric Thanner for the late-night conversations and for time and time again proving himself a true friend, and, lastly, to all the new friends gained the past year for helping steady the ship. I owe special thanks to Andrea Cumbo for loyal friendship and enduring support. She has given the best pep talks, shared the longest laughs, and wiped the occasional tear. The book might not have been started without her faith and encouragement.

Lastly, my family has supported my career decisions in too many ways to list, and I appreciate everyone's support and understanding. Derek Boyd and Stacey Wisniewski Boyd listened to me talk about this project much longer than was really necessary. I thank them for listening and for getting me out of the office, and, especially to Stacey, for reminding me there was more to life than school. This project would have been impossible without the help of my parents. This certainly isn't the book they intended to read, but I am sure part of my interest in the topic is from my mother's fondness of Motown and *Soul Train* and my father's companionship during Richard Pryor and Gene Wilder movie nights as a child and his own interest in the Wayans Brothers' *In Living Color*. For your encouragement, love, and generosity, I am truly grateful.

Table of Contents

Introduction

K.A. WISNIEWSKI

It is rare that only two years after the original airing of its final episode, a television series may already be named a milestone to our culture. But *Chappelle's Show* is just that. In its two complete seasons, the sketch comedy has given its viewers more than a few short-lived laughs, though catch phrases such as "I'm Rick James, bitch" and "I smoke rocks" and sketches like the "Black White Supremacist" and "The Racial Draft" are hardly out of the public's memory. One of the best-selling TV series DVD sets of all time, the show has provided us with some framework regarding who we are, what we have achieved, and what issues are still challenging us and not only reflects its own time's mores but also serves as a rung on which future generations may climb.[1] This is only part of the legacy comedian Dave Chappelle offers us. Chappelle's canon of work, stretching beyond television and into film, stand-up, and even music, is truly an archetypal model for postmodern America, both in its successes and in its struggles. His comedy lives in the ecstasy of communication, for good and for bad, and Chappelle is quick to celebrate the hyperreality in which we live, to expose its tensions and absurdities, and to question and reject its meanings.[2] Although the show ended on such a controversial and anti-climactic note, today Chappelle is stronger than ever as demonstrated most recently in his early December 2007 record-setting stand-up performance at Hollywood's Laugh Factory, which lasted over six hours.

Like his comedy, Chappelle has enthusiasm, endurance. So it was quite a shock to this fans when in April 2005 rumors circulated throughout the media that not only had the comedian abandoned the set of the show during the taping of the third season but that he had also apparently left for Africa. Why would such a budding young star with a successful show walk out on a $50 million deal? The public could not understand, and gossip quickly turned into new reports that claimed drug abuse and mental instability as possible answers. It was a media circus that only Chappelle himself could quell, and, in February 2006, Chappelle gave a series of interviews from *Time* to *Oprah* that provided some answers to the public's bewilderment. Perhaps his most famous and compelling interview was with James Lipton in the program *Inside the Actors Studio*. (His offer to pay for the trip's expenses himself and his bright disposition throughout the taping despite a several hour flight delay — let alone the audience's eagerness to wait over five hours to hear him talk — are proof of the man's character and staying power.)

In the broadcast, Chappelle confessed that "the *fame* thing and being called crazy and drug addict and all of these things scared me ... being treated that way like I'm not a person anymore. To say this shit in front of my children.... The higher up I go, the less happy I am."[3] The honesty here is potent jab at our celebrity-driven culture and parallels the truths often masked throughout his comedy. The trip to Africa, he later explained, offered a chance to relieve the pressure imposed by the network, by the industry at large, by his fans, and by himself to maintain his own sense of morals and to be able to question his audience's responses to jokes. As Manohla Dargis suggested in one review, the comedian's interview revealed a "heart-melting glimpse into both the pressures of his fish bowl existence and what it can mean for a black man when he makes white people laugh."[4] Despite this fear and intimidation of a return to work, Chappelle cites his fans as an inspiring force. Recalling the audience's cheers at his first club appearance since his departure from his show, Cincinnati, Chappelle admitted getting "teary eyed just thinking about it. 'Cause this industry can say whatever they want but, man, people will hold you up, and — that crowd — man, my spirits were so low but they were holdin' me up. And I hadn't told jokes but that shit was just comin' back like *Karate Kid* again."[5] The interview also serves as a strong portrait of the mind and inter-workings of an artist. As silly and improvisational as the surface level of his work appears, Chappelle demonstrated a genuine sensibility and clear conviction concerning his creative process and the messages his work transmits.

Moreover, Chappelle revealed the deep-rooted interconnectedness between today's artist and the industry, which is reminiscent of Adorno's concept of "culture industry" and the systematic exploitation of the gulf between human beings and their culture. This opens up a broader discussion on the topic what constitutes entertainment in our culture and further questions how the audience reads, or at least is meant to read, a narrative. Chappelle's work paradoxically sits within both art and entertainment; it belongs to a culture of the after-image that is comprised of a wit and energy separate from high culture. It practices pastiche and parody and offers, if not a revaluation of mass culture, certainly an honest observation from within it. From the debut episode of *Chappelle's Show*, for example, the audience immediately realizes they are in store for something new.

From the dawn of television, networks maintained strict control over programming content. Sitcoms and live variety shows generally preserved a wholesome and family-friendly set of values. Producers believed in the philosophy that the less offensive the material was, the greater the potential audience. This marketing strategy was one directly borrowed from radio. But unlike network radio, television almost immediately included African American entertainers. According to J. Fred MacDonald, one of the pioneers of television (and one of the "most influential employers of black talent") during this early period was Ed Sullivan, who frequently invited black entertainers and celebrities onto his show. Sullivan's belief was that broadcasting these stars and introducing them to the American public would "undermine racism ... white adults and children seeing and appreciating black talent, would be forced to reassess racist stereotyping and their own prejudices."[6] Still, as MacDonald's study shows, blacks were often depicted in not only stereotypical and secondary roles in the upcoming decades but were also often depicted in a way that could be viewed as other or separate from both white performers and audiences.[7]

Perhaps more difficult to break were the standard formulas of primetime shows. But the 1990s saw such a change develop in *Seinfeld*, the self-proclaimed show about nothing. Using Jerry — a hard-to-place, quasi-fictional character himself — and his stand-up as the backdrop to its absurdist narratives, the series portrayed neurotic, cynical, and overall dim-witted characters that somehow won the attention, and hearts, of mass audiences. It is largely the use of Seinfeld's poignant social observations that fuel the show's witty repartee and edgy pokes at social institutions like work, the family and religion, and questions values systems surrounding human relationships in general. The show, in general, is a study of public culture. The pilot of the series, entitled "The Seinfeld Chronicles," includes an interesting scene in which Jerry and George attempt to define and analyze the array of potential greetings Jerry could receive from a lady friend at the airport. This sets the tone for future episodes that continually push the envelope with such previously taboo topics as masturbation and political incorrectness.

Seinfeld's humor is based on playing with definitions and social constructs and, in part, (re)constructing new stereotypes. The series is famous for introducing these catch phrases and labels into the popular vernacular: having "hand"; shrinkage; the high/low/close-talkers; the hipster doofus; and the stocky, slow-witted, bald man. The show specifically addresses the confines and stereotypes surrounding race and ethnicity with characters like Donna Chang, a Jewish woman who seemingly adopts every clichéd characteristic belonging to an Asian American cast from quoting Confucius to practicing acupuncture, and with scenes ridiculously avoiding the question as to whether or not Elaine's new boyfriend in "The Wizard" was black or George's desire to convince his boss that he *does* have a black friend (which he doesn't). But the most potent episode on race is "The Cigar Store Indian," in which Jerry's purchase of and powwow with a "kitschy" life-sized wooden Indian offends this episode's romantic interest, Winona, a woman of Native American descent. Several scenes' portrayal of an insensitive Jerry spurs the lead character to cautiously overthink every word around her. The hyperbolic scenes that follow eventually lead Jerry to his melting point and perhaps to the claim of the episode: "Aren't we all getting a little too sensitive?"

While *Seinfeld* was rising in popularity, Chappelle, too, was climbing in status, gaining a strong reputation with audiences in his supportive roles on the big screen. While none of these roles were necessarily astounding performances, they did, as Bambi Haggins points out, "establish him as a young black comic with *possible* crossover appeal ... [and his] ability to 'work the material.'"[8] From his 1994 role as Ahchoo in the Mel Brooks' comedy *Robin Hood: Men in Tights* to his character as Tom Hanks' friend and employee in the romantic comedy *You've Got Mail*, Chappelle has shown his versatility and growth as an actor and comic; each of these roles exposes glimpses of the voice and personality that later made Chappelle famous. Ahchoo's Malcolm X–inspired monologue to the Sherwood Forest recruits, for example, easily belongs beside Chappelle's later impersonations of Nelson Mandella and Samuel L. Jackson. Similarly, Tulley, the ex-partner of a diamond heist con man played by Martin Lawrence, shows a certain naïveté or vulnerability that is fully gelled in both his stand-up and in *Chappelle's Show* sketches like the "Wayne Brady Show." But Chappelle also gracefully played the exaggerated archetypal roles as a "two-bit Negro crackhead" in *Con Air* and the ridiculously over-the-top and cruel comic Reggie Warrington in Eddie Murphy's remake of *The Nutty Professor*. Haggins refers to his period of Chappelle's career as being mostly comprised of "buddy" roles and notes that the most prominent feature of all of these roles is Chappelle's crafted delivery that simultaneously plays and parodies the assigned stereotype.[9]

This play with social structure and stereotype reaches a simmer for Chappelle in the 1998 "buddy" film *Half Baked*, which he co-wrote with co-creator of *Chappelle's Show* Neal Brennan. The film loosely revolves around a plot that forces three friends to sell marijuana stolen from a medical laboratory in order to bail their friend out of jail. The story parallels *Seinfeld* in its use of satirical critique of semiotics in the everyday, thus exposing the inconsistency of such identities within subculture. Like *Seinfeld*, labels and archetypes are clearly defined by the Chappelle's character Thurgood. The cheeba smoking world alone consists of personalities such as the enhancement smoker, the scavenger smoker, the historian smoker, the MacGyver smoker, the afterschool fathers and sons smokers, and the nursing home granny smokers. Here, race, class, age are all irrelevant, interconnected by the thread of drug culture. Concurrently, however, difference also is maintained: the "scientist" is portrayed as an older white man, while Thurgood — a young African American — holds employment as "the janitor." This paradox is the very thing that would make Chappelle's series so edgy five years later.

The film's humor transcends fun with these stereotypes and creates games from sexual innuendoes and puns, pop culture references and subversions, and even deep-seated historical allusions. While the crude insinuations of sex — I am thinking specifically of the "pearl necklace" sequence — and the outrageous naming of the female lead Mary Jane Potman are clear to the audience, subtle references like Thurgood's mention of this grandfather's participation in the "Tuskegee experiments" are easily missed. But the film's own spin on popular culture staples is unmistakable in parodies of films like *Jerry Maguire* and *The Shawshank Redemption* and with appearances by Willie Nelson, Snoop Dogg, and Janeane Garofalo. Even *Full House*'s squeaky clean dad Bob Saget breaks his pop culture image by harassing Thurgood for attending a counseling session without having ever performed oral sex on a man for coke.

While the film is not the cinematic achievement it might have been, Chappelle suggests, had the original, "more adult" script been used, it certainly fares better than the banal comedy seen in *Dude, Where's My Car?* and maintains a much larger audience than Ice Cube and Chris Tucker's 1995 film *Friday*. Recreating the 1970s Cheech and Chong films, *Half Baked* appeals to a new emerging culture that is not bound by typologies of class or race. The buddy portraits established in the film reveal a contradictory or changing morphology of youth cultures comprising of a "series of temporal gatherings characterized by fluid boundaries and floating memberships."[10] This is best seen in the cultural awareness of the socially-deemed "slacker" quartet. And this is where the brilliance of *Chappelle's Show* emerges. The double-consciousness, here, orbits beyond that of African American identity or even American identity; using the diversity and mobility of the Generation X and Y cultures, Chappelle examines both new and old tensions and finds humor in the momentary coalescence of the subcultures within these larger paradigms. His humor, like the culture he observes, exists in a liminal space where nothing is constant, operating within ruling class frameworks and yet distinct from it. He is the voice for an emerging culture.[11]

With the arrival of the new millennium, many scholars and critics have postulated a new class in America. Most often dubbed Generation Y or the Millennium Generation, most critics envision this contemporary, or "postmodern," culture as a polyethnic society — of polyethnic cultures — shifting away from industrial production and towards consumerism. Moreover, this new group is riding the wake of high technology, in which information technology, the service industry, and the mass media (especially marketing and advertising) triumph through consumption and the pre-eminence of commodity imagery above all else. It seems as if Baudrillard's fears have become a reality. But, of course, opinions about the character of this group raised within this hyper-reality vary. Whereas Paulina Borsook's take is obvious from the title her book *Cyberselfish: A Critical Romp Though the Terribly Libertarian Culture of High Tech*, David Brooks' work *Bobos in Paradise: The New Upper Class and How They Got There* argues that the 1990s integration of a host of values traditionally in opposition allowed a new class, comprised of education instead of privilege, to surface.[12] While both sides may be argued, it is clear that postmodernism has shaped or even created this new class in America.

While many critics are concerned that simulacra of television and mass-market films are replacing social and political engagement of youths, placating this new generation and diverting them from issues more critical than the winner of *American Idol* or the gripping conclusion of MTV's *Real World*, such work should also be interpreted as a politicizing force with potential to create dialogue and propel activism and commitment. The lack of linearity and teleology in the MTV/Reality Show generation makes sense for Gary Newman, co-president of 20th Century Television, who asserts that "for a lot of young people, the sitcom format feels retro and tired."[13] And, on January 22, 2003, *Chappelle's Show* debuted on Comedy Central and delivered something new to American television, a hybrid of live comedy and recorded sketches that both celebrated and crucified the kitsch that was dominating the ratings. As Chappelle demonstrates, this kitsch, this popular culture, acts as more than a mirror through which marginalized groups become aware of social hierarchies and dynamics, but it is also, as Foucault asserts, an exercise of and struggle for power.

For Chappelle, one the most mimicked and criticized elements of our society is consumerism. Through film, radio, television, telephones, music, computers, video games, and the Internet, images of commodities are flooding our lives, circulating and recirculating in a variety of forms. While such advertising can both entertain and annoy their viewers, Chappelle is aware that his audience comprises of an image-conscious, complex reading people who are aware of what's popular and what's being aired and the range of attached meanings. The opening sketch of the first episode of *Chappelle's Show* sets the tone for the comedian's assessment of the absurdity of advertisements. Parodying a commercial promoting a Mitsubishi Eclipse, Chappelle appears driving a white woman dancing absurdly to a techno beat in the seat beside him only to replace her with a woman who *can* dance — not coincidentally a black woman who naturally flows to the hip hop now beating from the sound system. Besides laughing at the "coolness" of the original and its trendy, white middle-class audience, it may also be read in terms of its objectification of women in advertising.[14] Similarly, in the debut episode of Season Two, Chappelle introduces Samuel L. Jackson beer, parodying not only the New England lager Samuel Adams but also embellishing the loud cinematic image of the aforementioned actor. What is even more interesting in discussions of the postmodern is Chappelle's recruitment of celebrities like Redman and Wu Tang Clan to endorse other fictional products ranging from toiletries to banking investment counseling. And the interesting turns into the eerie when Chappelle's impersonations of the real are, in fact, tête-a-tête with the real in cases like Rick James, whose interview is cut to juxtapose the re-enacted story, and Lil' Jon, who mirrors and interacts in real time beside Chappelle's Jon. For Marx, the citation and imitation of such "commodity language" can be read as a form of resistance.[15] The act of miming its character transforms the commodity into a sign that deconstructs its social reading as a product. Therefore, distance is created between the audience and the structure in which the commodity was originally defined, thus allowing the audience to envision the system itself.

A large part of this commodity culture is the Internet. It is not enough to say the Internet has changed habits of learning, shopping, communicating; it is postmodernism realized. And Chappelle fully embraces the digital culture in which he lives. His sketch transforming the hyper-real or virtual world of cyberspace into a physical space is a good example of how Chappelle uses the converse of a sign to highlight the misperceptions surrounding the concept. Typical for his humor, he plays on the duality of the Internet: it can be a place of freedom, amusement, and community, but it can also lead to restrictions, dangers, and isolation. For Chappelle, the Internet, here, represents more than opportunities for exchange (and corruption) of goods and ideas. The "disgusting and intolerable" mall-like world he explores exposes a host of activities, from the immoral to the just plan irritating, that includes a series of sexual links leading to the latest Paris Hilton sex tape and a video of bestiality, which Dave just can't ignore; an array of spam and pop-up adds advertisements that in one scene becomes superimposed over previous copies of itself; and two sites for downloading music, a quiet kiosk where one man patiently stands waiting to pay the posted 99¢ per song and a shop adjacent to the kiosk offering free downloads that appears as if it were being looted with masses of people frantically running with cases of music. (The scenes are a good reminder of the "state of fascination and vertigo" that Baudrillard mentions.) But the sketch insinuates more than the potential dirtiness of the virtual community; it reveals the irregularity of identities living in a place-less time of simulation and artifice, where subcultural identity may be pur-chased over the counter and, in fact, what appears may be a far cry from reality. This is revealed when a seemingly beautiful woman is transformed into a sleazy, penis-enlarging salesman during Dave's visit to a chat room.

One of the most compelling elements of Chappelle's comedy is the way he consistently uses such shared experiences to challenge the rigidity of social reality and the binary epistemology that is typically employed in television narratives. And nothing is left sacred in the series. Chappelle critiques the popular dramas like *Law & Order*, hidden camera shows (represented by his sketch Zapped!), and reality shows like *Trading Spouses* just as quickly as he jeers such staples as the classic miniseries *Roots*, the image of Nat King Cole, and the depiction of history in the media as seen in his sketches on the History Channel and the Atlantic slave trade. By holding and exaggerating these binaries, the comedies reveal the malleability of such constructs. Moreover, it reveals the blurring of high and mass cultures. The last decade has witnessed a new phenomenon in scholarship on globalization and polyethnicity. Chap-pelle embraces this ethnically diverse and culturally aware group. For Gen-erations X and Y, MTV and celebrity culture are as necessary or relevant as and often overlap with highbrow art and world politics. In fact, Chappelle's focus on "cool places" like bars, nightclubs, and the Internet match the grow-ing trend in cultural studies that has shifted away from research on educa-tion and labor (production), which are also reviewed by Chappelle, and towards popular culture topics on music and films (consumption).[16] Read-ing Chappelle, it becomes clear that dialogue on these matters need to opened even further.

If high-tech, hyper-real post-industrialization is the context within which these emerging generations are situated, polyethnicity and diaspora is the blanket that covers and unites them. In his book *The American Kaleido-scope: Race, Ethnicity, and the Civic Culture*, Lawrence H. Fuchs creates the metaphor of an "American kaleidoscope" to underscore the interaction between a diverse group of constituents varying in ethnicity and class. He explains, "When a kaleidoscope is in motion, the parts give the appearance of rapid change and extensive variety in color and shape and in their inter-relationships."[17] Interestingly, Chappelle employs a similar image in his first season of *Chappelle's Show* when between sketches he reminds us, the televi-sion viewer, that the audience is more than just "a bunch of black people." Like America, he reminds us, it is comprised of a "multi-ethnic, multi-cul-tural patchwork." He then directly addresses the white audience watching at home: "I want to promote conversation and dialogue." An anecdote then leads to "Ask a Black Dude," a skit reminiscent of Jay Leno's "Jay Walking" outings, in which people of the street are allowed to ask comedian Paul Mooney a question centered on stereotypically black behavior. And it is for these racially charged sketches that Chappelle has received the most attention. One of the final sketches in the debut episode — and perhaps the most controversy during the time of its airing — is a sketch about black, white supremacist Clayton Bigsby. Haggins thoroughly summarizes the sketch in her own reading of Chappelle and stresses the question that the sketch raises, "Who *is* the Other, anyway?"[18] Here, the *N-word* is fully realized as both an empowering and marginalizing agent. It is still attached to the history of racial hierarchy and the black degradation, but it also maintains its contemporary social hip-hop context so that being reprimanded and addressed as niggers propels the suburban white people to cheer and congratulate themselves with high fives.[19] For Leon E. Wynter, this is an example of the end of "white" America as mainstream culture. He asserts,

> As far as Gen-Y knows, hip-hop is not just black culture; it's the most distinctive characteristic of their generation. Boomers can act out their American dreams in color today because, starting in the 1980s, commercial popular culture began catching up to America's transracial collective unconscious. But Gen-Y's multicolored vision is its collective consciousness as well as the national id. Even if he is white, lives in an all-white community, and identifies with mostly white celebrities, the Gen-Y consumer is acutely aware of the fact that his preferences, his very whiteness, are not preeminently American, and in some contexts are not even average.[20]

Despite its white attraction and mass popularity, other critics, like Greg Tate in his *Everything But the Burden*, see this as the appropriation of black culture where whites often take the entertainment without the attached responsibility while African Americans still remain seriously disadvantaged socio-economically, thus perpetuating degrading stereotypes and racist myths.

This is the American paradox that Chappelle examines. Who can use the word nigger and in what context? What meaning or energy does the word carry itself? Chappelle's work reminds his audience of Edmund Morgan's pinnacle work *American Slavery, American Freedom*, in which the historian writes, "[T]o a large degree it may be said that Americans bought their independence with slave labor.... The paradox is American, and it behooves Americans to understand it if they would understand themselves."[21] Whether it is in the characters of Clayton Bigsby and the Niggar Family or in sketches like "I Know Black People" and "The Racial Draft," Chappelle demonstrates the powers and problems surrounding stereotypes. As demonstrated in early 2007 when radio shock jock Don Imus referred to the Rutgers women's basketball team as "nappy-headed hos" and when Michael Richards, famous for playing Kramer on *Seinfeld*, shouted "nigger" at two hecklers during a comedy routine, social boundaries need to be set and dialogues need to be opened.[22]

It is in this American paradox that Chappelle's comedy lies: diversity, unity, and the fear of difference. Chappelle's work has the capability to not only reveal and define the racial and ethnic dynamics at work in America but also to maintain, deconstruct, and create a new set of cultural myths. American history is a complex epic chronicling the ebb and flow of democracy and opportunity, oppression and slavery, allocation and exploitation, and unity and segregation. It is never an easy story to tell, but it is the story we need to hear and to examine if we are to understand ourselves and to work towards an improved future. Upon reflecting about the show and his departure from it, Chappelle recently confessed, "I was doing sketches that were funny but socially irresponsible."[23] This further demonstrates how each of us needs to find our own social boundaries and self-identity. Still, Chappelle continues to vehemently attack social taboos in his stand-up act. He admits that while on stage, "I get real happy up there. Maybe that's the only time in my adult life that I feel like myself. You're standing up there, you know what I mean, like a gladiator...."[24]

Yes, Chappelle can make people laugh. But he is also fighter, promoting conversation and dialogue. That, too, is the mission of this collection. If it may be agreed upon that Chappelle's work may be read as the expression of a new, emerging class, the cultural manifestation of late capitalism's Generation Y audience, the chapters that follow formalize themselves around the challenges, successes, and limitations of both Chappelle's work and the postmodern culture itself. They will examine Chappelle's borrowing from different epochs and cultures, his reliance and deconstruction of rigid typologies and "meta-narratives," his critique on traditional values and explorations into social taboos, his claims on representation and authenticity, and his investigations of identity. Like Chappelle's canon, this collection is a truly interdisciplinary effort to use Chappelle to explore and to understand the interrelationships between classes, races, and generations and to examine how various cultural or better yet structural processes impact our lives.

As its polar opposite, laughter — that is, comedy — is deeply rooted to the tragic. On one hand, as Samuel Beckett points out, "Nothing is funnier than suffering"; of course, Eugene Ionesco asserts, "We laugh in order not to cry." So the ideas complement each other, completing a cycle that is much more complex than a simple cause and effect model or push-and-pull dichotomy. There is something cathartic in comedy, in the open expression of laughter. In his work *Jokes and Their Relation to the Unconscious*, Freud positions laughter (and the response to that laughter) at the center of the collective unconscious. For Freud, it is one of the most honest of human emotions. But philosophers including Plato, Hobbes, Descartes, and Kant have for centuries also tried to come up with a clear theory for the essence of comedy and laughter.[25] In his outline of the variety of theories on humor, Christopher P. Wilson notes one spot of consistency among philosophers: incongruity. There is a moment of tension and release, of stress and release. Reviewing Leach's and Fiebleman's theories, he highlights how the theories "contrast the forces of order and intelligence with those of the random and chaotic. For Leach, humour expresses the tension between symbols and the things to which they refer. According to Fiebleman, humour contrasts the world as it is with the world as it ought to be."[26] Moreover, this sentiment is further complicated in the postmodern state where language is a temporal process and meaning will never stay quite the same from one context to the next. Reading the undoing of reason — and the joke is already soaked in ambiguity — becomes more difficult. Jerry Aline Flieger attempts to explain ways in which the comic may be in the postmodern text relying heavily on psychoanalysis. In his efforts to deconstruct ideological assumptions, the author does maintain one conclusion: "the conclusion that the comic is somehow poetic ... [that] they will continue to question social convention by criticizing existing institutions and to expose repressive or automatic habits of thought."[27]

The opening essays of this collection specifically address the consequences of Chappelle's comedy. Richard J. Gray II and Michael Putnam's "Exploring Niggerdom" re-addresses the complex nature of the N-word drawing on Bahktin's thoughts on laughter and Randall Kennedy's extensive studies on the word's history and current connotations. While they hold that the comedian is able to defuse difficult subjects of discussion, Novotny Lawrence in Chapter 2, "Comic Genius or Con Man?," investigates how Chappelle's use of the N-word could also be more problematic than initially considered and, in fact, create conflict. This chapter and the subsequent one by Andrea Cumbo also examine the portrayal of gender and sexuality, specifically in *Chappelle's Show* sketches "It's a Wonderful Chest" and "A Gay World." With discussions of race and gender already on the table, Graham Chia-Hui Preston's essay "Dave Chappelle, the Wu-Tang Clan and Afro-Asian America" presents an analysis of nationality and ethnicity in the show. Observing the roles of actor Yoshio Mita and hip-hop artists Wu-Tang Clan, Preston opens a new conversation with Afro-Asian America.

The following three essays are dedicated to Chappelle at the height of his success. In Chapter 5, "Laughing Whiteness," Brian Gogan critiques the *Lost Episodes*, the third season that was completed without Chappelle, and explicitly focuses on the rhetoric and consequences of "Racial Pixies" sketch.

Meanwhile Julia Round's "Impersonating Hollywood," takes a step back: How significant is celebrity culture—the culture the comedian himself tried to leave behind—to Chappelle's comedy? *Chappelle's Show*, she argues, offers much to the discourse on the "real" versus the "inauthentic" and, thus, reveals one avenue, one system, for constructing identity. Riley Snorton, in Chapter 7's ethnographic look in Chappelle's *Block Party*, builds on this idea of commodification and authenticity and the role of the media in an urban setting. In fact, in some fashion, these motifs carry into the following three essays as well.

As Chapter 7 reads Chappelle as a valuable "native ethnographer," in Chapter 8, Amarnath Amarasingam views Chappelle as one of Gramsci's "organic intellectuals" and attributes Chappelle's departure to the pressures of the industry and the sense that they were pushing him to betray his community. This idea of the sellout is reprised in the following two essays by Katherine Lee and Kimberley A. Yates, respectively. While the former argues that Chappelle is guilty of selling out to the industry, not necessarily intentionally but perhaps because this is the nature of the capitalistic system and finding success within it, the latter author reads the comedian as a member of the Black Arts Movement and, as such, someone who is able to transcend stereotypes. In fact, Chappelle, here, is read not as a part of mainstream culture but rather as one who resists it.

The final essays of this collection concern history, memory, and remembrance. So much of this book is concerned with the uses and abuses of power and authority and the social conflict that plague our society. Many of these conflicts are the result of our nation's turbulent past. Eric Hobsbawm has argued that the invention of new traditions is an essential part of creating continuity with the past. In Chapter 11, Francesca Gamber explores the history of carnivalesque humor and its traditions and how Chappelle uses this tradition to subvert traditional roles and to further push his very political comedy. Chiwen Bao's essay "Haunted" analyzes Chappelle's work for racial paranoia and how performing race commercially has potentially dangerous consequences, serving as a reminder of past and present enslavement. The conclusion develops Gamber's and Bao's claims, specifically examining memory, that is how Chappelle interprets, or reinterprets, history. But the final essay is also a reflection of the entire collection and includes final comments on race and ethnicity, on the celebrity, on authenticity, and on food. Its mission is not to find resolution in any reading of Chappelle's comedy but to ask "So what?" Its target is to analyze the role of comedy in America and how Chappelle not only exposes a cultural obsession with the pollution of ideas, to borrow from Mary Douglas, but also serves as a way to deconstruct (or reaffirm) systems of power.

If the comic is in fact read as a poet, we must remember Keats' proclamation that "[t]he poetry of earth is never dead." At the start of this collection, *Chappelle's Show* has been on for nearly three years. And yet it doesn't feel that long. The show is still being aired not only on Comedy Central but also on a host of other networks as late-night reruns. If the legacy of Pryor was passed to Chappelle, the comic did his job. The torch is now up for grabs. One show strongly supported by Comedy Central the past three seasons after the loss of *Chappelle's Show* is *The Sarah Silverman Show*, which addresses topics similar to its predecessor. Silverman, who received a lot of media attention in 2001 for her "I love chinks" joke, has not backed down from prodding issues deemed sensitive to the public. Like Chappelle, she works towards differentiating a racist joke from a joke about racism and struggles as a comic no longer positioned as an underdog.

Chappelle's Show was groundbreaking for its time. It highlights its creator as a man of his time, trying to understand the tension and conflict that exists within the human experience and those that also shape the American people in general. He is as aware of the past as he is own cultural milieu. His version of sketch comedy offered something new to the American public, ridiculous and funny and yet grounded by the seriousness of the issues it stirs up. Whether or not each of his viewers are seriously considering the meanings and ramifications of his work, the work shows Dave Chappelle himself is thinking about these issues. The essays collected here survey some of these contradictions. They explain how, and attest to the fact that, Dave Chappelle and his comedy offer new social arenas through which our culture may be examined.

1

Exploring Niggerdom
Racial Inversion in Language Taboos

RICHARD J. GRAY II
and MICHAEL PUTNAM

"Sir! I'm going to make this clear. I'm in no way, shape or form involved in any *Niggerdom*." This is the response of the character Clayton Bigbsy to a question posed to him by Kent Wallace, host of *Frontline*, in Dave Chappelle's sketch entitled "Blind Supremacy," taken from the first episode of his successful *Chappelle's Show*. *Niggerdom*, a term appropriated by Chappelle, is loosely defined as "of or related to the actions of African Americans."[1] *Niggerdom*, in principle, draws illusions to words such as "kingdom" and "dukedom," suggesting that this term is part of a larger, more powerful order. In fact, *Niggerdom* encompasses elements that are stereotypical of the black experience that are either frowned upon or despised by the white majority, including hard-core rap, menthol cigarettes, malt liquor drinks like Colt 45, tinted windows and kickin' car stereos, gangstas, ebnonics, or any other aspect of African American life that Whites almost randomly choose to deplore. *Niggerdom* is a realm of its own which also denotes the slaves peoples from which African Americans emerged, a rebellious piece of property that has never found a way to integrate or assimilate to White society.

In *Chappelle's Show*, Dave Chappelle plays upon traditional and stereotypical African American roles and values that continually function within the realm that he calls *Niggerdom*. In this chapter, we explore racial identity and the concept of *Niggerdom* in the language of Dave Chappelle as illustrated in the sketches "Black White Supremacist" (Season One; Episode 1), "The Niggar Family" (Season Two; Episode 2) and "I Know Black People" (Season Two; Episode 8). Our analysis illustrates how Chappelle utilizes his comedic sketches to defuse complex and often volatile cultural topics within the domains of racial identity and interracial relations. The aforementioned sketches from *Chappelle's Show* best illustrate the intricate engagement and interplay of cultural and linguistic taboos in Chappelle's comedy while simultaneously maintaining market appeal to a mass interracial audience.

This chapter will focus on the inversion of racial roles in the aforementioned sketches, while paying particular attention to the strategic use of racial slurs, taboos, and the recasting of cultural stereotypes in Chappelle's sketches. In "Blind Supremacy," we encounter a black white supremacist who is unaware of his own skin color, while, in contrast to the former, "The Niggar Family" is cast in black-and-white reminiscent of sitcoms such as *Leave it to Beaver* and *The Patty Duke Show* starring white upper-class suburban family with the last name "Niggar." Lastly, in "I Know Black People," Dave Chappelle plays the role of a game show host who quizzes contestants of various ethnic backgrounds (African Americans included) on terminology frequently used and underground habits often undertaken by "black people." Through our exploration of *Niggerdom* in *Chappelle's Show* sketches, we show how Chappelle's comedy addresses interracial relationships and stereotypes as well as linguistic taboos within the framework of comedy sketches, which gives him carte blanche unattainable in most public venues.[2] Chappelle relies strongly on the concept of racial inversion — a variant of Bertolt Brecht's *Verfremdungseffekt* (alienation effect)— where the stage and audience is drastically disassociated from one another. This encapsulates the core tenet of our thesis of what makes Chappelle's racially charged sketches so damn funny: What makes Chappelle's sketches funny to the American public is that his racial humor in many regards "intensionally" represents alternative worlds and scenarios that are simply too far-fetched to possibly be true.

Since the appearance of *Chappelle's Show* in 2003, Dave Chappelle has continually been compared to the late, great Richard Pryor, who entertained audiences on the comic stage as well as on the silver screen. Such comparisons remain relevant, given the social backdrops and contexts against which and from which each comedian's material emerged. In his 2007 article entitled "Is It Something He Said: The Mass Consumption of Richard Pryor's Culturally Intimate Humor," Evan Cooper underscores the fact that "despite Pryor's complex invocation of African American stereotypes, Black and non–Black viewers generally viewed Pryor's comic representations of African Americans through the lens of dominant stereotypes, especially when a working-class milieu was signified."[3] We can make this same general claim with regard to the work of Dave Chappelle, a claim which resonates most loudly in the three sketches that we are examining here.

Chappelle's television series is a deconstruction of racial discourse that saw its genesis in programs such as *All in the Family* and *The Cosby Show*.[4] In their 1992 study entitled *Enlightened Racism: The Cosby Show, Audiences, and the Myth of the American Dream*, Jhally and Lewis argued that *The Cosby Show*'s means of portraying a successful upper middle-class African American family, which, for any American family regardless of color seemed utopian, suggested that discrimination against blacks had ended by 1984.[5] Chappelle proposes a contrary point of view that is based on his own dystopian life experience. Chappelle grew up in Washington, D.C., in a household that he has cleverly described as the "broke Huxtables," a parallel, complementary one to that which was portrayed by Bill Cosby.[6] The vision that Chappelle offers in his comedic descriptions, a less "warm and fuzzy" comedic approach to racism than that of Bill Cosby, may cause some viewers to disengage.[7] Evan Cooper continues,

> Given the frequent obliqueness of a contemporary African American comic form like *The Dave Chappelle Show*, audience reception of satirical humor is likely to be fraught with selective perception. Though a genre like the family situation comedy can rely on humor based on misunderstandings and gentle mocking of children's delusions and adolescent hubris, comic forms are generally not the ideal vehicles for idealistic representations or social uplift.[8]

We would maintain, however, that in the case of *Chappelle's Show*, selective perception of Chappelle's satirical humor is likely caused by a failure on the part of certain audience members to completely relate to the scenes that Chappelle depicts more than a deficiency in the comic form itself.

Our analysis of these three episodes from Chappelle's series necessitates an understanding of the theoretic foundation of comedy, the foundation of which is laughter. We will consider two complementary theoretical bases: firstly, Mikhail Bahktin's theory on *carnival* and laughter described in his monumental work *Rabelais and His World* and, secondly, Henri Bergson's theory on laughter outlined in his work entitled *Le Rire: Essai sur la Signification du Comique*. On a more basic level, our analysis will answer the following questions: Is there anything humorous about Clayton Bigsby, a black white supremacist who is unaware of his own skin color? What is so amusing about a middle-class "Leave It to Beaver-esque" family named the "Niggars"? Why do we find the game show "I Know Black People" funny? In general, why do we laugh at Chappelle's comedy sketches?

Why Do We Laugh at These Sketches?

There is arguably no study on the comedic aspect of literature more important than Mikhail Bahktin's study of *carnival*, this topsy-turvy world, the grotesque and laughter in François Rabelais' literary works. Mikhail Bahktin, the Russian philosopher, literary critic, and semiotician, wrote some of the most powerful works of literary and rhetorical theory and criticism of the 20th century. In *Rabelais and His World*, Bahktin deconstructed the real world that Rabelais painted in literary form in an effort to better understand the role that laughter and humor played in that world. For Bahktin, Rabelais' *carnival* was associated with the collectivity. Those attending a carnival did not merely constitute a crowd; rather the people were seen as a whole and organized in a way that defied socioeconomic and political organization. Chappelle's studio and television audience function in the same collective fashion. Regardless of social or political strata, this audience participates in the sketches together and hears Chappelle's message initially through the collective experience before moving to individual understanding, or, as Bahktin explains, "The wholeness of the world's comic aspect is destroyed, and that which appears comic becomes a private reaction. The people's ambivalent laughter, on the other hand, expressed the point of view of the whole world; he who is laughing also belongs to it."[9] Both through the individual and through the collective experience, laughter serves to help us to defeat those things which we fear the most, for according to Bahktin, "Fear is the extreme expression of narrow-minded and stupid seriousness, which is defeated by laughter.... Complete liberty is possible only in the completely fearless world."[10] If we fear racism and if we fear the scourge that has been created by gross misappropriation of the N-word, we can only defeat our fear through laughter, as Chappelle suggests in his sketches.

Laughter itself has a significance that was arguably first defined during the Renaissance. Laughter serves as a means to understand both what is found in the world and what is found within the individual. Bahktin summarizes, "Laughter has a deep philosophical meaning, it is one of the essential forms of the truth concerning the world as a whole, concerning history and man; it is a peculiar point of view relative to the world; the world is seen anew, no less (and perhaps more) profoundly than when seen from the serious standpoint. Therefore, laughter is just as admissible in great literature, posing universal problems, as seriousness. Certain essential aspects of the universe are accessible only to laughter."[11] Laughter, therefore, gives each individual access to truth, albeit an internal truth more than an external truth. In a sense, laughter is also a defense mechanism against external realities that contradict our inner truths. Laughter keeps the dialogue moving and gives he who laughs a stake in the larger social discourse.[12]

In *Le Rire: Essai sur la Signification du Comique*, Henri Bergson defines laughter as a biological, intellectual, social function.[13] The central idea of Bergson's work is that laughter serves as a corrective of society. Laughter makes it possible for people to live in society and for the society to function.

Bergson explains that "[o]ur excuse, to take our shot at answering this question, is that we do not seek to enclose comic fantasy in a definition. We see in it, before anything, something living. We will treat her, as delicate as she might be, with the respect that we owe to life. We will limit ourselves to watching it grow and blossom. From form to form, by imperceptible gradations, it will complete unusual metamorphoses before our very eyes."[14] This "something living" is human life itself, which "presents itself to us like an evolution in time and complexity in space."[15] Therefore, we tend to laugh at people when they appear to be too *mechanical*, too rigid to reflect humanity, for "any arrangement of actions or events is comical that gives us, one inside the other, the illusion of life and the distinct feeling of a mechanical organization."[16] Therefore, to laugh at someone, is to expect the individual to curb the behavior and operate in a way more in conformity with the rules established by our society. When someone shows the inability to curb a behavior, laughter reveals our disapproval. The comic writer uses different tools to create characters that fail to check their behavior. One of the most common and useful is the inversion of roles, the topsy-turvy world to which Bahktin also refers.[17] This comic technique (inversion) is evident in the three sketches from *Chappelle's Show* upon which this study centers. Chappelle's use of inversion, in particular with regard to the role that his characters play, gives Chappelle's characters new agency in the larger social (and comedic) discourse.[18]

Chappelle's comedic discourse enjoys a salutary quality as well. In *Laughing Mad: The Black Comic Persona in Post-Soul America*, Bambi Haggins writes,

> Although Chappelle is a storyteller, who, with casual and almost lackluster candor, pulls you into his world and his logic, the content of his humor often has the sly righteousness and progressing radicalism of [Dick] Gregory and the outlandish inner truism and gut-busting honesty of [Richard] Pryor. Yet Chappelle's comic voice — and the dualities in his comic persona — reflects the dynamic, complex, and conflicted nature of sociopolitical discourse in the post-civil rights movement.[19]

In the sketches from *Chappelle's Show* that we will examine here, Chappelle's sociopolitical discourse serves both to examine and to exorcise the N-word of its denigrating and demeaning connotations. Through the comedic, Chappelle succeeds in reappropriating a terminology that had previously been held within the hands of whites. By using language for his own purpose, with his own nuances and intentions, Chappelle takes back the power that whites had originally given to that language. Chappelle's comic genius is polyvalent to the extent that it can be read and understood at two different levels: at an audience or street level and at the academic level. In order to laugh at Chappelle's work as illustrated in these sketches, we must, either as spectators or as scholars, connect at some intellectual level to the words, expressions, and scenes that Chappelle employs.

The N-word, Racial Stereotypes and the Exploitation of Other Taboos

Erasing negative connotations associated with the N-word is the subject of study of an entire host of academic books and articles, the most significant of which include Randall Kennedy's *Nigger: The Strange Career of a Troublesome Word* (2002) and *Sellout: The Politics of Racial Betrayal* (2008). In *Nigger: The Strange Career of a Troublesome Word*, Kennedy explores the very notion of "nigger" by posing such questions as, "What is the definition of the word *nigger*? Who has the right to use this word? Is there any historical connotation to the word that should, for some reason, be maintained? Why does *nigger*, when employed in certain contexts, produce reactions that range from anger to all-out violence? How can we rid the word of its destructiveness?"[20] In *Sellout*, the Harvard law professor examines accusations of favoring white interests over those of blacks. Labeled a "sellout" himself after the publication of *Nigger: The Strange Career of a Troublesome Word*, in *Sellout: The Politics of Racial Betrayal*, Kennedy examines the history of sellout rhetoric from a legal perspective, which he argues is sometimes found in blacks who supported white supremacist ideology (à la Clayton Bigsby in *Chappelle's Show*). He also examines the role of sellout rhetoric in unifying the black community against racist ideologies. Kennedy maintains that "nigger" can have a wide variety of meanings. In hip-hop, for example, "nigger" represents a neutral or friendly greeting shared among some African Americans, "an ironic gesture of solidarity."[21] Kennedy concludes that although "nigger," which has been a derogatory term for centuries, has recently gained additional meanings created by the black community, in general, the N-word is off limits to any individual who is not African American. Its use is, in fact, nearly always questionable. The historical connotations of the word will forever remain, and there may be little that anyone can to do reduce the potentially destructive power of the word.

Clearly, the cursed N-word is a linguistic taboo, a fact that Chappelle obviously plays to his advantage. Taboos are open to beneficial exploitation. The notion of taboo is more than ritual and prohibition and avoidance. Although the use of some taboos can be dangerous to individuals and their respective societies (leading even to death), milder forms of taboo do exist and often result often in lesser penalties of corporal punishment, incarceration, or social ostracism or mere disapproval. Furthermore, the concept of an "absolute taboo" does not exist: Nothing is taboo for all people, under all circumstances for all times. Although the N-word conjures up strong feelings of social, economy and political oppression as well as violence towards African Americans, exactly what the N-word means for one generation to the next is dynamic and ever-changing.

The restriction on language is much like a ban on weapons; both prohibitions function as a "forbidden fruit" of sorts and enhance their respective attractiveness for use. As pointed out by Allan and Burridge, "Criticisms of monarchs, heads of state and other persons of rank is often severely censored, particularly in times of national instability."[22] One could argue that the identity of African Americans in the post–Civil Rights era is, and continues to be, in a state of flux. For example, in his book titled *Post-Soul Nation: The Explosive, Contradictory, Triumphant, and Tragic 1980s as Experienced by African Americans (Previously known as Blacks and before that Negroes)*, critically acclaimed journalist Nelson George chronicles the advances and, in many instances, the continual struggle for racial equality in the 1980s. As evidenced by the title of the book, George examines the successes and failures of African Americans during the 1980s. Interestingly, and perhaps not intentional on the part of George, he regularly comments on the semantic change that has taken place since the 1960s in lexemes such as "soul" and the various positive and negative connotations that accompany that word today.

In a technical sense, the N-word can be formally classified as a *dysphemism*: a word or phrase with connotations that are offensive either about the denotatum and/or to people addressed or overhearing the utterance.[23] Dysphemisms are often used by people to vent frustration towards people and situations that annoy them. To take things a step further, dysphemisms can be employed as a linguistic weapon to humiliate and degrade others who have previously caused them harm or have angered them in some way. As such, "Dysphemisms are therefore characteristic of political groups and cliques talking about their opponents; of feminists speaking about men; and also of male larrikins and macho types speaking of women and effete behaviors. Dysphemistic expressions include curses, name-calling, and any sort of derogatory comment directed towards others in order to insult or to wound them. But they also serve as a way to let off steam, for example, when exclamatory swear words alleviate frustration or anger."[24] Here, we wish to explicate the crafty method that Chappelle's use of the N-word gains in his comedy. Put simply, the N-word becomes a weapon in these comedy sketches, in situations that could not be real in any possible world, that actually poke fun at true racists who actually harbor and support these racist doctrines. For the white audience, Chappelle's tactful use of the N-word in the sketches analyses in this paper (as well as a host of others) endows them with a sense empowerment and sense of self-worth: Chappelle's white audience can walk away with the assurance that, although racism persists in modern society to a greater or lesser extent, they are at the very least not that racist in their views towards blacks and other minorities.

Be that as it may, one question continues to be a point of extreme controversy surrounding the use of the N-word is, quite simply, the question of who is allowed to say it and within what contexts. Is it only to be used by those in the black community? This, too, is a point of controversy; prominent African Americans such as Bill Cosby, Oprah Winfrey and the late Richard Pryor (later in his career) have publicly expressed their opinion that the N-word should never be used, even by African Americans.[25] This same controversy has also been a mainstay within the hip-hop community since its conception. Whereas politically active rappers such as Public Enemy's Chuck D have always denounced the use of the N-word, others such as Boogie Down Production's KRS-One have interpreted the use of the N-word as a source of black empowerment.[26] To paraphrase, KRS-One envisages the adoption of the word N-word in standard vernacular speech patterns of blacks as a source of linguistic empowerment; by removing the stigma that white Americans have encapsulated within this word for centuries, those blacks who actively use this term in their speech and sphere of reference have taken back the term and put a positive spin on quite arguably the most damaging and degrading lexeme used to label African Americans.

Regardless, it still does not address the "stewardship" issue; i.e., are only blacks allowed to use this term or can "some" whites also use this term in certain situations? Perhaps more pertinent for the topic at hand, when and why can the use of the N-word, especially by whites (or those who think or wish or are positioned as white), be regarded as funny? Contemporary animated sitcoms provide parallel (and relevant) examples to the sketches analyzed in this paper. We mention this here not to detract from the main argument of our paper, but to illustrate how other instances of the dysphemic N-word in popular sitcoms bear striking similarities to Chappelle's usage of these controversial linguistic terms.

In the animated series *The Boondocks*, the character known as Uncle Ruckus continually bemoans the fact that he is black. As a matter of fact, he regards his black skin as the result of a disease and supports white supremacist ideology.[27] Uncle Ruckus is the voice of much diatribe in the form of exploitations of negative stereotypes of African Americans. He openly uses the N-word in a negative way toward fellow African Americans but argues that overuse of the term has received a positive connotation in some circles: "I say, next time you gonna call a darkie a nigger, call that coon a jungle bunny instead!" (Season Two; Episode 11). To better understand this quote, we have to return the primary context of the episode at hand ("The S-Word") during which Riley Freeman, a third-grader who frequently uses the N-word, is called a "nigga" by his teacher, Mr. Petto. Mr. Petto, a middle-aged White elementary school teacher, attempted to use the N-word in a positive connotation, however, the public perceived it as a racial slur.

Another television show that continues to push the envelope when it comes to political correctness and public acceptability is *South Park*. In the episode entitled, "With Apologies to Jesse Jackson" (Season Eleven; Episode One), Randy Marsh is a contestant on the game show *Wheel of Fortune*. The puzzle he is given to solve is entitled "People Who Annoy You." Randy is presented with N _ G G E R S, and only needs one vowel to complete the puzzle. Although he has an answer in mind (N I G G E R S), he hesitates to provide the answer right away because he clearly recognizes it to be a dysphemism. When he finally shouts out the answer ("NIGGERS"), the entire studio is overcome with silence and disbelief. When the host reveals the correct answer (NAGGERS), the director immediately chooses to cut to "bars and tone."

From a purely theoretical point of view, *Chappelle's Show* set a trend in breaking taboos in cable comedy sketch writing. Chappelle's series also combines ideas that Kennedy expresses in his work with those expressed by John Limon in his book entitled *Stand-up Comedy in Theory, or, Abjection in America*. Limon argues that stand-up is characterized by a focus on the abject, or, those aspects of the comedian's identity that are offensive to him or to his audience. By abjection, Limon means "a psychic worrying of those aspects of oneself that one cannot be rid of, that seem, but are not quite, alienable — for example, blood, urine, feces, nails, and the corpse."[28] Limon furthers his thesis by stating that "What is abject is that which one wants to cleanse oneself of, but ultimately cannot. When comedians proudly perform their abjection, it becomes comic."[29] Performing their abjection is a way of simultaneously owning it and attempting to temporarily escape it, despite its inevitable return. This represents a dialectic shift, an allusion to the topsy-turvy world that is often expressed through the comedic. Thus, there is a transformation that happens when comedians like Chappelle attempt to push away qualities of themselves that they cannot really push away.

Elizabeth Ludwig furthers Limon's theory of abjection when she says that "clearly, if comedy is an expression of abjection, then it must be an expression of one's own abjection; otherwise, the performer is likely to be perceived as merely perpetuating the abjection of others. For the performer to make jokes at the expense of a minority group to which he or she does not belong is to take on a power position at the expense of othering."[30] This was certainly the case with Michael Richard's performance at the Laugh Factory in

West Hollywood, California, on November 17, 2006, when addressing a group of black hecklers, a cell phone video captured Richards shouting "Shut up" to a heckler in the audience, followed by "He's a nigger!" to the rest of the audience.[31] Michael Richards was criticized for using the N-word because he is not black. As John Strausbaugh explains, "White people joking about Black people is almost automatically treated as hate speech."[32] Therefore, Chappelle is performing his abjection on stage and in his sketches. This does not, however, suggest that Chappelle is repulsed by the fact that he is black. It simply means that he has the "ethnic license" to look at his own race from the white man's perspective.

In his sketch entitled "Black White Supremacist," a spoof of the PBS series *Frontline*, Dave Chappelle plays the role of a blind white supremacist who is unaware that he is black. This sketch is set in the South and contains heavy KKK overtones. At the beginning of the sketch, Kent Wallace, host of the program, arrives at the home of Clayton Bigsby in search of an exclusive interview of the White supremacist leader and is stunned to learn that Bigsby is, in fact, black. Wallace asks Bigsby what is the overall message of his books, to which Bigsby replies, "My message is simple. Niggers, Jews, homosexuals, Mexicans, A-rabs, and all kinds of different Chinks stink! And I hate 'em!" Wallace attempts to further the dialogue by asking Bigsby exactly what problem he has with African Americans. Bigsby answers,

> They're lazy, good for nothin' tricksters, crack smokin' swindlers, big butt havin', wide-nose breathin' all the White man's air.... They eat up all the chicken, they think they're the best dancers, and they stink. Did I mention that before? ... Matter of fact, my friend Jasper told me one of them coons came by his house to pick his sister up for a date. He said "look here nigger, that there is my girl. If anyone is going to have sex with my sister, it's gonna be me!"

It is clear that the Clayton Bigsby character is a composite of racial and ethnic prejudices. Beneath Chappelle's "Bigsby" humor is a rich social commentary on race relations in the United States that is based upon a smorgasbord of stereotypes, for which the preceding examples taken from his sketches provide evidence. In their article "When the Truth Hurts, Tell a Joke: Why America Needs Its Comedians," authors Roger Cohen and Ryan Richards argue that

> [W]hile comedians will make everyone uncomfortable at some point, good comics are playing an important function in society by holding up a mirror and forcing us to confront realities that we would often prefer to ignore. For minority groups, humor also serves as a tool to

neutralize the power of stereotypes that obstruct their path to equal participation in society. Stand-up comedy can give social critique and instigate transformation in a way that leaves many audience members wanting more.[33]

This is exactly the type of stereotype neutralization that Chappelle performs in "Blind Supremacy." The effect of this sketch, however, is much more widespread than simply neutralizing stereotypes of African Americans. In the previous quotes, the Clayton Bigsby character slurs six different groups, and not all of them are racial or ethnic groups. Bigsby makes no distinction between racial/ethic groups and homosexuals, throwing the latter in the same lot as the former: "Don't let the liberal media tell you how to think and feel. If you have hate in your heart, let it out. *(pauses)* If you don't like Will and Grace, that doesn't mean there's something wrong with you. Means there's something wrong with Will! He's a homosexual."[34] The Clayton Bigsby character is one of the richest of Chappelle's characters for he at the same time quite literally casts a blind eye toward all groups that do not belong to the one to which he thinks he belongs and represents a model that is not at all possible in American society.

Kent Wallace continues his interview of Clayton, ultimately informing Bigsby that he is, in fact, an African American. In denying his participation in *Niggerdom*, Bigsby means, of course, that he does not participate in any of the behaviors that have caused African Americans to become such a hated racial group. When Bigsby is harassed by skin heads at the gas station, the blind white supremacist leader thinks that they are harassing someone else. Bigsby exhibits a total disconnection from the environment of hate that he himself has worked to forge. His blindness prevents him from being able to hold up a mirror to society and judge the actions that are permitted to perpetuate. The inversion of roles in the Clayton Bigsby character, such as defined in Bergson's work, is complete when Clayton rolls through town with his friend Jasper and meets a group of White teenagers cruising down the street in a convertible blasting hip-hop music. "Hey, niggers!" yells Bigsby. "Turn that jungle music down!" The teen driving the car has a different understanding of the N-word, which is immediately revealed in his response to his friends in the car: "Did he just call us niggers? ... Awesome!" These adolescents perpetuate the stereotype of "Wiggers" and "Wannabes." A "Wigger" is defined as "a young white who desperately wants to be down with hip-hop, who identifies more strongly with black culture than white."[35] The "Wannabe," in contrast, is "someone uncomfortable being himself or herself and fanatically trying to be someone else. Long used in Black American colloquial language to describe an outsider aping insider behavior and popularized among the younger generation by the 1988 Spike Lee film *School Daze*."[36] Whether "Wigger" or "Wannabe," these adolescents long for the life of a young, black man: a life full of struggle and controversy.

When Bigsby finally learns that he is, in fact, black, he suffers an identity crisis of epic proportions, which creates what is the greatest irony of the entire sketch: "In the past few weeks," ends Kent Wallace, "Clayton Bigsby accepted the fact that he is a black man. And three days ago, he filed for divorce from his wife. When we asked 'Why after 19 years of marriage?' He responded, 'Because she's a nigger lover.'" Clayton Bigsby's unwillingness to accept the fact that he is black mirrors that of society's unwillingness or lack of preparedness to accept that African Americans are a vital group within the United States. In this particular sketch, Chappelle's humor is contained within this irony, an irony which somehow implicates each and every one of us who has, sometime in the past, discriminated against another racial or ethnic group, and who has, perhaps, been discriminated against as well. Chappelle extends his discussion of discrimination to include homosexuals, Asians, Arabs, Mexicans, rednecks and white teen "Wannabes" who desire to emulate the apparent "awesome" nature of the African American world.

In his sketch "The Niggar Family," Chappelle introduces us to an upper-class white suburban family who happens to have the last name "Niggar." The sketch is set in black and white and appears to strongly resemble 1950s and '60s sitcoms and their pristine portrayal of Americana. The sketch employs countless references to negative stereotypes often placed on African Americans. For example, Mr. Niggar, the family patriarch, refers to his son (Timmy) as "one lazy Niggar" for sleeping in, and when showing his wife a picture of his new nephew, his wife comments "he sure does have those Niggar lips." Chappelle openly embraces these stereotypes himself when he appears as Clarence, the Niggar's family milkman (and wearing a clean, white uniform). Immediately after Clarence's entrance, Mr. Niggar refers to Clarence as "our colored milkman" which is clearly a racial dysphemism. As a matter of fact, one could possibly argue that Chappelle embracing the role of a milkman — a profession typically undertaken by those of a lower socio-economic class — is an instance of type casting and blaxploitation. Entering the family kitchen, Clarence greets them with "Mmmm ... mmmm. Somethin' sure smells good. You Niggars cookin'?" He makes other allusions to racial stereotypes by stating that he "knows better than to get between a 'Niggar' and their pork" because he "might get his fingers bit." In similar fashion, Clarence reminds Mr. Niggar that he forgot to pay his bill last week and "he knows how forgetful you 'Niggars' are when it comes to paying bills." Mr. Niggar immediately pays Clarence, apologizes and states that "it slipped my mind," to which Clarence replies "Nigga, please, Nigga please!" The greeting/exclamation "Nigga please!" is not the only instance of Clarence making use of the N-word as a form of greeting. Before exiting the kitchen, Clarence leaves the room by saying "Peace, nigga." He then quickly returns to the kitchen to shout out "Niggars."[37]

Outside of the Niggar family home, other negative stereotypes about African Americans are introduced and interwoven in this masterfully calculated paradoxical world of the Niggar family. At the home of Jenny Halstead, the girl who will go out with Timmy Niggar later that evening, the father of the family reacts with a sense of terror and urgency when he discusses that his daughter "has a date with the Niggar boy from school," to which he exclaims, "Oh God! No!" Jenny quickly quells his fears by explaining that "Niggar" is the boy's name. The father quickly retorts, "I like that 'Niggar' ... he's so well-spoken and such a good athlete. That family's going places. We're rich, but their nigger rich." The positive attributes listed by Mr. Halstead are clearly those that Whites are often regarded to seek in blacks who exhibit "white-like" characteristics. The comments on Timmy Niggar's well-spoken manner and prowess as an athlete contrast with some of the more negative stereotypes delivered in the scene in the Niggar family kitchen discussed above. Be that as it may, these positive racial characteristics here are just as, if not more offensive than the former situation. The message here is simple: 'Niggars' that "know how to act right" are acceptable, while the rest of them are a menace to society.

The concluding segments of the sketch find both Timmy Niggar and his date waiting to be seated at the same restaurant where Clarence and his wife wish to dine. When the host announces that "Niggar, party of two" may now be seated, Clarence interprets this remark incorrectly as a racial gibe, until he sees Timmy and greets him as "little Niggar." Clarence introduces the young couple to his wife as "the 'Niggars' from work that I was tellin' you about," to which she quickly responds in a sassy tone asking Timmy if he was "the nigger who broke the bottle over her husband's head at a dice game." Clarence immediately reprimands his wife by clarifying her interpretative error by stating that Timmy is not "that nigger" but "the 'Niggar' from the milk route." Here his wife completed changes her demeanor and is no longer pointing her finger directly at Timmy with an aggressive tone of voice; rather, she embraces a humble manner and wishes that young couple a pleasant time out. This quick about-face change in behavior of blacks towards whites also shows a stereotype of (traditional) norms of behavior that blacks should be subservient and obsequious in their interactions with whites. This, of course, alludes to the master-slave dialectic which Chappelle manipulates to his own end. The sketch concludes as the Niggar family hosts a dinner party with Hispanic guests, whose name happens to be the "Wetbacks."

This, of course, returns us to some of the key (aforementioned) questions raised by Kennedy regarding the usage and stewardship of the N-word. We maintain that whites can (apparently) only use the N-word in situations that are so far removed from reality — such as Chappelle's comedy sketches — that a mixed audience interprets their remarks purely as sarcasm inducing a comedic effect. Pursuing the issue of whether the N-word can potentially be stripped of its negative connotations is a red herring. Chappelle's comedy does reveal that when a person uses the N-word, they develop a platform through which racial taboos and controversial topics can at least be exposed if not discussed. In other words, Chappelle's humor reveals that racism is still alive and well in our society. However, the comedian also demonstrates that humor can also exploit this fact and serve as a way to discuss, to analyze, and to critique such ways of thinking.

The final sketch from *Chappelle's Show* that we will use to illustrate the principal claim of this essay is "I Know Black People," a game show in which contestants answer a series of question that tests their knowledge of African American culture. Hosted by Chappelle himself, contestants include a white African American studies and history professor, a white female police officer, a TV writer for the *Chris Rock Show* and *Chappelle's Show* (Chappelle's friend and co-writer, Neal Brennan), a Korean grocery store worker, a DJ, a social worker, a high school student, and a black barber from Brooklyn. The people that Chappelle chooses as contestants reveal as much about the racial stereotypes as the questions that Chappelle, the host, asks. Chappelle makes use of archetypal, theatrical personas that automatically provide all the background information that the audience needs to understand how the game show is going to unfold. The audience would expect the professor to fare well in the competition, as they would the television writer, but it appears that Chappelle's purpose for choosing these people speaks as much to the stereotypes associated with their "walks of life" as it does to their knowledge of African American culture. The social worker and the Korean grocery worker quickly emerge as the least savvy with regard to African American culture. It is a bit of a paradox that the social worker is so disconnected with a society which contains a racial group that is reputed for putting a strain on the American social and public systems. The Korean grocery worker, for his part, encapsulates the myth of the Korean worker who gets a job at the corner grocery store and who takes advantage of America's resources without "assimilating" into American society. Further, the Korean grocer is the "new immigrant" who has replaced the African American in "the neighborhood." The Korean grocer is also stereotyped as an impatient, skeptical, money-grabbing proprietor: "Hurry up and buy!" This scene adds another layer to Chappelle's racial discourse, as he underscores the fact that these "new kids on the block" have supplanted African Americans as the most hated racial minority in the United States.

In the character of the black barber from Brooklyn, Chappelle plays upon the stereotype of the barbershop, a place where it is less about the haircut than the lively discussions that take place there. As an audience, we cannot help but think of Tim Story's film *Barbershop* (2002), which starred Ice Cube, Cedric the Entertainer, and Anthony Anderson. The film centers on social life in a south Chicago barbershop in which the characters discuss both trivial and serious issues. One of the most important issues discussed in the film is the significance of Rosa Parks' contribution to the Civil Rights movement. Chappelle alludes to this scene when he asks the contestants, "Will black people ever overcome?" In response to this question, the white female cop repeats, "Ummm, will they ever overcome?," to which Chappelle responds, "That is correct!" The characters in *Barbershop* also discuss whether black people need (or deserve) reparations as a result of the Civil War, which is another acceptable answer to the final question in the sketch "I Know Black People." Other questions from *Barbershop* that surface in "I Know Black People" include discussions on white people who act "black" and black people who act "white" (which we also saw in "Blind Supremacy") and whether being educated makes a black person "better" than his own racial group or better than uneducated whites (also a reference to "Blind Supremacy"). The series of rhetorical questions that Chappelle poses gives evidence to the fact that the dialogue on racial equality of African Americans within a predominately white American society must continue. Chappelle seems to suggest that as African Americans have been marginalized within American society, they have also been forgotten within that marginalization. They are left in an abyss of misunderstanding.

One of the prime aims of this investigation is to arrive at a clearer idea of what exactly *Niggerdom* in Dave Chappelle's *Chappelle Show* actually denotes. In the sketches analyzed here, we see how Dave Chappelle plays the role of exposing the American public to the racism that still exists towards African Americans in society today. In some instances, like those during "The Niggar Family" sketch at the Halstead home, Chappelle interjects aspects of racism that African Americans still encounter today in the form of what we call a positive dysphemism. To recapitulate, *Niggerdom* is probably best understood as the collective negative stereotypes that persist even today in America regarding African American culture, speech and customs.

How is Chappelle able to effectively deliver these potentially volatile messages in a comedic format? We suggest that some of his success can be attributed to the fact that Chappelle himself is an African American. With Dave

Chappelle, there is no question regarding his authenticity as an African American. However, the Whites that use the N-word in his sketches are so far removed from any semblance of reality that the question of their racial authenticity does not come into play. Nonetheless, this clearly is not the only reason that he is successful in delivering his punch lines. As mentioned in the introduction, Chappelle relies strongly on the concept of racial inversion — a variant of Bertolt Brecht's *Verfremdungseffekt*— where the stage and audience is drastically disassociated from one another. This, of course, gains him the distance between reality and the alternative worlds that his sketches are supposedly set in. What's so funny about the notions of *Niggerdom* that persist in Chappelle's sketches is that we find people who still actually harbor these strong racist ideologies as existing far outside the norm. In short, Chappelle's form of humor helps us feel better about ourselves, because at the end of the day we realize that we are at least not *that* racist and socially inept.[38] Chappelle was a calculated risk taker who found great success in this form of humor and blazed a trail in many regards for other cable comedy sitcoms such as *The Boondocks* and *South Park* that benefited tremendously from Chappelle's pioneering work in manipulating 21st century inter-racial barriers and converting them into laughs.

Chappelle's Show critiques the illusion of America as a happy melting pot. In the three sketches that we have investigated here, we have shown how Chappelle's comedic writing illustrates the interplay of cultural and linguistic taboos through a deconstruction of the N-word. In the end, Chappelle's exploration into the realms of *Niggerdom* through his sketches helps inform us, the American public, as much about ourselves as it does Chappelle's abrasive form of comedy. And what is really cool is that we can laugh while we think about his work.

2

Comic Genius or Con Man?

Deconstructing the Comedy of Dave Chappelle

Novotny Lawrence

Dave Chappelle is perhaps one of the most well-known and influential comedians of his generation. Often infusing his comedy with critiques of politics and race, Chappelle has used motion pictures, television, and the stage as a platform to provide entertaining and insightful commentary about the black experience in America. Prime examples include his role in *Undercover Brother* (2002) as "Conspiracy Brother," an angry black male obsessed with exposing "The Man's" covert attempts to oppress blacks, as well as *Chappelle's Show* (2003–2006) skits, such as "The Black White Supremacist," "The Racial Draft," and "I Know Black People." While the aforementioned work is significant, Chappelle's comedy is often complicated by his performance of a black masculinity that relies upon misogynistic and homophobic rhetoric, as well as an over-reliance upon the highly controversial word "nigger." Specifically, *Chappelle's Show* skits "It's a Wonderful Chest," "A Gay World," "The Niggar Family," and segments of his stand-up performance in *For What It's Worth* (2004) serve as examples of some of the comedian's more sophomoric and offensive material.

When critiqued for its sociopolitical value, the dichotomy that exists in Chappelle's comedy is glaring. The comedian's material focusing on the exploration of the black experience in the U.S. illustrates his knowledge of the manner that racism continues to permeate contemporary society, demonstrating that he is socially and politically aware. Although Chappelle is masterful at critiquing and exposing America's racial injustices, his ruminations on women and gays and lesbians lack similar insight and often perpetuate common stereotypes that characterize members of the groups. Hence, aspects of Chappelle's comedy serve to reinforce the oppressive hierarchy that exists in the U.S., thus, positioning him as part of a longstanding and enduring tradition. Taking these contradictions into account, this chapter utilizes methodologies from African American, gender, and queer studies to deconstruct Chappelle's comedy in the attempt to answer the question, "comic genius or con man?" The chapter begins with a brief discussion of the comedian in relation to stereotypes that have historically circumscribed black performers and continues with an examination of his crossover appeal which affords him the opportunity to critique America's social, economic, and political structure in front of a multicultural and multigenerational audience. The second half of the examination focuses on Chappelle's misogyny, homophobia, and use of the "N-word," demonstrating how these factors devalue the significance of his more relevant material.

Chappelle as Comic Genius

At first glance, Dave Chappelle is reminiscent of quintessential coon, Stepin Fetchit. Like Fetchit, his head is nearly or completely shaved, he is tall, thin, and often speaks in an excited, albeit exaggerated, tone to emphasize the punch lines of his material. At times Chappelle also widens his eyes for comic effect, harkening back to the days when the coon was the most prominent representation of black masculinity on motion picture and television screens. However, these attributes are a unique feature of Chappelle's comic persona that he uses to the fullest. As Mel Watkins notes in *On the Real Side*, "Black American humor is nearly as dependent on a delivery that incorporates black America's generally more expressive and flamboyant style as it is on wit."[1] While Chappelle's hyper-frenetic manner is reminiscent of cooning, he is armed with an intelligence that transcends the one-dimensional stereotype, positioning him as a dynamic comedian and an insightful cultural commentator.

In *Open Mike: Reflections on Race, Sex, Culture, and Religion*, Michael Eric Dyson contends, "The comic-as-cultural-critic-and-social-commentator does not merely celebrate or valorize the culture from which he or she emerges. Such comics enable us to understand our culture as they honestly explore it and thus help explain black culture's internal contradictions, stress its positive features, and acknowledge its detrimental characteristics."[2] Chappelle's role as comic-as-cultural-critic-and-social-commentator is highly influenced by his childhood experiences. Significantly, the comedian spent his adolescent years in Yellow Springs, Ohio before relocating to Washington, D.C. As Bambi Haggins notes in *Laughing Mad: The Black Comic Persona in Post-Soul America*, there is a "dual nature of his black experience — identity formation in predominantly black and predominantly white spaces....

Chappelle enjoys a sort of dual credibility — his comic persona is inflected by both the Afrocentrism of the black hip-hop intelligentsia and the skater/slacker/stoner ethos."[3] This presents Chappelle with a large fan base, allowing him to entertain and challenge the status quo on behalf of the "Gen X and Gen Y subcultures in both the black and white communities."[4]

Chappelle's connection to the skater/slacker/stoner ethos is reflected in his appearance in *Half Baked* (1998), which he co-wrote with his writing partner Neil Brennan, and *Chappelle's Show* skits like "First Black Man to Use a White Toilet." *Baked* is the epitome of the Gen X slacker film, chronicling the story of three unintelligent, marijuana smoking friends who come up with a series of outrageous schemes to free a friend from jail. Chappelle plays Thurgood, whose "throwaway jokes reveal how racially and sociohistorically aware a slacker can be — in a fairly sardonic and self deprecating way."[5] For example, after volunteering to be a guinea pig in a medicinal marijuana study, Thurgood comments, "My grandfather was a Tuskegee Airman, you know." As Haggins explains, "This seeming non sequitur, which actually invokes the unethical Tuskegee Research project rather than the barrier-breaking freedom flyers, is delivered with a certain degree of insolence for authority, in general, and white authority, in particular, and purposefully provides an off-kilter condensation of African American history."[6] "First Black Man to Use a White Toilet," is presented in a similar fashion. At the heart of the sketch is a sociopolitical commentary about Jim Crow laws in the South; however, that message is diluted in favor of entertaining the viewers with gross out humor that relies upon flatulence and the phrase "mud butt" in recounting the historic event. Although the comedy in *Baked* and "First Black Man to Use a Toilet" is not Chappelle's most significant material, it speaks to a segment of his fan base and perfectly illustrates the comedian's crossover and cross-generational appeal.

In stark contrast are Chappelle's film roles, sketches, and stand-up routines that demonstrate his connection to the black community and to hip-hop culture, which heavily informs his comedy. According to Tricia Rose, hip-hop music "attempts to negotiate the experiences of marginalization, brutally truncated opportunity and oppression with the cultural imperatives of African American and Caribbean history, identity, and community."[7] Its origins can be traced back to rap music which in the 1970s emerged as a platform for the socially, politically, and economically disenfranchised minority youths to critique America's patriarchal society. During that time "DJ's and MCs took two turntables and microphones creating music from borrowed beats of soul, funk, disco, reggae, and salsa, overlaid with lyrics reflecting their alienated youths."[8]

Chappelle's upbringing in Washington, D.C., exposed him to similar conditions to those that rap pioneers and contemporary hip-hop artists often address in their music. Specifically, upon arriving in the nation's capital he found "the culture of Washington had changed significantly for its black residents: 'crack had come out.'"[9] In an interview with Terry Gross on *Fresh Air* in 2004, Chappelle spoke about the drug epidemic facing D.C., commenting, "Selling drugs was like a legitimate job in the high school that I was going to.... It was that context [that] kind of isolated me — initially, and then when I started doing stand-up, it was like I thrived all over again."[10] Stand-up comedy was Chappelle's alternative to entering illegal activity, but not a means to avoid confronting the realities of black life in his D.C. neighborhood. As Haggins notes, Chappelle's comic persona is "imbued with hip-hop sensibility — the aesthetic and the politics of the musical genre are inextricably linked to his own."[11] While rappers such as Kanye West, Dead Prez, Blackaliscious, and Talib Kweli use their rhymes to expose American injustice, Chappelle positions himself alongside the performers, using his film roles, stand-up routines, and TV series as a platform for address pressing social, economic, and political issues plaguing the black community.

Chappelle's role as Conspiracy Brother in Malcolm D. Lee's *Undercover Brother* (2002), serves as a prime example of his ability to imbue his film roles with critiques of America's racial politics. *Brother* is a parody of 1970s black exploitation or blaxploitation films, which are defined as "movies made between 1970 and 1975, by both black and white directors alike, to exploit the black film audience."[12] The films are characterized by a black hero or heroine, a predominantly black urban setting, black supporting characters, a white villain, plot themes that relate to the black experience in America, strong displays of black sexuality, excessive violence, and funky rhythm and blues soundtracks.[13] Popular titles include *Cotton Comes to Harlem* (1970), *Shaft* (1971), *Superfly* (1972), and *Cleopatra Jones* (1973). Emerging as a result of the Civil Rights Movement, blaxploitation films are significant because they represent a period in movie history when a plethora of black performers were bona fide stars and the time when black audiences were first seriously considered a viable segment of the movie going audience.

Brother both parodies and pays homage to blaxploitation cinema, telling the story of "The Man's" attempt to derail a black candidate's presidential campaign. The arch villain meets resistance from Undercover Brother (Eddie Griffin) and his fellow secret agents who seek to put an end to the scheme. As previously noted, blaxploitation films include social, economic, and political commentary about the black experience in America. In *Brother*, Chappelle's Conspiracy Brother humorously provides that insight by trying to expose anything and everything as a scheme perpetuated against blacks by "The Man." For example, during their initial meeting, Undercover greets

Conspiracy with a warm "Good morning." The comment garners immediate mistrust from Conspiracy who in return labels Undercover a spy, emphatically explaining, "Good is an ancient Anglo-Saxon word meaning the absence of color.... When I hear good morning all I hear is I'm going to kill your black ass in the morning!"

While Conpiracy's hypotheses and subsequent tirades are unfounded and over the top at times, there are occasions when the character provides insightful commentary into the black experience. For instance, in another scene, Undercover responds to one of Conspiracy's tirades telling him that he needs to calm down and suggesting that he take in a movie. Conspiracy responds, "Why, so I can fall in love with some cute black man who teaches a white man everything he knows about the shrimping industry before they kill him thirty minutes into the movie?" On the surface, Conspiracy's comment is simply a reference to the relationship that Forrest Gump (Tom Hanks) shares with Bubba (Mykelti Williamson) in the Academy Award winning film *Forrest Gump* (1994). A closer examination reveals that the line is actually a poignant critique of Hollywood's male interracial relationships. In *Masculinity and the Interracial Buddy Film*, Melvin Donalson explains, "Throughout the twentieth century, men of color in Hollywood features—with black men being the most prevalent — have been juxtaposed with white male characters to accentuate and enhance the latter; in short, the characters of color have been rendered to make white males appear more courageous, tolerant, heroic, intelligent, etc., in the narrative."[14] This relationship is highly visible in *Gump* as well as the *Lethal Weapon* series (1987–1998), *Die Hard* (1988), *Die Hard With a Vengeance* (1995), and the *Men in Black* films (1997, 2003) among others. It is also a paradox that Chappelle faced firsthand in *Robin Hood: Men in Tights* (1993) and while working on his short-lived sitcom *Buddies* (1996).

Significantly, a similar construction of interracial relationships between white and black men is also visible in Hollywood's practice of portraying blacks as what columnist Christopher John Farley refers to as Magical African American Figures (MAAF).[15] In "Hoodoo Economics: White Men's Work and Black Men's Magic in Contemporary American Film," Heather J. Hicks explains, "An important similarity among most of what we can call the MAAF genre is ostensibly directed toward helping and enlightening a white male character."[16] A plethora of films released over the past 10 years, including *What Dreams May Come* (1998), *The Green Mile* (1999), *The Legend of Bagger Vance* (2000), *Bruce Almighty* (2003), and *Hancock* (2008), illustrate Hollywood's continued reliance upon the MAAF. Thus, in the role of Conspiracy Brother, Chappelle calls attention to one of the stereotypical roles that black performers are relegated to in contemporary Hollywood fare.

In addition to his role in *Brother*, *Dave Chappelle's Block Party* (2006) also illustrates the comedian's ties to the black community as well as hip-hop's intelligentsia. Depicting a "block party" hosted by Chappelle in Brooklyn, the comedian "envisioned the film as *Wattstax* for the new millennium."[17] *Wattstax* (1972) chronicles the 1972 Watts Summer Festival, a celebration of black life and music, culminating in a concert at the Los Angeles Coliseum. Richard Pryor, who at the time was emerging as one of the most significant comedians of his generation, emceed the event. Discussing Pryor's comedic discourse Bogle notes that the comedian spoke "in comic and frequently moving terms for a vast underclass of the dissatisfied and the disenfranchised in the ghettos of America. His was ethnic humor, infused with brilliant new insights, sometimes blistering with pain and pathos and trenchant comments on the social system."[18] Pryor's appearance in *Wattstax* alongside prominent R&B artists such as Isaac Hayes, the Staple Singers, and Luther Ingram,[19] further highlighted his connection to the black community. Like Pryor in *Wattstax*, Chappelle emcees *Party*, using his position as one of the most influential comedians of the day to create an authentic and unique experience. The film depicts Chappelle recruiting guests from Ohio and New York to attend the party and the preparation for what he describes as "the concert that he always wanted to see." These events are intercut between performances by Mos Def, Common, Erykah Badu, Kanye West, Talib Kweli, Dead Prez, and The Fugees, among others.

In *Party*, Chappelle demonstrates his love of hip-hop, but more importantly, he aligns himself with the politics of several of the aforementioned performers, who due to their political lyrics typically enjoy success on the fringes of mainstream culture. This is highlighted in one of *Party*'s most memorable sequences which intercuts Dead Prez's performance with an interview of Chappelle who discusses the rapper's lyrics, concerning the murder of Biggie Smalls.[20] Chappelle's discussion of the song is an indictment of corporate domination of the music industry, which emphasizes the manufacturing of "safe" music in the attempt to turn a profit, in favor of the production of more socially relevant compositions. Specifically, Chappelle notes, "You'll never hear that shit on the radio. Never in a million years will you hear somebody say on the radio, 'I'm up for running up on some crackers in city hall.'"[21] Chappelle continues observing, "People have stopped asking who shot Biggie Smalls. But if you're in show business and black, you would wonder about that every day, cause they might get you too."[22] Here, the comedian uses Biggie Smalls's death as a means to point out the value that is placed on black life in America. In Chappelle's assessment, the failure to solve the case or express continued interest in finding the slain rapper's killer sends the message to other high-profile black celebrities, and the black community at large, that their lives are insignificant. This observation is more glaring when considering the fact that the 1996 murder of JonBenet Ramsey continues to make headlines,[23] while the predominantly black population of New Orleans that continues to suffer as a result of Hurricane Katrina, receives little to no media attention.

While *Half Baked*, "First Black Man to Use a White Toilet," *Undercover Brother* and *Block Party* serve as examples of material that seems to be directed at different segments of his fan base, Chappelle's crossover appeal allows him to engage in important social critiques that appeal to his multicultural constituency. His ability to traverse both audiences while exploring significant themes is perhaps best displayed in the *Chappelle's Show* skit, "White People Can't Dance Experiment" (season two; episode 3). In this sketch, Chappelle seeks to expose the longstanding stereotype that white people cannot dance as false. His theory is that "it's not that white people can't dance, but that they respond to different musical instruments." Thus, Chappelle posits that whites love the electric guitar, which he contends, "Speaks directly to the soul of the white person." To help him test his theory, Chappelle recruits John Mayer, who equipped with an electric guitar, will play a crucial role in testing the hypothesis.

"Experiment" proceeds as Chappelle and Mayer visit multiple staged locations, beginning with a corporate boardroom and an upscale restaurant, to see if the whites inhabiting these spaces will respond to the electric guitar. In both instances, Chappelle instructs Mayer to begin playing, which results in the white people uncontrollably breaking into dance. After visiting the boardroom and the restaurant, Chappelle informs viewers that every experiment needs a control so he and Mayer venture to an inner city barber shop where all of the inhabitants are either black or Latino. As Mayer begins playing the electric guitar, the people become visibly annoyed, glaring at him until one of the patrons eventually instructs him to stop. At this point, Chappelle has proven that whites respond to the electric guitar; however, he is not finished. He contends that all blacks respond to the drums while all Latinos enjoy the electric piano. He is joined by ?uestlove Thompson and a fictitious Latino performer that he calls "Sanchez," who play the drums and electronic piano, respectively. Chappelle's theory is again validated when the blacks dance and rap to the drums, while the Latinos begin to Salsa upon hearing the electric piano.

This concludes the experimentation portion of the skit, which cuts to Mayer and Chappelle, standing on a street corner summarizing their research where they are approached by two police officers, one black and one white. The white police officer informs Chappelle that he needs a permit to film on the street. He quickly turns to Mayer and tells him to do something to get them out of the situation. Mayer begins playing Poison's "Every Rose has its

Thorn." The white officer, unable to resist the sound of the electric guitar, becomes distracted and breaks into a dance. Much to Chappelle's dismay, the black officer joins in. When Chappelle confusedly asks the black officer how he knows the song, he responds, "I'm from the suburbs man; I can't help it." The sketch ends with a montage of all of the "participants" in the experiment reacting to the various instruments as title cards read, "People of Earth. No matter what your instrument. Keep dancing."

In "White People Can't Dance Experiment," Chappelle's comic genius is on full display. His appearance with John Mayer and ?uestlove further emphasizes his connection to a multicultural demographic. Furthermore, he focuses the skit on a commonly held stereotype often perpetuated by whites and blacks, alike. When uttered by whites the stereotype is harmless self deprecation, while for blacks it functions as a positive stereotype. In short, black denial of whites' ability to dance serves as validation that African Americans have the market cornered on rhythm, promoting a they can't/but we can binary. Chappelle challenges the "white people can't dance stereotype," attributing the ability to dance on cultural differences. He initially engages in an expanded form of stereotyping concluding, all whites love the electric guitar, all blacks love the drums, and all Latinos love the electric piano. However, in the final scene, Chappelle deconstructs his entire sketch, demonstrating the ridiculousness of stereotyping, by having the black police officer respond to the electric guitar. Attributing the officer's appreciation of the song to his background is significant because it highlights the importance of individual experience. Hence, the sketch demonstrates that ethnic groups are not monolithic and, therefore, should not be characterized by narrow stereotypes.

Ruminations of a Con Man

Chappelle's critiques of America's inherent racism are indeed significant. However, while his comedy is often poignant, the sociopolitical commentary is often neutralized by his reliance upon offensive material, which is at times imbued with the worst aspects of the hip-hop culture that influences his style. Although the comedian's politics are more in line with less visible hip-hop artists, like Dead Prez and Talib Kweli, Chappelle also appears to be influenced by more mainstream stars like 50 Cent and Snoop Dogg, whose lyrics and music videos are often sexist, homophobic, and racially offensive.

In many aspects, the pitfalls of Chappelle's comedy mirror those of hip-hop, which has been the subject of scrutiny for a number of years. Concerns about rap music's portrayal of women were articulated as early as 1993 when "Congresswoman C. Delores Tucker initiated congressional hearings against rap, and became a leader in a national moral movement against it (particularly the lyrics of Tupac Shakur). As a staunch defender of minorities and women, she took a moral stance against the misogyny and sexism of gangsta rap, which, she argued was exemplified by its emphasis on violence, sex, drugs, and criminal behavior."[24] Despite Tucker's efforts, there has been little change in hip-hop's portrayal of women since 1993. Today, artists' lyrics remain misogynistic, seemingly referring to women as "bitches" and "ho's" in each verse. The videos that promote the rappers' songs on the airwaves of MTV, BET, and VH1, are equally objectionable, depicting women as booty shakin,' erotic objects whose sole purpose is to validate the performers' masculinity. As a result popular artists such as Snoop Dogg, Dr. Dre, Eminem, Nelly, and a host of others have been criticized for degrading women. While hip-hop cannot and should not be blamed for all of the sexism that permeates the fabric of American culture, it does play a role in perpetuating narrow and subjugated images of women.[25]

It is easy to provide specific examples of hip-hop's derogatory treatment of women. The hyper-sexualized video vixen gazing into the camera as she performs is practically a cry for critics and scholars summations' of the genre. In comparison, Chappelle's comedy seems less detrimental in its subjugation of women in part, because he rarely focuses on women at all. For example, Chappelle spends a significant amount of time examining racism, yet he rarely, if ever, seriously explores its impact on black women or the gender imbalance that exists for them in America. Positioning black femininity as either nonexistent or a secondary cause in the struggle for equality in favor of salvaging black masculine identity, neither begins nor ends with Dave Chappelle. The comedian is part of an ongoing problem that has historically manifested itself in varying forms. For example, the typical discussion of the Civil Rights movement often focuses on the exploits of Malcolm X, Martin Luther King, Jr., and John F. Kennedy, with little to no mention of the involvement of black female activists, Fannie Lou Hamer, Diane Nash, or Septima Clark. Describing her time as activist, Clark recalled, "I found all over the South that whatever the man said had to be right. They had the whole say. The woman couldn't say a thing."[26] Additionally, Calvin Hernton asserts that the "masculine perspective itself, concerning the manhood of the black race, has always occupied center stage in the drama of Afro-American literature."[27] The notion that women's rights are secondary to black males' was sometimes appropriated by black females. For example, when asked about her appearance as the seemingly pro Women's Liberation title character in the blaxploitation film *Cleopatra Jones* (1973), Tamara Dobson responded, "I don't believe in that for black people. We're trying to free our men."[28] As these examples illustrate, Chappelle's failure to recognize black women's needs continues to reinforce a longstanding hierarchy that warrants change.

Not only does Chappelle fail to seriously acknowledge the struggles of black females, when his material does addresses the opposite gender, it is often a disservice to all women regardless of their ethnicities. As Haggins notes, "Women, in general, don't occupy a significant space in Chappelle's comedy except as ironic foils and punch lines."[29] Hence, the material is frequently sophomoric and insignificant, with an undercurrent of "boys will be boys." *Chappelle's Show* sketches "It's a Wonderful Chest," and "New York Boobs" serve as prime examples. In the former, Chappelle depicts a young woman who after cursing the size of her chest, realizes the error of her ways when an angel (Chappelle) appears, showing her how difficult her life would be if she had a smaller bust. In "New York Boobs," Chappelle again displays his childish obsession with breasts, paying homage to New York women with large cup sizes. Unfortunately, the easygoing manner, in which Chappelle presents such skits to his largely male fan base, seems to excuse them for their misogyny.

In addition to relying upon juvenile themes when focusing on women, Chappelle's sketches and stand-up routines are permeated with the word "bitch." He regularly uses the slur with little to no regard given to its sexist connotations. The most prominent examples are his oft imitated catch phrases "I'm rich, bitch!" and "I'm Rick James bitch!" While these lines can be humorous in their respective contexts, the over-reliance on the word "bitch" sometimes deemphasizes the point of Chappelle's significant material. For example, in *For What It's Worth* (2004) Chappelle jokingly expresses his reluctance to criticize the Bush Administration's policies, citing the controversy that surrounded the Dixie Chicks when as a protest against the War in Iraq, the group's lead singer (Natalie Maines) told a London audience, "Just so you know, we're ashamed the president of the United States is from Texas."[30] In discussing the severe backlash that the group encountered as a result of the comment, Chappelle refers to the Dixie Chicks as "bitches who can sing." Although the bit was supposed to call attention to the dichotomy that exists between whites and blacks in America, the derogatory comment detracts from the point, potentially offending women and progressive men, alike.

In addition to engaging in misogynistic behavior, Chappelle also perpetuates homophobia, which is rampant in popular entertainment and American culture at large. In *The Celluloid Closet: Homosexuality in the Movies*, Vito Russo chronicles gay and lesbian representation in motion pictures, defining three prominent archetypes that have historically circumscribed members of the marginalized group. His paradigm includes the "Sissy," the

"Victim," and the "Villain."[31] Of these stereotypical characters, the "Sissy" or the comical, effeminate male character has been most the most evident. As Russo explains, the "Sissy" perpetuates negative stereotypes about gay men because "it is supposed to be an insult to call a man effeminate, for it means he is like a woman and therefore not as valuable as a 'real' man."[32] The "Sissy' is visible in early motion pictures like *The Soilers* (1923), *The Front Page* (1931), *His Girl Friday* (1940), and countless others.[33] The archetype successfully made the transition from the silver screen to television and currently remains a staple of both forms entertainment. For example, *Queer Eye for the Straight Guy* (2003–present) *Will and Grace* (1998–2006), *The Break Up* (2006), and *Ugly Betty* (2006–present) all present variations of the "Sissy." In each instance, the effeminate male characters function as comic relief rather than serious explorations of gay life.

In addition to films and television programs, homophobia is pervasive in hip-hop lyrics. In fact, it is commonplace to hear terms such as "punk," "faggot," "bitch nigga," and "bitch ass nigga," which are used to emasculate men in the same manner as the "sissy" archetype. In the documentary, *Hip-hop: Beyond Beats and Rhymes*, director Byron Hurt comments, "You know what I think is deep? Just the fact that you hear so many brothas calling other brothas 'bitches,' and bitch ass niggas. It's amazing that we haven't really talked about it more, cause to me, that's just as pervasive as the misogyny."[34] However, when considering the hyper-masculinity that dominates hip-hop culture the fact that homophobia is so deeply entrenched in the genre is actually not surprising at all. As Michael Eric Dyson explains, "The greatest insult that a man might imagine for another man is to assume that he's less than a man and to assign him the very derogatory terms that one associates with women."[35] Thus, rappers such as 50 Cent, JaRule, and Eminem, among others, who are constantly engaged in the process of reaffirming their manhood through sex, violence, and misogyny, employ homophobic rhetoric as a means to further validate their own masculinity.

The significance of David Chappelle's comedy is hindered by his homophobia, which manifests itself in much the same way as it does in the hip-hop culture that influences his comic persona. Given the fact that Chappelle belongs to an ethnic group that has been historically subjugated, it would seem that the comedian would be above participating in the marginalization of another group. Nevertheless, there are instances in his comedy where he assumes the position of the oppressor. For example, in the opening of *For What It's Worth*, which was filmed at the Filmore Hotel in San Francisco, Chappelle is met with a lukewarm reaction from the crowd when he begins his performance lamenting, "Thanks for makin' a nigga feel welcome in the gayest place on earth. I didn't really think it was that gay at first and then I wandered into that Castro and I was like, this is America's anus right here. This shit is deep!" While terms like "That's so gay" and "Gaydar" have become chic phrases in the national lexicon, they perpetuate homophobia. Chappelle's usage of the phrase "the gayest place on earth" to describe San Francisco, functions in a similar manner and is offensive. He also takes his insult further by alluding to gay sexual relations between men, which he openly admitted that he felt was gross during a *Chappelle's Show* monologue.

Perhaps the most disturbing example of the comedian's homophobia occurs in a *Chappelle's Show* episode dedicated to airing clips that Comedy Central network executives initially considered too controversial for TV. Given *Chappelle's Show*'s runaway success, the powers that be were ultimately persuaded to allow Chappelle to air the segments. Among the material is a Frontline piece titled, "A Gay World" (Season Two; Episode 11), which depicts a society where everyone is gay. Chappelle's vision of a gay utopia only includes men and falls back upon the "Sissy" archetype. The first vignette presents a gay department of motor vehicles where patrons pose for their driver's licenses as if they are at a photo shoot. The skit ends with a worker speaking in the stereotypical exaggerated lisp often associated with gay men stating, "Congratulations your license is so ready!" He hands the customer his new personalized plate that reads, "ASS MILK." Other portions of the skit depict a butcher who chops meat while wearing nothing but his underwear and an apron, a leather clad landscaper who dances behind a moving lawnmower, and a pair of effeminate prizefighters weighing in before a "gay" boxing match. Also included is a sketch featuring a gay chapter of the KKK, which Chappelle acknowledges is offensive to both gays and blacks when introducing the skit. The vignette opens with a Klansman removing his hood to speak with the Frontline reporter, commenting with the "gay lisp," "It's hot like the dickens. As I was saying, we hate, too, but we do it differently. We do it in a special way. We do it with compassion." The sketch then cuts to a clip of the Klansman approaching the front door of a black couple as they are exiting their home. He greets the couple commenting, "Good morning. I'm with the KKK. We had a meeting and we were talking and we'd be more comfortable if you guys left the neighborhood. Have you considered going back to Africa?"

While screening the "A Gay World" sketch for the audience, Chappelle makes it a point to repeatedly emphasize the fact that the skit was created in fun. However, when considering the comedian's comments in San Francisco as well as his sentiments about sex between gay men, it is difficult to view the sketch as mere fun or as a satire about the ridiculousness of homophobia. In *Prime Time Closet: A History of Gays and Lesbians on TV*, Stephen Tropiano outlines several social myths that are commonly held about gays. The popular misconceptions include, "Homosexuals are identifiable on the basis of their appearance and behavior, All gay men are effeminate, and All gay men ... are interested in one thing: sex."[36] While Tropiano seeks to expose the absurdity of primetime television's perpetuation of these social myths, the humor in Chappelle's "A Gay World" is derived from reinforcing them. Significantly, all of the actors in the sketch use stereotypical speech patterns and engage in effeminate behavior, which are clearly meant to code them as gay. Furthermore, an undercurrent of perverse sexual yearning is apparent in some of the actors' performances. Thus, instead of providing a poignant critique of homophobia in manner comparable to his examinations of racism, "A Gay World" exposes Chappelle's inhibitions about gays and lesbians.

In addition to perpetuating homophobia, Chappelle's comedy also relies heavily upon the use of the word "nigger," which is often at the center of conversations regarding America's racial politics. Derived from the Latin word for the color black (niger), nigger "did not originate as a slur but took on a derogatory connotation over time."[37] According to Randall Kennedy, author of *Nigger: The Strange Career of a Troublesome Word*, "No one knows precisely when or how "niger" turned derisively into "nigger" and attained a pejorative meaning. We do know, however, that by the end of the nineteenth century, "nigger" had already become a familiar and influential insult."[38]

Since emerging as a derogatory term, "nigger" has been used as a tool of subjugation on multiple fronts. First and foremost, the term has been historically used by whites to suppress blacks since the days of slavery. However, whites often also used the term to denigrate other whites by reducing them to the same status as blacks. Hosea Easton explains that "often the earliest instruction white adults gave to white children prominently featured the word 'nigger,' reprimanding them for being 'worse than niggers'" and often disciplining them, telling them that unless they behaved they would be "consigned to the 'nigger seat,' which was, of course, a place of shame."[39] Other disturbing examples of this include the following phrases that rely upon "nigger" as a means of insult:

> *Niggerish*: Acting in a lazy and irresponsible manner.
> *Niggerlipping*: Wetting the end of a cigarette while smoking it.
> *Nigger luck*: Exceptionally good luck, emphasis on undeserved.
> *Nigger rich*: Deeply in debt but flamboyant.
> *Nigger tip*: Leaving a small tip or no tip in a restaurant.
> *Nigger work*: Demeaning, menial tasks.[40]

In addition to the aforementioned uses of "nigger," the term has a long-standing tradition in American popular culture. As Kennedy points out, "Throughout the 1800s and for much of the 1900s as well, writers of popular music generated countless lyrics that lampooned blacks."[41] Songs such as

"I Guess It Wasn't De Niggas Dis Time," "Who's Dat Nigga Dar A-Peepin?," "Niggas Get on the Boat," and "He's Just a Nigger" serve as prime examples. In the latter title the chorus begins, "He's just a nigger, when you've said dat you've said it all."[42]

Despite its cultural baggage, the "N-word," as it has come to be called, continues to be used today. The word is so powerful that when uttered by racists toward blacks, it can evoke a range of emotions including fear, hurt, sadness, and rage. However, when used by blacks in social relationships, the word can be used to debase or as a term of endearment. In the former context, a phrase like "bad niggers" can refer to blacks that are in trouble with the law, while in the latter context the same phrase elicits pride by pointing out blacks that bravely confront the laws of white patriarchy.[43] In popular culture, the variant of the "N-word," "nigga," which is used in phrases like "That's my nigga," or "What up nigga?," is considered a friendly salutation and is prevalent in the lexicon of the hip-hop generation and the black community at large.[44]

This brief history of the "N-word" provides insight into the controversial nature of the expression, which in the author's opinion, should not be discounted by those who include the word in their vocabulary. In a *60 Minutes* interview, Dave Chappelle demonstrates an understanding of the power of the "N-word" commenting, "If you could sum up the story of America in a word, ['nigger'] might be the word. It has connotations in it that society has never dealt with."[45] Even with a deep understanding of the power of the "N-word," Chappelle constantly utters the term in his stand-up routines, movie roles, and on *Chappelle's Show* as a term of endearment and as a comic device. As the comedian notes, "[It] used to be a word of oppression. But for me it feels more like an act of freedom."[46] Indeed, Chapelle's usage of the "N-word" is seemingly in line with Professor Clarence Major's assertion that among black people "[it] is a racial term with undertones of warmth and good will—reflecting ... a tragicomic sensibility that is aware of black history."[47]

The *Chappelle's Show* skit "The Niggar Family" (Season Two; Episode 2), which centers on a naïve white family—Fred, Emily, and Tim—whose last name is a play upon the "N-word," perfectly illustrates the comedian's use of the expression in the aforementioned context. A parody of 1950s sitcoms like *Father Knows Best* (1954–1960) and *Leave It to Beaver* (1957–1963), the sketch is shot in black and white and depicts the Niggar family as oblivious to the negative connotations surrounding the sound of their surname. Consequently, part of the skit's humor derives from the Niggar family's inadvertent perpetuation of black stereotypes while engaging in every day conversation. For example, the sketch opens with Fred showing his wife Emily a picture of his sister's newborn baby daughter. She looks at the photo and cheerfully responds, "She's got those Niggar lips." Next the father asks if their son Tim is still asleep. When Emily informs him that he is, Fred replies, "He sure is one lazy Niggar." Chappelle joins the skit, doing his best Eddie "Rochester" Anderson impersonation as Clifton, the colored milkman. Much like Jack Benny's Rochester always seemed to know the score, Clifton is fully aware of the dual meaning and the cultural implications behind the family's last name. For example, when Clifton informs Fred that he has forgotten to pay his bill he comments, "I hate to bother you about this, but, well you didn't pay your bill last week and I know how forgetful you Niggars can be when it comes to paying bills." Furthermore as he leaves Clifton quips, "Peace Niggars!" The remainder of the sketch continues in this manner using "the 'N-word' as a means to list every possible stereotype about 'niggers' in an off-kilter context."[48]

"The Niggar Family" is an interesting example of the way that the "N-word" can be used to critique racial politics. The sketch relies on the use of a homonym, as well as the audience's familiarity with stereotyping. The combination of the two, lend to the sketch's shocking and significant humor while calling attention to America's past and present race problems. The skit's appearance on *Chappelle Show* is significant because it critiques 1950s sitcoms, which were either devoid of black performers or presented them as one-dimensional caricatures. At the time "The Niggar Family" aired, Dave Chappelle was one of the most prominent figures in the entertainment industry and a symbol of black success. On the other hand, the audience's understanding of the jokes is predicated upon the knowledge that the "N-word" remains a loaded and controversial word. Exploring it in a comical manner exposes the ridiculousness of stereotypes, while demonstrating just how deeply racism continues to permeate the fabric of American society.

As effective as "The Niggar family" is as a commentary, the skit's significance is negated by Dave Chappelle, who commented that he and his writing partner "just thought it was funny."[49] It is disturbing that a word with such deep connotations that it has been described as "the nuclear bomb of racial epithets, the most obnoxious racial epithet in contemporary American lexicon, and the filthiest, dirtiest, nastiest word in the English language,"[50] can be toyed with so casually by someone who at times acknowledges the cultural baggage attached to the term. Perhaps Chappelle is given too much credit. It should be noted that the comedian asserted, "I'm not concerned when black intellectuals say the 'N-word' is awful. If people stop saying the 'N-word' is everything going to be equal? Is a rainbow going to come out of the sky, and all of a sudden things are going to be better for black people?"[51] The response to Chappelle's query is a resounding "No!" This critique is not meant to suggest that eradicating its use will bring an end to America's race problems; however, keeping the word's sociohistorical legacy in mind will perhaps make certain that it is not abused. At the present time, Chappelle uses the "N-word" far too casually, distorting the significance of sketches like the "Niggar Family" as well as his other more political comedic material.

The purpose of this chapter has been to critique the comedy of Dave Chappelle, with the intent of highlighting the brilliance and the shortcomings of the comedian's stand-up routines, film roles, and groundbreaking series. Deconstructing the comedian's work is indeed a complex task. However, an answer to the question posed in the title of this chapter, "Comic Genius or Con Man?" is hopefully now more apparent. As Bambi Haggins contends, "In order for the comedic discourse produced by the black comic to be effectively edifying, it must be self aware *and* self reflexive — able to elicit thought along with laughter."[52] As this examination reveals, Chappelle's comedy is self aware *and* self reflexive. The analysis of *Undercover Brother*, *Block Party*, and "White People Can't Dance Experiment" illustrate that Chappelle's material often combines humor with relevant critiques of America's racial politics, eliciting thought among his multigenerational and multicultural audience. However, taking Haggins's summation into account, Chappelle's comedy often fails at times because, as this discussion articulates, instead of uplifting people, it at times marginalizes women and gays, while offending critics of the "N-word." The discussion of *For What It's Worth*, "A Gay World," and "The Niggar Family" perfectly illustrate how Chappelle's misogyny, homophobia, and contradictory comments about the "N-word" can complicate readings of his work. Thus, the answer to the question at the present time is that Chappelle traverses the line functioning as comic genius and con man, both critiquing necessary societal evils, while perpetuating others.

Despite the shortcomings of his comedy, there is hope for Chappelle. Significantly, laughter from a white crew member that seemed inappropriate during the filming of a skit called "The Nigger Pixie" prompted Chappelle to reconsider his racially infused humor and played a role in his subsequent departure from *Chappelle's Show*. It is this kind of recognition that leads to true change. The hope is that Chappelle will eventually consider the misogyny, homophobia, and his use of the "N-word" through a similar lens and redefine his politics.

3

The Comedian Is a "Man"

Gender Performance in the Comedy of Dave Chappelle

ANDREA CUMBO

"No one will notice," the woman in workout attire says to her friend who has forgotten to wear a sports bra for their jog that day. But, of course, all the men *do* notice, making comments like "Look at those knockers" and "Whoo-Eee" as she jogs past, her ample bosom bouncing almost to her chin. Humiliated, the woman runs, crying, into the locker room, where she encounters a man in a white outfit (played by Dave Chappelle) who asks her what is wrong. She tells him she wishes she had smaller breasts, and he — the good "angel"— shows her what life would be like without her big boobs. So begins the skit "It's a Wonderful Chest" in the first season of *Chappelle's Show*.

The current fascination with political correctness may lead many individuals to think that this skit was offensive to women, particularly to those of us who consider ourselves feminists— and perhaps these people are right. Perhaps Dave Chappelle *is* setting women back forty years, just as many of his critics charged him in regard to African Americans when he aired the sketch "The Black White Supremacist" (Season One; Episode 1). But I don't think so. While Chappelle's comedy skits and stand-up performances *seem* to reify the traditional and stereotypical notions of gender that much feminist debate has attempted to disrupt, his work actually helps to defy the hierarchical ordering and dualistic theory of gender and undermines stereotypical concepts of gender roles and gendered identity. This disruption and undercutting is achieved through three equally important elements of Chappelle's writing: his role as commentator, the use of humor, and the utilization of repetition. Thus, Chappelle's comedy destabilizes the very stereotypes and dualities that he seems to reinforce.

For decades, feminists have been laying out the complex theoretical and social underpinnings of popular gender constructions, seeking to break down the traditional duality of "man" and "woman" and to destroy the phallocentric, patriarchal hierarchy of men as more focal to human existence. Laura Mulvey's 1975 seminal work "Visual Pleasure and Narrative Cinema" posits that film complicates, but reinforces, the male as viewer and female as viewee. Going far beyond highlighting a woman's to-be-looked-at-ness, cinema builds the way she is to be looked at into the spectacle itself ... cinematic codes create a gaze, a world and an object, thereby, producing an illusion cut to the measure of desire. It is these cinematic codes and their relationship to formative external structures that must be broken down before mainstream film and the pleasure it provides can be challenged.[1] Thus, Mulvey began a long conversation on performativity and the role of the gaze in gender formation.

Judith Butler, in the early 1990s, continued this conversation in such works as *Gender Trouble: Feminism and the Subversion of Identity* and "Imitation and Gender Insubordination," challenging the notion that not only should the male gaze not subjugate women but also that such binaries of gender — "man" and "woman" — are false in and of themselves. She contends, "It may be that the very categories of sex, of sexual identity, of gender are produced or maintained in the *effects* of this compulsory performance, effects which are disingenuously lined up within a causal or expressive sequence that the heterosexual norm produces to legitimate itself as the origin of all sex."[2] According to Butler, all gender is a drag performance, a putting on of identity rather than a revealing of identity.

Using Butler's theory as a grounding, Diane Elam then argues, in her work *Feminism and Deconstruction: Ms. en Abyme*, that theories of feminism must be set against theories of deconstruction so that each theoretical impetus can tease apart and complicate the other, breaking down all theory into its practical and often political pieces. She states:

> No more authoritative deconstructions of literary texts, no more authoritative statements on the essence of woman. To speak without recourse to the meta-language of authority is to speak as singularities, to attempt to do justice in singular cases, rather than just once and for all. It is this dispersal of the modernist horizon of social justice that feminism and deconstruction work for.[3]

Her work becomes a call for social action that takes theory beyond the walls of the academy and into the singular existences—the streets of Dave Chappelle's world.

If a viewer examines Chappelle's work closely, it becomes apparent that his humor is breaking down, not reinforcing, those very dichotomies that

Mulvey, Butler, and Elam challenge. First, his comedy conflates viewer and viewee, dissolving the space between audience and performer and calling overt attention to the performativity of all communication. Secondly, he plays with conceptions of gender through the use of persona and humor i.e. his satirical portray of Prince. Finally, his sketches and stand-up routines tease out complex questions of identity using the tools of deconstruction and the language of popular culture.

To understand the complex rhetorical and political action that takes place in Chappelle's humor, it's important to comprehend the reaction that many viewers assume of so-called feminists and gender-theorists and to conceive of that very assumption as itself sexist and biased. This is easily seen in Chappelle's "It's a Wonderful Chest" skit. To the "average" viewer (who we'll define as an educated, middle class individual of either gender or any race), this skit is funny simply because it plays on both the stereotypes of women and men — women for their willingness to accept their role, as Mulvey puts it, as image and men for their unquestioning acceptance as spectator. The average viewer understands that this sketch is poking fun at these stereotypes (and also, perhaps, at the truth that lies deep beneath them) and, thus, finds the sketch funny as he/she sees himself/herself in that sketch as either the big-breasted woman or the male and female acquaintances — audience becomes participant.

These same viewers, however, may not be able imagine that a person who is a feminist would ever find these ideas funny because perhaps that feminist would be too "offended" to appreciate the humor. Herein lies the bias — that average viewers may assume that those who are not average by their standards (a bias in and of itself), those who are more educated, more radicalized, more "political," even, more angry — could not appreciate the humor in stereotype or caricature. The feminist intelligentsia becomes humorless activists, unable to appreciate a good joke.

But perhaps there is something to the conceptions of the "average" viewer. Perhaps some cannot see the humor in a sketch about breasts, the very part of female anatomy that is so often — along with the vagina — the central focus of the male gaze; the ability to laugh is an act of power, the very thing that is often stripped of women when they become "object" rather than subject. But it is in the inversion, and eventual decimation, of this dichotomy that Chappelle's comedy shows its strength. By pulling the discussion of this binary out of the academy and "taking it to the streets," and by using the act of actual performance to highlight the performativity of gender roles, Chappelle opens up this theoretical discussion to the public, becoming a philosopher of the people. As he says to Maya Angelou in their episode of *Iconoclasts*, "I'm a pop culture figure."[4] The comedian of the public becomes the comedian of the theoretical sphere; the space between popular culture and academic culture dissolves in brusque humor that is stripped of academic jargon.

The most crucial element of Chappelle's deconstruction of gender stereotypes and systems is the comedian's persona itself. He is actor, commentator, and object of commentary, implicating and self-implicating. He plays part of both teacher and student, performer and audience member. Chappelle's role as emcee and commentator is never absent from his performance. Before each sketch in *Chappelle's Show* and every joke in his standup routines, Chappelle establishes his role as the viewer's surrogate in the sketch; the audience member is to see what he sees, not necessarily what the audience member's actual perspective on the situation would be, if it were "real." This position as surrogate is crucial, according to Mulvey, for in film or — in the case of *Chappelle's Show*— television the viewer, on one level, looks for his or her surrogate on the screen. Thus, a man might ally himself with Sidney Poitier's character in *Raisin in the Sun* (1961), a woman with Ruby Dee. In the case of Chappelle's comedy, his introductions ally the viewer, regardless of their biological sex, with Chappelle; thus, each audience member takes on Chappelle's viewpoint on the situation, and, because Chappelle gazes with an eye to humor, the humor is what the audience sees.

Take, for instance, his introduction to "Nat's Holiday Special," where he explicitly refers to hip-hop's objectification of women and says he tires of hearing talk like this is a "new thing" (Season One; Episode One). The Cole sketch exemplifies the comedian's point that men have been objectifying women for decades. By highlighting what he wants to reader to note, by calling it out using the language of oppression — "the objectification of women" — and by using the forum of comedy, Chappelle sets the reader up to see the sketch as laughable and, thus, unacceptable as typical male behavior.

In another example, Chappelle introduces his stand-up bit about women's attire, dubbed on the ubiquitous YouTube as "Hoes Uniform," by saying, "The only thing in our society that bothers me the most is that men and women don't get along no more."[5] And here we see, explicitly, the most crucial element that makes humor work as a deconstructive tool: the narrator. Chappelle is priming the audience (as most comedians do) and bringing them to his perspective. He gains their trust, elicits their affection, and contextualizes the joke, thereby pulling it out of the world of actuality and bringing it into the world of performativity.[6] Therefore, nothing he says is meant to be taken as reality — or as that which can be seen as appropriate for everyday interaction. Instead his comedy becomes pedantic (but not pedestrian) and expository (but not moral). His act of setting up the joke brings the humor to a level above the norm, making it a meta-narrative experience.

Returning to "It's a Wonderful Chest" (Season One; Episode Three), we can see Chappelle's role very clearly. Not only does he, on the set of *Chappelle's Show*, set up this sketch, he also appears in the sketch itself as a seemingly innocent and benevolent participant who only, in the end, identifies himself as a man, a man with a motive. But throughout the sketch, it's his distance from the social situation that establishes the remove at which viewers participate in the situation — he is a guide, not a man or a woman. At the end of the piece, where he comments directly on the woman's breasts, he still is acting in a meta-narrative capacity as he calls attention, once again, to the complex levels of degradation inherent in the situation. Ultimately, his role in this skit — as both guide and man — becomes completely undermined as his character confesses to not having taken this trip as either guide or man but simply as a person "high on crack." His lesson becomes delusion. Chappelle's only static role is as deconstructor of not only gender hierarchy but also story itself. The skit implies that no one's role is static; no one is always what they seem. This movement with the sketch coupled with Chappelle's preceding commentary increases the levels of complexity and the places of self-implication for the audience. Nothing and no one stays the same or is beyond the reach of this commentary.

So with his complex position as writer, actor, commentator, and citizen intact, Chappelle begins to crack apart the phallocentric hierarchy that places one of the sexes above the other. In "Hoes Uniform," Chappelle highlights the difference in perceptions between men and women. He describes a woman dressed up for her night at the club with her friends— with "half her ass hanging out of her skirt" and her "titties all pushed up together." He points out that men at the club begin to think of this kind of woman sexually (to put it slightly more academically than Chappelle does) and the woman reacts by quipping, "Just because I am dressed this way does not make me a whore." He continues the bit by saying, "Gentlemen, that is true, just because they dress that way, doesn't mean they are a certain way. Don't ever forget it. But ladies, you must understand that is fucking confusing." He then illustrates his point by conjecturing what would happen if he dressed as a police office and wondered why people mistook him for one: "Just because I'm dressed like a police officer, doesn't make me a police officer." He closes the joke by saying, "Fine, you are a not a whore, but you are wearing a whore's uniform. So misunderstandings can happen." Here again, Chappelle plays out the games of appearance as they do and do not reveal identity. The uniforms of human lives, the skit shows, lend no clue to human nature ... just because he looks that way.

What is also noteworthy in this sketch is the work that this performance (a performance both literally, for he is on stage in front of an audience, and politically, for he is deconstructing standards of gendered behavior) works to deconstruct who is "right" and who is "wrong" in this sketch. Men are not free from culpability in their sexualization of women, nor are women free from the behavior that often brings on such sexualization. Consequently, the hierarchy — of men as objectifiers of women and of women as simple victims to this situation — is collapsed — no one is right here. Most importantly, the women are held culpable for the behavior of men, a fact which may seem in opposition to the feminist movement where women seek no longer to be objectified in anyway, but a fact which is, actually, empowering for it gives women a place to act (or not to act) to remove their own subjugators.

Take another example: "New York Boobs" (Season One; Episode Four). The premise of the sketch, as established by Chappelle in his introductory monologue, is that he has found a great way to comment on women's breasts without offending them — he awards them ribbons for "great New York boobs." (It's vital to note here that he is even further deepening the level of commentary by calling attention to the very offense that women might take from the clip that follows.) A camera crew on the streets of New York City follows Chappelle around in his persona as a flamboyant man with an ambiguous sexual orientation, and the character compliments women's breasts, pinning ribbons to their chests as they grin awkwardly. Both the nature of Chappelle's preceding commentary, which calls out the perceived tendency of men to look at breasts and the corresponding practice of women to react defensively, and the sardonic, satiric nature of the sketch itself lend a place and space for commentary about the ways that men and women respond to the "other" gender when playing out their traditionally-conceived roles as gazer and object of the gaze. There, Chappelle calls out the stereotypical hierarchy for comment. But it is at the end of the sketch where Chappelle pins a ribbon on the chest of man — a moment that is brief and perfunctory but important — that the true absurdity of such gender binaries is called out. Chappelle's choice to highlight this particular anatomical feature on a person who is biologically male calls out the arbitrary and socially constructed nature of gendered, anatomical fascination. Thus, by taking on the role as what Mulvey terms "the surrogate," Chappelle guides the viewer's gaze away from the traditional binary of gender into the genderless world of humor.

According to linguist Thomas C. Veatch, in his article "A Theory of Humor," "humor occurs when it seems that things are normal (N) while at the same time something seems wrong (V)."[7] In other words, humor develops when a viewer sees a situation that seems commonplace or normal but also sees that norm violated or disrupted by satire, exaggeration, ridicule, or absurd repetition. Take, for example, the "It's a Wonderful Chest" sketch. In this skit, two women are jogging together, and one person forgets an important piece of attire; this woman is, therefore, ridiculed and gawked at. This situation may seem sad or embarrassing to some because it elicits sympathy for the braless woman on some levels, but it should also seem normal to many viewers. Most people know themselves to have been, at one time or another, the gazer or the object of the gaze. This ability to identify with both parts of the signifier/signified relationship is particularly strong for women or other oppressed people groups such as homosexuals or people of color, for it is historically only the white male in America who seems able to see himself beyond the signified, a man creating his own destiny. Even so, both roles— object and subject — are played out in the sketch; thus, most viewers understand the event and emotion of teasing and ridicule.[8] Therefore, the viewer perceives this situation as commonplace, something they could witness or participate in during their normal course of existence. As Veatch contends,

> Situations in which nothing seems wrong to the perceiver are not perceived as funny. Note that the perception of a subject moral violation in a situation, V, is a function of both the situation and the perceiver. That is, a somewhat different situation may have no apparent violation [i.e. it may seem quite normal to someone with delusions to see an angel appear in a locker room] and thus lose its humor.[9]

Thus, normality is in the eye of the beholder. Therefore, women, who may perceive such behavior by men and other women as normal, may find this situation not humorous simply because it is the norm.

This sketch, however, violates that norm, just as Veatch's theory requires, when it begins to venture into ridicule — i.e., the men's boisterous statements about the woman's breasts such as situation would seem normal only in the most traditionally masculine of environments where women have been deemed only as objects for admiration, not living beings— and then into satire as it takes on the flavor of the popular film *It's a Wonderful Life* (1947). As the sketch progresses, the framework of normal existence fades away, normality is violated, and a place for humor is created. The everyday first becomes cause for laughter, which in return allows, or creates, room for contemplation and even discussion.

But our "average" viewers could wisely argue that not all people will find such a violation of the norm to be humorous. Take, for example, a woman with large breasts who has wished for just such a breast reduction, perhaps even had a surgical procedure to do so—could she or would she find a spoof on something that may be a very painful part of her life to be funny? Veatch accepts the possibility that she might not find humor in this situation as part of the nature of humor — not everything is funny to everyone. He states, "a

different perceiver, who may have different views on the way things are supposed to be, or different affective commitments to those views, will consequently perceive humor differently. Thus humor perception is doubly
subjective, not only in that it is a psychological event in a subjective perceived, but also in that different subjects may differ in their perceptions."[10]
An individual person's subjective experiences determine that which they feel
is normal or that which they feel is overtly violatory. If either of these require-
ments is not reached — if the situation is too far-fetched or too offensive or
taboo for an individual — then a given individual will not find the situation
humorous. Therefore, our "average" viewers are right — some people will not
find Dave Chappelle humorous.[11] To play out this idea on the level of gender
binaries, it can be assumed, then, that an individual who finds the disruption of traditional gender roles to be either too obvious or too transgressive
will also find this sketch, and most of Chappelle's humor, less than humorous, perhaps even offensive.

To illustrate, let's return to "Nat's Holiday Special," where Chappelle
spoofs Nat King Cole while ironically claiming to condone the objectification
of women as seen in the hip-hop industry. Interestingly, Chappelle — a self-
professed lover of hip-hop — seems not only to be commenting simply on the
objectification of women here but particularly of this objectification as seen
in hip-hop. Given the context of comedy, his comments that may seem, at
first glance, to be about the victimization of hip-hop for something that is a
much larger social issue, actually indict hip-hop as well, leaving no one,
including himself, beyond the pale of critique.

In this sketch, there are many things that seem conventional — the black
and white images of Dave Chappelle dressed at Nat King Cole, the setting
with a wide curtain in that backgrounds as viewers would expect of TV shows
from that era, the smooth music in the background. To most, this scene is,
in some ways, what is expected of a Nat King Cole special. But in this same
sketch, the violations that produce humor are myriad: the language of Chappelle's character including expletives like *bitches* and *fuck*; slang that is both
anachronistic and seemingly unlike the popular concept of Cole, the overtly
sexualized treatment that Cole shows to the woman in the sketch when he
pours champagne over her and tells her where to rub it into her body. These
obvious violations, while funny for many, may indeed cause offense and even
anger in those who revere Cole or who see this treatment of women, even in
comedy, as heinous and beyond the pale of reasonable entertainment. Additionally, and at a deeper level, individuals who hold hip-hop and the treatment of women that Chappelle is ridiculing here as unique, acceptable or
even valuable may also find this reference offensive and, therefore, not
humorous. Thus, the very transgressions that produce humor may, indeed,

also incite disgust or anger depending on the viewer's own experience or worldview.

According to Veatch, it is also possible that humor will fail if the viewer considers the content too commonplace. Therefore, if by chance an individual viewer thinks the act of pouring champagne on a woman and asking her to rub it into her skin is normal and not taboo in the public sphere, then the affect of having this scene be part of what is obviously — by rhetorical situation — an attempt at humor also undermines the belief that such practices — be they exaggerated or seemingly normal — are acceptable. The person who takes the scene as normative transforms from simply a member of the audience into a target of the commentary — witness becomes participant. Chappelle's comedy "free[s] the look of the camera into its materiality in time and space and the look of the audience into dialectics and passionate detachment."[12] The humor subverts the practices that it seemingly purports to support and draws in the viewer just as Mulvey hoped it would, leaving no one outside the purview of commentary or critique.

Not only does his comedy implicate the viewer, Chappelle's metanarrative breaks down the socially accepted binary system of gender: Man And Woman. Again, at first blush, it may seem he is reifying the differences between men and women, calling apart "what men do" as different from "what women do." But in fact, since these differences are highlighted in the midst of a comedy performance, they are also collapsed, leaving a vacuum and a void where people can define gender without the binaries. Here the work of theorists Judith Butler and Diane Elam becomes vital. In *Gender Trouble*, Butler claims that to displace gender norms it is essential NOT to ignore the traditional binary of men and women or to try to speak of that binary in terms that do not take it into account, but instead to interrogate the binary directly through repetition of terms and ideas. She puts her claim this way:

> The task is not whether to repeat, but how to repeat, or indeed, to repeat and, through a radical proliferation of gender to *displace* the very gender norms that enable the repetition itself. There is no ontology of gender on which we might construct a politics, for gender ontologies always operate within established political contexts as normative injunctions, determining what qualifies as intelligible sex, invoking and consolidating the productive constraints on sexuality, setting the prescriptive requirements whereby sexed or gendered bodies come into cultural intelligibility.[13]

It is this "cultural intelligibility" that Chappelle is interrogating. He takes as normative these very differences that he calls out and by calling them out over and over again breaks them down and takes down with them the "nor-

mative injunctions" that political thought puts into place. His repetition of
the "difference" disintegrates the two-gender theory of identity.

Again, reference to a sketch seems necessary for illustration. In the stand-
up bit, "What Women and Men Want," Chappelle notes that women often
say, "Chivalry is dead." And then, he points out — to boisterous audience
laughter — that "women killed it."[14] He continues by saying, "We're just not
going to see eye to eye on this issue; we're just not. Our tests in life are different. A woman's test in life is material; a man's test in life is a woman." Here,
again, it would be easy to say that Chappelle is simply playing off stereotypes
to get a laugh, but in fact, if we consider Butler's argument for repetition, it
is this very restatement, reemphasis of these ideas that begins to break them
down. In this piece, Chappelle even goes so far as to say "men are hunters,"
an idea that most people would dispel, at least outwardly. But by calling it
out repeatedly — and by calling out those people who believe it — he begins
to disrupt the thought patterns that support this binary. The repetition of the
binary leads to its destruction, an overused assumption breaking down.

Diane Elam, in her book *Feminism and Deconstruction: Ms. En Abyme*,
plays out this idea of repetition as deconstructive force by using the concept
of a *mise en abyme*, a visual device where "the 'whole' image is represented
in part of the image. Thus, the Quaker Oats man appears on the Quaker Oats
box holding a small box, which depicts the Quaker Oats man holding a box
with a Quaker Oats man ... and so on *ad infinitum*."[15] Her point in calling to
mind this device is to point out that repetition teases apart a representation,
making it susceptible to further, more complex understanding. Therefore, any
representation of women and even the idea that *a* woman can be representative of the whole breaks down into every smaller piece as it is brought forth
again and again in the public eye:

> To think of feminism in these terms would be to suggest that each new
> attempt to determine women does not put an end to feminist ques-
> tioning but only makes us more aware of the infinite possibilities of
> women. That is to say, women may be represented, but the attempt to
> represent them exhaustively only makes us more aware of the failure
> of such attempts. Hence the infinite regression that [she] specifically
> call[s] "*ms. en abyme*."[16]

If we apply this concept to Chappelle, say in his "Whore's Uniform" narrative, we see his comedy representing women who are representing themselves
as women (not whores) who are representing women who are dressed like
whores (but are not whores) who are representing women who are dressed
like whores (and who are prostitutes) who are representing what they think
men want and so on, ever into more levels of complexity and representation.
Chappelle's comedy drags this *ms. en abyme* onto the stage, adding on-stage

performance as one more level of representation but doing so in the public eye, where scrutiny is unavoidable. The repetition of the stereotype, the reinforcement of the binary, only works to break it down further.

As another example, consider Chappelle's remake of the Mel Gibson film *What Women Want*, which Chappelle has entitled "What Men Want" (Season One; Episode Eight). In the sketch a woman enters an elevator full of men, and the men's thoughts are all grossly sexual, including those of a little boy who thinks, "I'll put a hurtin' on that bitch." By playing out, in exaggerated form, the beliefs that the viewers may have about men — that they are oversexualized creatures who only think about women in sexual terms — Chappelle's comedy becomes part of Elam's *ms. en abyme*, where the satire of the original film calls into question not only the stereotypes represented in the original version but also those represented in this clip itself. The clip becomes a veritable funhouse of mirrors, reflecting the distorted shapes of stereotype and traditional conceptions of gender.

Some may argue — perhaps our "average" viewer who understands the underlying impetus of feminist theory but has not been privy to the complexities of linguistic conversation that rise out of that impetus — that simply using the language of the binary, i.e. referring to men and to women, does not disrupt stereotypes but instead reinforces it; he or she may argue that to break down these ideas one must step beyond the language that helps to reinforce them. But as Butler notes above, such a sidestepping of linguistic norms is impossible for the norms exist only within the language.

Elam stresses that "women's complaints make no sense within the terms of patriarchal language," pointing out that such language — with terms like chairperson or doctor almost always leading to the conjecture that the person in question is a man simply because of the patriarchal idiom surrounding the term — will always be insufficient and, thus, we need a new system of language.[17] But this invention or creation of a new language or linguistic system, while highly valid and important, is not the role of the comedian. Again, he is, as Chappelle himself notes, a popular culture icon. His work is to tease apart the identity of the culture, creating it from the inside, not imposing new systems from outside as would someone — many might argue — from the academy. Thus, Chappelle operates with the terminology available to him and perhaps makes room for new signifiers to come into being.

One other point about language needs to be made here and that is one about the gendered word choices that Chappelle takes on in terms like "boobs" and "bitches." Here, perhaps, is the area of the greatest potential offense and objection. Take, for example, the word *bitch*. This word has been taken — like *queer* by some members of the gay/lesbian community or *nigger* by some members of the black community — by some women to be a reappropriated term that is used affectionately — as in "Hey, bitch, how's it going?" when a woman speaks to a good friend. Many women are quick to point this out — that this word isn't always meant derogatorily. However, these same women, myself included, are quick to emphasize that most men, gay men usually excepted, cannot use this term, at least in direct address to a woman, without the woman taking great offense. The same is true if a woman "calls" another woman this name in spite or anger. These uses of these charged words are unacceptable when employed from a position of real or perceived power.

So how then does Dave Chappelle, a man who presumably does not know the women — be they real or imaginary — that he refers to with this term, get away with using this language. Again, we return to his role as both commentator and performer. His words here have a complexity of meaning, calling forth their slang usage (as obviously viewers know he is not speaking of female dogs here) and at the same time commenting on that very usage. Additionally, he is not using the terms with a mind to power; instead, he speaks them from the level playing field of comedy.

The same complexity is true of his use of sexualized terms such as "boobs" or "ass." Here the commentary is the important part, not the sexualized usage. Take, again, as an example his skit "New York Boobs." In this scene, because of both Chappelle's preceding commentary and the satirical nature of the format, Chappelle sidesteps the potential for offense to women — both as "awardees" and viewers. In this moment and this setting, it is okay not only to refer to a woman's breasts in public but to refer to them with a slang term: "boobs." Language, for those whom such terms may be somewhat normative, then is neutralized, making it part of a humor sketch and not an act of oppression or even every day dialogue.

No conversation on Chappelle and gender is complete without at least a cursory note about his depiction of homosexuality. While this topic occurs far less frequently in Chappelle's comedy than do discussions of race or gender, he does venture into the topic in sketches such as "Ask a Gay Guy" where, using the same model as in his famous "Ask a Black Dude" sketches, he asks individuals on the street to pose questions about gay people to gay actor Mario Cantone (Season One; Episode Six). Cantone, then, responds to these questions, usually with a fearsome bit of mock anger, thus dispelling the stereotype directly. For instance, when hip-hop artist Bazarre Royal says, "I just got one question for all your fruity pants out there ... what is the rainbow about?" Cantone answers by saying, "Fruity pants? Let me tell you something, I'll put a band aid over your left cheek and make you my Nelly." By calling out the derogatory name and responding to it harshly, but still with humor and an undermining of the stereotype of the passive, feminized man who doesn't stand up for himself, Chappelle again complicates and inverts the stereotype around sexuality.

However, it is important to note the scarcity of these discussions of homosexuality in Chappelle's oeuvre and to call to mind his comments about cross-dressing on *The Oprah Winfrey Show*, where he talked about his apparent discomfort with being asked to wear a dress as part of a film shooting.[18] He claims his discomfort comes from the hackneyed racism that "they put every black man in the movies in a dress," but his refusal to wear a dress coupled with his relatively rare discussions on homosexuality do call into question his ability to interrogate the continuum of sexual orientation as successfully as he has those of race and gender. Perhaps, as a straight man, he feels no space to appropriate that discussion, or perhaps he simply has little material to create comedy from. In any case, he has chosen not to delve into that area as fully as some might wish; thus, his deconstruction of various levels of gender and sexual identity remains incomplete.

In this sphere of comedy, where the perceived can become the actor, an object can become a subject and vice versa, and audience can become implicated, Chappelle creates space where contemplation and awareness occur. Here, the laughter and the moments of silence around it expunge the normalities of gendered interaction, leaving a vacuum where perceptions can be changed, beliefs altered, and stereotypes challenged. For it is in the audience's reaction where the real power lies, where the final blows to stereotype and hierarchy are felled. In the act of laughing together — across boundaries of gender (and race, class, and sexual orientation) — with each other and with the perpetrator Chappelle (for he is often the most amused perceiver of his own humor), differences collapse under the weight of humor. In many ways, Chappelle's role as social commentator comes as much from his choice to assume the role of comedian as it does from his comedy itself and as much from the audience's willingness to be *audience* rather than citizen.

4

Dave Chappelle, the Wu-Tang Clan and Afro-Asian America

GRAHAM CHIA-HUI PRESTON

Chappelle's Show speaks to and with a diverse, nuanced and complex American cultural and racial landscape. While most of the program's sketches deal explicitly with many of the absurdities inherent in modern Black-White relations, the show also makes note of the place of Asian America within the racial framework of the United States. That is, although it should not be surprising to see Asian American faces on the screen, the sheer volume of Asians on the show *is* unusual in a popular culture that is marked by a lack of an Asian American presence or, perhaps worse, an existence as a token model minority being folded into White America.[1] In other words, Asian Americans on *Chappelle's Show* are plainly *visible*, and their presence should be seen as neither a product of just tokenism or stereotypes, although both effects are alternately deployed and critiqued in the show, but as an unavoidable part of the America of *Chappelle's Show*. Asian Americans play scientists, copy shop customers, "Playa Haters," sweatshop workers, neighbors, soldiers, the Asian delegation to the Racial Draft, world class dice players, corner store employees, and, mirroring real life, Chappelle's wife.[2]

When one considers the breadth and centrality of the roles to the sketches, these parts cannot be seen simply as a deployment of stereotypes for cheap laughs. For example, in the "Playa Haters Ball" sketch, Mr. Roboto (Yoshio Mita, an actor who has, by far, played the most Asian characters on the show) is billed as the "Least Understood Hater" of the Playa Haters, a flashily dressed group of men who trade sharply worded insults and commit hate-worthy acts for prizes (Season One; Episode 7). The fact that Mr. Roboto is an Asian Playa Hater is accepted as fact; a hater named Beautiful (Donnell Rawlings) insults him in Korean and English, thereby engaging with Mr. Roboto on *both* their linguistic terms. The point here is that Mita plays a role far from usual stereotypes of Asian Americans, a part that is quite different

60

than expectations of usual television roles for Asian American actors and a character that is in clear discussion, however venomous, with the African American Playa Haters. Furthermore, Mita's presence in the sketch is a conspicuous and quotidian reality of the world of the Playa Haters and, more broadly, *Chappelle's Show.*

This chapter seeks to build an understanding of Asian America in *Chappelle's Show* that consciously elides a strict categorization of Asian Americans actors and their roles on the show but instead looks into specific strategies and aesthetic tropes in what one could call Dave Chappelle's version of Afro-Asian America. Moreover, this chapter thinks through the place of Asian Americans on the show specifically in their relations with other racial groups, most notably African Americans. These discussions should be thought of as an antiphonal exchange that transforms both sides of the conversation. Drawing upon and adapting Paul Gilroy's notion of the importance of antiphony (call-and-response song) to Black Atlantic music and art, this essay considers the racial, social and cultural resonances of the Wu-Tang Clan, a hip-hop group who are central to Dave Chappelle's conceptions of Afro-Asian America, and a number of Afro-Asian American sketches on *Chappelle's Show*, including "Racial Draft 2004," "Blackzilla," and the "Racial Pixies."

The first section of this chapter will explore a few theoretical approaches to Afro-Asian America. These approaches include Paul Gilroy's notion of antiphony in concert with a brief reading of theories of globalization and polyculturalism. The chapter will then examine the Wu-Tang Clan's antiphonal appropriation of aspects of Asian and Asian American cinema, music and art. The hip-hop group is important for Chappelle in that they present a useful model for the program's "racial conversation" with Afro-Asian America. This importance is underlined by their many appearances— as guests and as reference points— on the show. I will then turn towards a number of close readings of the aforementioned *Chappelle's Show* sketches before considering the larger valences of this form of antiphony.

"We Are a Kindred People": Afro-Asian America, Antiphony, and Polyculturalism

In *Margins and Mainstreams*, Gary Y. Okihiro notes, "[w]e are a kindred people, African and Asian Americans. We share a history of migration, interaction and cultural sharing."[3] Okihiro continues with a list of shared historical concerns, alignments and dangers— slave and cheap labor, for example — but what is notable about his list is the repetition and continual emphasis he places on what the two groups may share. It is in this *sense* of sharing that Afro-Asian America emerges. Simply put, Afro-Asian America is an imaginary space of exchange, dialogue and, at times, transformation between African and Asian Americans. It is a space that also does not subscribe to dichotomies between Black and White, or even trichotomies (Black-White-everyone else) but instead emphasizes the real *and* imagined interactions between previously geographically and culturally disparate groups. *Chappelle's Show* and the Wu-Tang Clan's music are clear examples of racial dialogue, as well as Afro-Asian America itself, and it is a conversation that involves Asian Americans not just as tokens but as important elements in the exchange. The Clan's reliance on Asian (American) signifiers and the visibility of Asian Americans on *Chappelle's Show* bear this point out.

In one sense, Chappelle, the Wu-Tang Clan and Afro-Asian America are neat examples of the result of the global flows of Arjun Appadurai and specifically of his notion that "the imagination has become an organized field of social practices, a form of work ... and a form of negotiation between sites of agency (individuals) and globally defined fields of possibility."[4] One could account for the interactions with Asian (American) culture as a result of the "organized field of social practices" that emerges out of the global reception, appreciation and appropriation of Asian cultural practices. The imagination here is linked with Benedict Anderson's notions of the social construction of the idea of community through collective imagination.[5] But, the situation is more complex when one considers and recalls the complicated history and diffuse racial politics of African and Asian American culture. Additionally, an explanation based solely on Appaduraian model of global flows and the social practices of imagination curiously elides specific aesthetic tropes and strategies involved in the production and dissemination of Afro-Asian American music and art.

Polyculturalism (as refined by Vijay Prashad) is an insightful approach that ultimately also shares the latter critique. In his landmark *Everybody Was Kung Fu Fighting*, Vijay Prashad, building upon a notion from Robin Kelley, proposes that one should think of the racial and cultural history of the United States as a profoundly polycultural experience. Prashad notes that "polyculturalism uncouples the notions of origins and authenticity from that of culture. Culture is a process ... with no identifiable origin. Therefore, no cultural actor can, in good faith, claim proprietary interest in what is claimed to be his or her authentic culture."[6] Instead of cultures that exist as distinct entities, as in theories of multiculturalism, polyculturalism celebrates how cultures are irrevocably linked and how they share the similar influences and even trajectories.

Prashad tells us that "polyculturalism draws from the idea of polyrhythms—many different rhythms operating together to produce a *whole* song, rather than different drummers doing their own thing."[7] While

Prashad's work is useful, insightful and engrossing, polyculturalism's flaw is found in this metaphor. There is a restricted sense of dialogue (and especially the possibility for transformation) here and the drummers are forever producing the whole song from distinct and perhaps unchanging sources. I do not though want to entirely dismiss polyculturalism as its central idea — the decoupling of origin and authenticity — is insightful and an important point when thinking of Afro-Asian America as a site of dialogue and transformation that does not rely upon the proprietary nature of authenticities. My major critique though is focused on the lack of a specific aesthetic trope or mechanism in this decoupling.

As a means of describing such a specific aesthetic mechanism, Paul Gilroy's articulation of the role of antiphony and call-and-response song in the music of "the Black Atlantic" is especially useful here. Originally used to describe a practice of a choral ensemble, antiphony here refers to a reliance on a form of African call-and-response song, which Leroi Jones (Amiri Baraka), for example, has found formal residues in gospel and blues music.[8] Furthermore, and building upon Jones' trajectory, it can be found as a guiding form in most the genres of music that have followed on blues practices such as jazz, rhythm and blues, rock 'n' roll and, ultimately, hip-hop.[9] For Gilroy, "[a]ntiphony (call and response) is the principle formal feature" of Black Atlantic music practices and aesthetic traditions such as "mimesis, gesture, kinesis, and costume."[10] It is also notable for "supplying, along with improvisation, montage and dramaturgy, the hermeneutic keys to the full medley of black artistic practices."[11] Additionally, and this is the key resonance of antiphony, "[l]ines between self and other are blurred and special forms of pleasure are created as a result of the meetings and conversations that are established between one fractured, incomplete, and unfinished racial self and others."[12] In the call-and-response of antiphonal art, ultimately *identities* are put into direct play and, at times, conflict with each other for the pursuit of a sort of affective pleasure. Antiphony then suggests an underlying mutability of the self, which may be quite unsettling.

It is in the call-and-response that differing voices are overtly put into direct discussion and it is also then the site of possible slippages and productive (if sometimes traumatic) exchange on or of racial, ethnic and aesthetic identity, especially when one notes that global flows of culture are making it "harder to locate" the original call.[13] Gilroy notes, "[T]he globalization of vernacular forms means that our understanding of antiphony will have to change."[14] Thus, while Gilroy quotes Ralph Ellison's idea that "jazz is an art of individual assertion *within* and against the group,"[15] one should note that, with the rise of regimes of globalization, the antiphonal assertion can often be located *outside* the group and brought into the conversation through processes such as sampling, interpellation or appropriation. With globalization, antiphony becomes a process that can be applied to the conversations of Afro-Asian America.

As a technique, antiphony opens up onto other strategies and forms such as appropriation and it also connects to other forms of art such as literature, comedy or television, rather than just music. In terms of comedy, antiphony could be seen as a basis for playing the dozens, where sharply worded insults are traded for laughs, comedy sketches that feature the dozens (the Playa Haters, for example) or even sorts of stand up comedy that demand audience interaction. In any case, Gilroy makes this link explicit when he quotes an interview he conducted with Toni Morrison in *Small Acts*. Morrison comments,

> My parallel is always the music because all of the strategies of the arts are there. All of the intricacy, all of the discipline.... Music makes you hungry for more of it. It never gives you the whole number. It slaps and embraces, it slaps and embraces. The literature ought to do the same thing.... I don't imitate it, but I am informed by it. Sometimes I hear blues, sometimes spirituals or jazz and I've appropriated it. I've tried to reconstruct the texture of it in my writing.[16]

The key phrase here that links antiphony with appropriation is "slaps and embraces," which speaks to the discursive and sometimes fraught nature of borrowing across media, especially within this framework of mediation between self, others and racial identity. Through her repetition of the phrase, Morrison gestures towards the teasing, almost always incomplete and heavily allusive nature of antiphonal appropriation. One "call" may be countered in turn by an unexpectedly fierce *or* loving response. The antiphonal exchange is unequal in that one side may have more power than the other. Antiphony then is not a utopian idea — the call and response can be dangerous in its slap and embrace. In the *Small Acts* interview, Morrison speaks about antiphony's relationship to her writing practices, but the ideas presented here can be applied as easily to other media, such as the television sketches of Dave Chappelle or the music of the Wu-Tang Clan. His comedy then does not just simply recapitulate antiphony but instead uses it as a "texture" in how it presents Afro-Asian America.

Shaolin Finger Jab: The Wu-Tang Clan's Afro-Asian America

Formed in the early 1990s in the Staten Island borough (known in the group's lexicon as Shaolin) of New York, the Wu-Tang Clan initially consisted of 9 emcees including Ol' Dirty Bastard, Method Man, Ghostface Killah, the GZA, Raekwon, Inspectah Deck, U-God, Masta Killa and the RZA (who also leads the group and produces nearly all the group's material). The group's sheer size and organization was unique and, instead of boasting one star, according to Nelson George, "with [the Wu-Tang Clan] the *posse* is the star."[17] In 1993, they released their debut record *Enter the Wu-Tang: 36 Chambers*, which sold over a million copies and set a new standard for hip-hop lyricism, production and musical innovation. Particularly important are the RZA's dark, claustrophobic beats, which Kodwo Eshun describe as "phantasmic HipHop productions [that] induce visions in the ear. Every breath becomes a wince of pain like a knife being swallowed."[18] Eshun gestures here towards the almost cinematic nature of the RZA's music, which juxtaposes samples from soul artists like Isaac Hayes with the RZA's own jazz inspired (and sometimes out of tune) keyboard lines and the group's own voices.[19] The group has subsequently released four albums, a number of solo albums of varying critical and commercial success, film appearances, video games, a clothing label, a book, and a number of appearances on *Chappelle's Show* as musical guests and actors.

One of the elements that set the group's music apart from its contemporaries was the RZA's reliance on vocal samples from kung fu films—a trend in the group's music from its earliest recordings to its latest album, *8 Diagrams* (2007), which samples liberally, both in musical and conceptual terms, from the film *The Eight Diagram Pole Fighter* (1983). The RZA has often used clips from films that he had become "really hooked" on during his youth in the late 1970s.[20] The RZA would later comment that the samples were "perfect for what I was trying to say about my crew. That's how I felt Wu was— invincible."[21] The RZA uses these samples as a means of asserting facets of the group's approach and their collective strength.

Kung fu films have been enormously influential on Hollywood, which can be observed in films such as, most famously, *The Matrix* (1999). The films have also been widely parodied; in the "Racial Pixies" sketch, Dave Chappelle himself briefly satirizes Asian cinema. Accordingly, there has been much discussion in cinema studies circles of this transnational appeal. In her introduction to *Hong Kong Connections*, Meaghan Morris notes, "Hong Kong films are watched, copied, collected, discussed, pirated, re-made, parodied and appropriated in many different *viewing situations* all over the world."[22] While not to discount the visual aspect of the group's work (i.e., music videos, film appearances, live performances), I would add that the Wu-Tang Clan are a fundamental example of cinema's impact upon other artistic forms such as, in this case, hip-hop music. In other words, kung fu cinema has had an impact upon much more than just other visual art forms but has instead become a sort of collective repository of imagery.

While the films themselves were mostly produced in Hong Kong (though some had funding from Hollywood), the films that the Wu-Tang Clan watched were dubbed into American accented English (as evidenced by the vocal samples throughout the group's music). Stephen Teo notes, "The tactic of dubbing local kung fu films into English and other languages also meant that the narratives were slightly modified and the often quite bad dubbing practices led to unintentional humor in scenes."[23] The films' modifications then turned them into a sort of Asian/American form that resides in an indeterminate space between Asia and America.[24] But, the films would be seen and understood by the Wu-Tang Clan in terms of an imagining of Asia through an explicitly American frame of reference, which would sight/cite populations of Asian Americans, perhaps first and foremost.

The opening track from the 2000 album *The W*, "Intro (Shaolin Finger Jab)/Chamber Music," is a suggestive example of antiphony at play in Afro-Asian America. The song opens with a series of vocal samples from *Five Deadly Venoms* (1978). The RZA samples the voice of the dying master who warns his young student, "I must tell you that the Clan is a danger to the public ... but still for many men just to hear of the name fills them with hate and loathing." In the film, these lines establish a plotline (the student must find the various "venoms" of the Clan), but, transposed into this introductory track, they speak to the Wu-Tang Clan themselves and of both their danger and notoriety. In other words, the kung fu cinema sample is a call, which demands a response from the emcees of the Wu-Tang Clan. Four members of the Clan respond and their verses seek to mostly confirm the sentiment of the vocal sample. Raekwon cautions against ignoring the potentially deadly consequences of your actions while the GZA soberly notes his fear-inspiring skills as a rapper.[25] This song is a representative example of how the Wu-Tang Clan usually treats their vocal samples from kung-fu cinema as something to respond to (the trend holds from 1993's "Bring da Ruckus" to 2007's "Campfire"). The end result of this use of this antiphonal appropriation is the central embedding of an element of Asian America within the key call-and-response song form.

"*The Asian Delegation Chooses ... the Wu-Tang Clan!*"

The Wu-Tang Clan's antiphonal conversations with Asian American culture are a model for how Dave Chappelle approaches Afro-Asian America. The integration of Asian American elements into an African American group's music is, I contend, one way to think about how Asian America functions within *Chappelle's Show*. The Wu-Tang Clan are clearly important to Chappelle; he devotes a number of sketches to them (including "Wu-Tang Financial" where the Clan advise suburbanites on financial decisions and the wisdom of purchasing a diverse portfolio of bonds), alludes to them in others and the GZA was one of the musical guests of the first season. Chappelle also uses the Wu-Tang Clan directly as a means to articulate a conception of Afro-Asian America in the "Racial Draft 2004" sketch.

On the second season premiere of *Chappelle's Show*, Dave Chappelle stages his version of what he calls the Racial Draft, which — modeled upon the amateur drafts of sports like football, basketball, baseball and hockey — consists of racial groups (Whites, Blacks, Latinos, Jews, Asians) selecting and naming an interracial individual as a member of their race (Season Two; Episode 1). As Chappelle notes in the "wraparound" segment that introduces the sketch, "we all mixed up. I mean genetically.... We need to just settle this once and for all. We need to have a draft. That's right I said it." Chappelle offers examples like Halle Berry, Derek Jeter and Tiger Woods as famous figures whose "mixed" racial and genetic makeup incites arguments and confusion between the races including within Chappelle's own family. He tells us that he and his Asian American wife argue over which part of Tiger Woods is doing so well at golf. The Racial Draft aims to defuse the debate and to settle upon a final answer for these interracial confusions.

During the course of this 8-minute sketch, there are seven selections, but, for the purposes of this chapter, I would like to only discuss the last choice. The Asian or Chinese delegation (the two terms are used here interchangeably) holds the final selection. In the climax of the sketch, the head Asian delegate, dressed in clothes vaguely reminiscent of 1960s Communist China fashion, cautiously approaches the microphone and exclaims, "The Asian delegation chooses the RZA, the GZA, U-God, Inspectah Deck, the Ghostface Killah: the Wu-Tang Clan!" The commentators declare that the Asian Delegation has made the shock pick of the night by choosing the exclusively African American hip-hop group, but the Wu-Tang Clan, as seen above, are well known for their appropriation and sampling of Asian (American) cinema and culture in their work and identity. The RZA and the GZA — the two de facto leaders of the hip-hop group — come up on stage to joyously accept the selection. The RZA exclaims, "This is big for us, yo, because we've always been a fan of the kung fu and the Chinese culture and shit." The GZA follows by reminding us to "diversify our bonds" (an allusion to "Wu-Tang Financial") before concluding, "Konichiwa, bitches!"

The moment is undeniably comical, but it also exposes a number of important issues about the construction and delineation of Asian and African American identity in popular American culture. While the sketch's humor derives ostensibly from the absurdity of naming an African American hip-hop group as Asian through the process of a "Racial Draft," the moment also gestures towards the deeper cultural and historical resonances—including a sort of racial mutability if not an antiphonal and transformative change inherent in the group's borrowings—of the group's use of and engagement with, to use the RZA's words, "the kung fu and the Chinese culture and shit." In its punch line, Chappelle's sketch foregrounds the group's reliance upon Asian American culture for its own innovations, musical palette and identity since the group's name and many of the individual emcees' names are all taken from kung-fu cinema of the 1970s. This privileging of the hybrid nature of the Clan over their lyrical (and, to a lesser extent, musical) subject matter, which locates the group primarily in the urban life of Staten Island, New York, is important in that it avoids any number of issues that the group deals with in favor of the group's artistic use of Asian cinema and culture. Cultural engagement becomes as important, if not more, than biology since the Clan are now "100% Asian" due to their cultural influences.

Through the sketch, Chappelle also highlights the Wu-Tang Clan's, to use Morrison's memorable phrase, "slaps and embraces" of Asian American culture through its underlining the group's cultural hybridity. That is, although on first glance the naming of the Clan as "100% Asian" may seem absurd, it still holds a kernel of plausibility, especially if we recall polyculturalism's decoupling of origin and authenticity. The hilarity of the moment is related to this sense of the dangers of a truly antiphonal exchange since, in antiphony, boundaries between identities are no longer strictly and clearly defined. The sketch draws our attention to the space of antiphonal exchange between African and Asian Americans as it stresses, however comically, the Wu-Tang Clan's inhabitance within Afro-Asian America.

Chappelle's Show does not only emphasize the Wu-Tang Clan's engagement with Afro-Asian America but also pursues its own antiphonal conversations with Asian American culture. One of the most prominent examples is the sketch "Blackzilla" (Season One; Episode 9). In a clear parody of the *Godzilla* motion picture franchise, Dave Chappelle casts himself as Blackzilla, a larger than life figure who towers over buildings and happens to be just an absurdly large African American man. Blackzilla terrorizes the presumably Japanese city, smokes its trees, fights with Godzilla and has sex with a volcano to end the segment. Throughout the sketch, Yoshio Mita turns up as nearly every Japanese character including a screaming woman.[26] On the commentary track, Dave Chappelle and co-writer Neal Brennan explain their rationale behind casting Mita. Chappelle tells us that they hired him because "this guy can barely speak English," while Brennan adds that he has been an Asian American "since 1965."[27] In other words, Mita's linguistic incompetence, despite his decades of life in the United States, was a determining factor in his casting. These comments must be considered in the context of the plain visibility of Asian Americans on the show rather than taken in isolation thus the highlighting of Mita's inability to speak English reflects the program's penchant for deploying stereotypes while also presenting a complex racial and cultural landscape.

Read in light of the commentary track, the sketch could be seen as purely stereotypical and perhaps even racist (especially in the casting of Mita), but it also engages in a productive conversation with Afro-Asian America. First, the sketch riffs on the *Godzilla* franchise in a similar fashion to the Wu-Tang's usage of kung fu cinema. Chappelle deploys the familiar if kitschy signifiers of *Godzilla* to celebrate and expand upon their humorous attributes. Second, the casting of and the comments on Yoshio Mita are illustrative of the difficulties inherent in Afro-Asian America; the conversation may be stilted, tricky and slow to develop because of linguistic issues even with people who have been Americans for over 40 years. The fact that Mita was brought back throughout the show's run and put in a diverse assortment of roles—later this episode, he returns as a Playa Hater, for example—suggests both an affinity for Mita and his inability to speak proper English and a gesture towards the visibility of Asian Americans on the show. In other words, Mita's numerous appearances in a variety of roles reflects the program's acknowledgement of Asian America itself as part of the racial conversation rather than just a silent element that is neither black nor white. Mita's inability to speak English also places him outside of the dichotomous racial conversation as an autonomous and unique individual in *Chappelle's Show*. Finally, one should note that antiphony both "slaps and embraces." It is not a utopian process or a conversation without dangers, slippages and possible victims. This traumatic risk though is one of its most productive and interesting elements.

The final *Chappelle's Show* segment that I would like to discuss in detail is the controversial "Racial Pixies" sketch (*Lost Episodes*; Episode 2), the sketch that has been blamed for Chappelle's sudden departure from his own show. In an interview in *Time*, Chappelle recalls that the laughter of a white man during the taping of the black pixie segment "made [him so] uncomfortable ... [his] head almost exploded."[28] The skit features several segments where members of various races (Blacks, Whites, Hispanics, Asians) are confronted with moments that reinforce cultural stereotypes. They demur, but a magical racial "pixie" appears (played in all cases by Chappelle) to persuade them otherwise. For example, the African American man is offered a choice of fried chicken or fish on a flight; he asks for the fish, but the blackface pixie hectors him to choose otherwise.

The Asian pixie scene, on the other hand, features the Asian American (Yoshio Mita) encountering Alani "La La" Vasquez, the beautiful young VJ from MTV, while in conversation with fellow cast member Charlie Murphy at a party. The Asian pixie advises on how to greet the woman — "Hello La La" but pronounced as "Herro Ra Ra" — but the Asian American instead greets her with an enthusiastic if inappropriate "Hello gorgeous!" The pixie, ashamed of Mita's words, yells out, "You have disgraced my family," commits suicide, and finally slides into La La's breasts to die. The Asian pixie is dressed in a fashion that is reminiscent of the master in *Five Deadly Venoms* and his dialogue clearly alludes to American English dubbed Asian martial arts films. The sketch lampoons the linguistic struggles of Asian Americans, a common theme on *Chappelle's Show,* Asian cinema and, intriguingly, interracial heterosexual desire. That is, Mita's linguistic slip is a reaction to his desire for La La. The Asian American's interest, however inept, is *sexual,* which contrasts with the long history of "feminization" and asexualization of Asian American males.[29] In one sense, the skit features an antiphonal confrontation in Afro-Asian America. The conversations between Asian and African Americans on the show gesture towards the antiphony between African and Asian Americans and the skit presents a dynamic encounter in Afro-Asian America.

When the sketch was finally aired, the studio audience was asked to comment on their impressions of the skit. Interestingly, there were no specific audience questions or comments on the Asian pixie and whether that part of the segment crossed the line from parody to outright racism. While unfortunate, this absence is not very surprising as most of the controversy focused on the Black pixie with his blacked-up face, costume, and dialogue which all clearly allude to the explosive racism and traumatic histories of blackface minstrelsy.[30] The silence on Asian Americans though is interrupted by a joke told by co-host Donnell Rawlings. Explaining that all people include himself have an "inner racism," Rawlings tells the audience that "if I see an Asian person, I say 'Where you from?' If they like 'Connecticut,' I'm like 'You know what I'm talkin' about!" Keeping in mind that it is an example of "inner racism," the joke subtly includes Asians as Americans. Rawlings asks about the Asian person's origin, but, when the answer trumps his expectations, he demands a new answer. It is this demand, a coupling of origin and authenticity, which is marked as racist. In other words, Asian Americans are included as part of the polycultural United States and as antiphonal participants in the racial conversation. While the joke is presumably Rawlings' own, it crystallizes *Chappelle's Show* approach to Asian America as a simultaneous slap ("Where you from?") and embrace ("You know what I'm talkin' about!").

Writing in 1972, cultural nationalist and polemical author Frank Chin suggests that "the success of the Chinese American minority is based on their being mightily, sincerely, definitely not black.... Blacks are a problem: badass.

Chinese Americans are not a problem: kissass."[31] Chin goes further when he notes, "We're hated by the blacks because the whites love us for being everything the blacks are not."[32] The contrast between the positions of the Wu-Tang Clan and *Chappelle's Show* and Chin is, in a word, striking, but it reminds one of the stark and unhelpful terms that have defined previous conversations between Asian and African America. Instead of clear cut dichotomies between kissass and badass, Afro-Asian America should be seen along the lines of a call-and-response song, a continual if indeterminate and negotiated exchange that carries risk, racism — inner or otherwise — and rewards. The work of the Wu-Tang Clan and Dave Chappelle must convince us of the latter.

5

Laughing Whiteness

Pixies, Parody, and Perspectives

Brian Gogan

[P]arody and its related forms serve to continue the conversation of the world, though its particular contribution is to ensure that the conversation will be usually carried on noisily, indecorously and accompanied by laughter.
— Simon Dentith, *Parody*[1]

In a May 14, 2005, *Time* magazine article entitled "Dave Speaks," Dave Chappelle explains why he rather abruptly ceased the production of the third season of his comedy show *Chappelle's Show*. Chappelle's explanation focuses on the November 2004 filming of a particular sketch, now known as the "Pixies" sketch (*Lost Episodes*; Episode 2). The sketch includes four distinct segments in which a raced male character — black, brown, yellow, white — finds himself in a situation in which racially coded practices may be enacted. In each segment, a raced miniature pixie appears and attempts to persuade the character to act in accordance with racially coded practices. Beyond each pixie's "racially combustible costume,"[2] each pixie's discourse invokes equally inflammatory racial stereotypes. When combined, the sketch's discourse and costuming position laughter as a particularly volatile response to comedy. According to *Time* writer Christopher John Farley, during the taping of the "Pixies" sketch, "one spectator, a white man, laughed particularly loud and long."[3] Chappelle, himself, recalls that spectator's laughter. "When he laughed," Chappelle remembers, "it made me uncomfortable."[4]

Although the white man's laughter made Chappelle "uncomfortable" with the "Pixies" sketch, I contend that the "Pixies" sketch constitutes a rhetorical arena which compels audience members to consider accountability as it pertains to United States racial discourse. In particular, the parodic repetitions presented in the two whiteness segments risk re-inscribing authoritative discourse on viewers and, therefore, require viewers to laugh conscientiously and listen carefully. To support this contention, I will: (1) define the "Pixies" sketch as parody; (2) distinguish parody's discursive position from laughter's discursive position; (3) outline *budding laughter*'s role in the "Pixies" sketch; (4) examine the "Pixies" sketch as a rhetorical enterprise; and (5) compare the accountability presented by the sketch's two whiteness segments.

The "Pixies" Sketch as Parody

The laughter that Chappelle heard in November, 2004, proves inextricably linked to racial discourse in the United States. As Mikhail Bakhtin contends, the universal principle of all laughter proves the "link[age] of laughter with time, with time's successive changes" and, as Farley notes in the *Time* article, United States racial discourse is, to some degree, changing.[5] "Racial divisions," according to Farley, "are becoming more complex, harder to understand, more challenging to discuss."[6] Additionally, Farley asserts that *Chappelle's Show* "worked because it talked about what America finds difficult to talk about: race."[7] Similarly, Danny Hooley of the *News & Observer* contends that *Chappelle's Show* treated "bold, fresh material that dealt mostly — hilariously — with race."[8] And Kevin Powell further claims, in a May 2006 *Esquire* magazine article, that "there was a razor-sharp racial consciousness to Chappelle's material — he had a keen eye for that gray area between social satire and pop culture."[9] Writing in the May 16, 2005, edition of *Newsweek*, Devin Gordon holds that Chappelle, by way of the sketches, "brought a rare cultural consciousness to the show."[10] However, this same consciousness also invites viewers to laugh at race through, what Farley calls, a "satiric take on race."[11]

Although *Chappelle's Show* clearly targets racial discourse, the categorization of *Chappelle's Show*, in general, and the "Pixies" sketch, in particular, as satiric proves problematic because of the invisible markings of the sketch. Here, the word *marking* refers to an act of reception; viewers receive a work of comedy as marked by the comedian. In other words, viewers infer that the comedian approaches his or her comedic target from a particular perspective. Subsequently, invisible markings refer to markings that, although present, are not received by viewers. Whereas satire possesses an obvious, or visible, marking, the "Pixies" sketch possesses no such marking. As Linda Hutcheon explains, satire proves a "kind of encoded anger" in which a "scornful ridicule is central to its identity."[12] Satire, according to Hutcheon, is visibly marked by a disdainful textual intent. Accordingly, satire cultivates a clear inference; the decoder of satire infers that that the text is intended to scorn its target. For Hutcheon, this inferred scorn marks or codes the text as satire in an obvious fashion.

Chappelle, however, repeatedly doubted the visibility of the markings attached to the third season's sketches. Chappelle felt that the white audience member received the "Pixies" sketch in a manner that contradicted his intent. *Chappelle's Show* co-writer Neal Brennan recalls a recurring scenario during the production process of the third season:

> He would come with an idea, or I would come with an idea, pitch it to him, and he'd say that's funny. And from there we'd write it. He'd love it, say, "I can't wait to do it." We'd shoot it, and then at some point he'd start saying, "This sketch is racist, and I don't want this on the air." And I was like, "You like this sketch. What do you mean?" There was this confusing and contradictory thing: he was calling his own writing racist.[13]

This "confusing and contradictory thing" to which Brennan refers positions *Chappelle's Show* sketches, like the "Pixies" sketch, outside of the realm of satire. To laugh at a sketch like the "Pixies" sketch is not to laugh at satire but instead to laugh at parody. Commenting on the received intent of a sketch, Hutcheon explains that "parody probably should be labeled as *un*marked, with a number of possibilities for marking."[14] Here, Hutcheon is not claiming that parody is void of intent; instead, she suggests that viewers of parody detect no obvious intent. Chappelle's reaction to his own writing and his own comedy indicates that *Chappelle's Show* sketches function without any visible intent and, therefore, could be viewed as invisibly marked. As such, the "Pixies" sketch could be received by viewers in multiple ways, ways that could subvert or support authoritative racial discourse. Moreover, parody's ability to target "[a]ny codified form" explicitly connects the general target of parody with the specific target of the "Pixies" sketch, for, as AnnLouise Keating and, in turn, Krista Ratcliffe remind, United States racial discourse establishes "a 'conditional' relationship" between coded people and coded practices.[15]

As parody, the "Pixies" sketch repeats the "conditional" relationship between people and practices while simultaneously providing difference.[16] In the "Pixies" sketch, each pixie attempts to persuade a particular person to enact a racially coded set of practices. The exchange between pixie and person illustrates the conditional nature of these relationships. In fact, the people in each one of the segments actually resist the coded practices endorsed by the pixies. For example, in the whiteness segment of the "Pixies" sketch, a white pixie coaxes a man to "hit [his three black friends] with their own vernacular," maintain an attraction to women with "pancake butt," and employ the twist on a dance floor. However, the man ignores the persistent urging of the pixie and acts otherwise. Since each segment of the "Pixies" sketch portrays a person ignoring the advice of each pixie, each segment therefore reveals the relationship between people, practices, and race to be conditional. In other words, individuals can reject these conditional relationships.

The Discursive Position of Parody and Laughter

Nonetheless, as parody, the "Pixies" sketch retains the ideological status of parody. As Hutcheon explains, "[t]he ideological status of parody is a subtle one: the textual and pragmatic natures of parody imply, at one and the same time, authority and transgression."[17] Whereas Hutcheon attempts to embrace the paradoxical, invisibly marked, nature of parody, Judith Butler seems to almost lament this same characteristic of parody. With a hint of exasperation, Butler persists: "[T]here must be a way to understand what makes certain kinds of parodic repetitions effectively disruptive, truly troubling, and which repetitions become domesticated and recirculated as instruments of cultural hegemony."[18] Both Butler and Hutcheon acknowledge that parody can be received as either complicit or subversive with regards to authoritative discourse. Authoritative discourse or "the authoritative word," to which Mikhail Bakhtin sometimes refers, "demands that we acknowledge it... [that] we encounter it with its authority already fused to it."[19] According to Bakhtin, authoritative discourse proves "the word of the fathers" whose "authority was already *acknowledged* in the past."[20] In United States racial discourse, the words, actions, and cultural practices "of our fathers" often prove the most disturbingly coded and racially bigoted ideologies.

Invisibly marked and coded, the parodic repetition of racial discourse in the "Pixies" sketch risks reinscribing authoritative discourse on viewers. Bakhtin holds that "[t]he degree to which a word may be conjoined with authority ... is what determines its specific demarcation."[21] Since parodic repetitions circulate with invisible marks and codes, decoders of parody might very well mark or code parody as authoritative discourse. In effect, such a move would interpret parody as simple repetition of authoritative discourse and simultaneously fail to recognize the difference crucially important to Hutcheon's definition of parody. Consequently, these viewers would respond to discourse in a manner predetermined by authority. Bakhtin reminds that "authoritative discourse permits no play with the context framing it, no play with it borders, no gradual and flexible transitions, no spontaneously creative stylizing variants on it."[22] Accordingly, viewers begin to understand Chappelle's concern that his comedy could be interpreted as racist. Chappelle, in other words, worried that viewers would interpret his comedy in accordance with authoritative discourse.

As parody, however, the "Pixies" sketch can transgress authoritative discourse. Parodic repetition puts authoritative discourse in a state of play wherein contextual shifts and stylized variants constitute difference. Thus, parody possesses a subversive potential; however, as Butler reminds, "[p]arody by itself is not subversive."[23] By extension, the comedy of Dave Chappelle, the "Pixies" sketch included, is not by itself subversive. Just as Butler emphasizes parody's dependence upon context and reception, the "Pixies" sketch also depends upon context and reception. Butler's emphasis on context and reception returns to a consideration of laughter, for Butler asserts that "parodic displacement, indeed parodic laughter, depends on a context and reception in which subversive confusions can be fostered."[24]

Although Butler illustrates parody's dependency upon context and reception, Butler's assertion proves problematic because it describes one result of parody's context and reception: laughter. Butler suggests that laughter's subversive potential, like parody's subversive potential, depends upon context and reception. Yet, this suggestion implies that viewers could return to the taping of the "Pixies" sketch in November of 2004 and listen to the laughter more closely, more intelligibly. Viewers could share in Farley's account of the situation: that the "laughter struck Chappelle as wrong, and he wondered if the new season of his show had gone from sending up stereotypes to merely reinforcing them."[25] A shared understanding of laughter would, in other words, clear up the confusion surrounding Chappelle's departure from his own show. A shared understanding of laughter would also avoid the speculations forwarded by individuals like Mark de la Vina of the *San Jose Mercury News* who describes the laughter as what "*allegedly* prompted Chappelle to abandon his show."[26] Similarly, a shared understanding of laughter would avoid the sardonic tone adopted by *New York Times* columnist Virginia Heffernan—"[Chappelle] has since said that a racist-sounding laugh by a white member of the studio audience set him off. The sound of that too-hard laugh—*at one of his own jokes*—led him to conclude, *in his own accounting*, that he was paying too high a moral price for his success"—drip with skepticism.[27]

Describing laughter as parodic, subversive, alleged, racist-sounding, and too-hard invokes conceptions of normative laughter from which other kinds of laughter may be distinguished and described. Problematically, these descriptions of laughter obscure laughter's extra-linguistic position. Whereas parody necessarily invokes and often repeats conceptions of the normative, laughter does not. Although parody's marking (its producer's intent) remains invisible, parody proves very much marked by language. As Hutcheon notes, "parodic codes, after all, have to be *shared* for parody—as parody—to be comprehended ... [w]hether parody is intended as subversive of established canons or as a conservative force."[28] Parodic codes are activated through language by an act of discursive exposition (i.e., describing a sketch as parodic or categorizing a sketch as parody) and, therefore, bound to language and the normative. Since parody is already imbricated within the strictures of language, the possibility exists that parody functions with, in the words of Bakhtin, "authority already fused to it."[29] Thus, the possibility exists that parody might exist as part of authoritative discourse, complicit in the promulgation of racially coded ideologies. Hutcheon even acknowledges this possibility while describing the feeling of active participation that decoders of parody receive: "In other words, being made to feel that we are actively participating in the generation of meaning is no guarantee of freedom; manipulators who make us feel in control are no less present for all their careful concealment."[30] On the contrary, laughter's subversive potential depends neither on context nor reception. While shared codes might spark laughter, laughter escapes language. Laughter cannot be read or written as parodic, subversive, alleged, racist-sounding, too-hard, or anything else for that matter, because laughter does not signify in any shared fashion. When it sounds, laughter breaks away from shared discourse.

Budding Laughter *and the "Pixies" Sketch*

When individuals hear laughter, they listen to sounds, which escape the strictures of language and, therefore, prove capable of subverting authoritative discourse and reviving dialogue.[31] Even in the most restrictive and contrived cultural arenas,[32] laughter possesses the ability to germ, sprout, and spring forth, in an uncontrollable, almost organic, manner. I call the point at which laughter breaks from authoritative discourse *budding laughter*. With fatigue as its fuel, budding laughter occurs when authority has laughed an individual silent. Budding laughter sounds from the voice of the individual. Budding laughter germinates; it is not manufactured by any authority — not by authors, such as Chappelle or Brennan, nor by industry magnates, like Comedy Central.

Budding laughter offers viewers a chance to maneuver in, about, and/or around markings, codes, and stylizations, for budding laughter does not fit a form, mold, or style. Unformed, unmolded, and unstylized, budding laughter is not reproducible and, therefore, not repeatable in parody or describable in language. Associated with an individual's voice, budding laughter is also associated with an individual's racial (dis)identifications. The acoustic difference in an individual's voice belies a discrete identity — one that cannot be reproduced through coded racial discourse or even parody. Accordingly, from among the masses of viewers searching for amusement, identities begin to emerge, shape, and sound. As a result, budding laughter begins a dialogue about coded discourse. No singular description possesses laughter;

instead, the authoritative discourse of a complicit culture now finds itself challenged by other voices.

Rather appropriately, then, guest co-hosts Rawlings and Murphy turn the microphone over to audience members and listen to the individual voices that emerge as a result of the budding laughter produced by the "Pixies" sketch. "As you may or may not have heard," Murphy explains, "Dave said he had some problems with the 'Pixies' sketch." Rawlings continues: "We didn't know if we should air the show or not, so we asked the audience what they thought about it."[33] One by one, audience members offer their own interpretations of the "Pixies" sketch. Taken together, these interpretations evidence the ability of the "Pixies" sketch to promote dialogue among viewers. As Michael Holquist notes, dialogue occurs for Bakhtin when "[a] word, discourse, language ... becomes relativized, de-privileged, aware of competing definitions for the same things."[34] In other words, viewers of the "Pixies" sketch are not simply repeating authoritative discourse. Instead, they are laughing at the racially coded discourse, stepping back, gaining some distance, distinguishing difference, and appearing to tacitly acknowledge the role of budding laughter in initiating dialogue.

Viewers repeatedly comment upon the ability of Chappelle's comedy to facilitate a different kind of dialogue — one in which budding laughter provides these viewers with a sense of familiarity, or comfort. In turn, this sense of comfort enables an exploration of race through discussion. For instance, one viewer comments, "I think that Dave has always [done] a good job of bringing race to the surface, because we all think about it, but he makes it comfortable to talk about and I've always appreciated that about this show." Another viewer agrees, "I like comedy and I like the show because it's kind of a relaxed way for other people to look at other races and see how people communicate." Both of these viewers seem to echo Bakhtin's assertion that the world becomes familiar through laughter.[35] This same sense of familiarity or comfort, however, comprises one viewer's source of discomfort. This viewer expresses discomfort around those who have become too comfortable with Chappelle's treatment of racial discourse. Although this viewer does note that "it is funny to hear Dave Chappelle do [the jokes]," this viewer contends that, "[s]ometimes [*Chappelle's Show*] makes people a little too comfortable where they shouldn't be comfortable." Other viewers emphasize a similar sense of discomfort produced by the "Pixies" sketch, yet even these viewers recognize the show's success in facilitating discourse. For example, one viewer declares, "[The 'Pixies' sketch] was intelligent, and it was uncomfortable, and I think that's the point of it. It's supposed to draw attention to people's stereotypes and talk about it and make it funny; that's why the show's successful."

The "Pixies" Sketch as a Rhetorical Enterprise

The point, or purpose, of *Chappelle's Show* attracts the attention of another audience member. This audience member speaks to the overall purpose of *Chappelle's Show*: "I don't think it's the responsibility of this show to educate everyone in the world. It's a comedy show, and, even if it is being a responsible comedy show, no matter how responsible you are, you're not going to be able to educate everybody in the world. So, I think you have to stick to what your true goal is— making people laugh." Like other audience members' responses to the "Pixies" sketch, this individual's comment embraces the rhetorical nature of laughing and listening and, as such, redefines *Chappelle's Show* as a rhetorical enterprise that raises issues related to responsibility and accountability. Yet, this individual's comment notably posits laughter at odds with responsibility.

Yet, if we examine the rhetorical nature of laughing and listening more closely, we discover that budding laughter and social responsibility are not mutually exclusive. Although budding laughter affirms both the "untamable aspect of language" and the untamable aspect of culture, we should not *necessarily* categorize budding laughter as irresponsible.[36] While budding laughter wrests individuals loose from extremely codified cultural and discursive practices, budding laughter does not *necessarily* wrest individuals loose from ethical considerations. As D. Diane Davis elucidates in *Breaking Up [at] Totality: A Rhetoric of Laughter*, laughter is not *necessarily* an irresponsible endeavor. According to Davis, "from a position that says 'let's talk' *and* 'let's listen' ... to the *laughter*, we will have found ourselves on the way to an/other 'responsibility.'"[37] Thus, a responsible rhetoric of laughter seems dependent upon a rhetoric of listening. As Ratcliffe explains in *Rhetorical Listening: Identification, Gender, Whiteness*, a rhetoric of listening facilitates accountability among individuals. In fact, Ratcliffe emphasizes that a rhetoric of listening asks listeners to consider different discourses and varying cultural logics in open arenas that foster engagement.[38] Acknowledging "that U.S. culture has few terms and even fewer protocols for discussing race," Ratcliffe contends that open engagement by way of listening will "help construct more terms and protocols to foster public debates."[39] Seemingly, parody constitutes one of the most engaging protocols for discussing race, for not only is parody's marking invisible, but also it fosters budding laughter through which individuals might consider their own markings, invisible or otherwise.

Accordingly, *Chappelle's Show* fuses a rhetoric of laughter with a rhetoric of listening. By inducing laughter, *Chappelle's Show* encourages the adoption of three functional rhetorical stances outlined by Ratcliffe and attempts "to turn denial into recognition, defensiveness into critique, and guilt/blame into accountability."[40] Indeed, the discourse that results from the "Pixies" sketch considers the rhetorical role of *Chappelle's Show* as parody, by focusing on accountability. "[A]ccountability," explains Ratcliffe, "offers forward-looking ways to address not just individual errors but also unearned structural privileges, which are grounded in the-past-that-is-always-present."[41] For instance, one viewer recognizes how laughter can breakdown the coded discursive barriers that exist among individuals. The viewer references the "Pixies" sketch and states, "It's funny that we can come together and laugh at each other like that." However, this viewer then explains how a parody like the "Pixies" sketch can become problematic. The viewer continues, "But, I think the problem lies in the ignorant people at home or possibly in here ... the problem comes in when people base their opinions on these jokes." Holding each individual viewer accountable for the sketch's interpretation, this viewer clearly recognizes parody's potential to reinscribe the coded authoritative discourse. Similarly, another viewer comments upon the rhetoric that a sketch like the "Pixies" sketch encourages among its viewers. This audience member asserts that "if [Chappelle] touches you to the point where you think about [racial discourse], I think the mission is done." Another audience member agrees, "You see a sketch like this and it gets people talking and laughing; so as long as we're thinking about it, it's a good thing." For this viewer, budding laughter grows into a rhetorical enterprise, an enterprise that leads to accountability.

The comments of two other viewers raise the issue of accountability with respect to the treatment of whiteness in the "Pixies" sketch. These two *Chappelle's Show* audience members criticize the initial whiteness segment of the "Pixies" sketch on the grounds that this segment treats its parodic target — whiteness — weakly. One audience member, for example, considers the "Pixies" sketch to be "derogatory to black and Spanish people." At the same time, this audience member feels that the "Pixies" sketch "plays on the good stereotypes of white people ... that they're educated and that ... they listen to rock music and that's not bad." For this audience member, the coded practices parodied by the "Pixies" sketch possess inherent value as either positive or negative, bad or "not bad." Moreover, in this audience member's estimation, the conditional relationship between coded people and coded practices examined in the initial whiteness segment almost proves complimentary.

Another audience member concurs. This audience member acknowledges that the "Pixies" sketch targets four different races, but, problematically, the sketch's repetition of whiteness proves inadequate. This audience member further explains that, because "the white race is seen as ... the generic race," the parodic repetition presented in the whiteness segment "doesn't really affect [people who identify as white] as much [as the sketch affects people who identify with one of the other three races parodied in the "Pixies" sketch]." For this audience member, the conditional relationship between people coded as white and practices coded as white requires a more parodic treatment than the other three races in order to produce an effect similar to that of the other three segments.

This audience member's comments speak to the paradoxical nature of both parody and whiteness. Just as Hutcheon notes the paradoxical ideological status of parody, Valerie Babb acknowledges the paradoxical ideological status of whiteness. In fact, Babb argues that the devices used to maintain the dominant ideology of whiteness actually "reveal the fundamental paradox of whiteness: the persistent need of non-whiteness to give it form and expression."[42] Like parody, whiteness, explains Ruth Frankenburg, maintains an unmarked (i.e.: invisibly marked) status.[43] Whereas comedic intent remains unmarked, or invisible, in parody, certain cultural practices remain unmarked as white racial practices. Evidently, a parody, like the "Pixies" sketch, that treats whiteness as its parodic target proves doubly paradoxical, for such a sketch relies upon practices and people coded as *both* white and nonwhite, all the while implying *both* authority and transgression.

Whiteness Repeated, Accountability Revisited

Doubly paradoxical, the "Pixies" whiteness segment calls for accountability and, indeed, an alternate parodic treatment. In fact, co-host Charlie Murphy seizes upon this last audience member's point that the whiteness segment "wasn't hard enough," that "it was the softest" of the four segments, and solicits further explanation. Murphy then proceeds to introduce an alternate whiteness segment to the studio audience. After the audience watches this alternate whiteness segment, Murphy asks: "Does that change anything?" While the studio audience indicates that the alternate segment (or even one hundred alternate whiteness segments) did not (and would not) change anything, the alternate whiteness segment changes, at the very least, one very substantial thing: The alternate segment renders whiteness— its uncritical logic and privileged vantage point — visible by holding whiteness accountable.

At first glance, both whiteness segments seem to render whiteness visible through the representation of a pixie — performed by a heavily costumed Chappelle — that embodies whiteness. In both segments, Chappelle appears in whiteface and wears a wardrobe — blazer, sweater, collared shirt, necktie, and slacks— of red, white, and blue. The very costuming displays what Babb refers to as the synonymity between whiteness and Americaness.[44] The white pixie literally wears his nationhood on his body. The costuming in the whiteness segments thus serves to "generate a ... recognition of the supremacy of whiteness and sanction the perception that whites intrinsically have more right to what is American than do other groups in the United States."[45] As Babb expounds, the notion that an intrinsic link exists between being white and being American proves outrageous (even more outrageous than the white pixie's costuming).

With no discernable difference between the pixie's costuming in the initial whiteness segment and the pixie's costuming in the alternate whiteness segment, viewers might be tempted to argue that no discernable difference exists between the whiteness depicted in both segments. Furthermore, viewers might cite the pixie's reaction to racially coded practices—particularly the fearful articulation of racial stereotypes—as additional evidence that the two segments represent whiteness identically. In both segments, whiteness's "principles of exclusion construct difference ... as something negative, something to be feared."[46] Indeed, the segments articulate racial stereotypes concerning music, dancing, television shows, income, sexual attraction, and physical endowment.

Yet, the claim that both whiteness segments depict whiteness similarly neither critiques the ideology of whiteness nor holds either segment accountable for the portrayal of whiteness. In effect, such an assertion merely adopts the first functional rhetorical stance that Ratcliffe describes. In other words, such an assertion only *recognizes* the presence of whiteness in the United States and the synonymity of whiteness and Americaness, all the while highlighting racial difference and fear of racial difference. Mere recognition, however, proves complicit with the ideology of whiteness, for it allows whiteness to function unquestioned. "Failure to question the impact of this ideology," contends Babb, "makes a nation of many peoples and traditions vulnerable to increased divisiveness."[47] Babb's contention emphasizes two very important points. First, it associates the professed unity of our nation with our (in)ability to critique. As Ratcliffe explains, "critique assumes the existence of multiple questions, multiple answers to each question, and multiple places from which to speak and listen."[48] Second, it illustrates that the ideology of whiteness assumes a lack of questions and an inability to critique. In other words, whiteness operates uncritically; it neither asks, nor anticipates, questions; whiteness is assumed, invoked, and declared. As Babb explains, the ideology of whiteness "encourages [those who identify as white] to fear contact with or feel a subtle, indefinable discomfort when in the presence of others not like them."[49] In Babb's estimation, "[e]ach encounter with someone from a different racial classification potentially necessitates a response to alleviate this discomfort."[50] Here, viewers of *Chappelle's Show* listen to the audible difference between the whiteness segments. The initial, "soft" whiteness segment employs questions in order to assuage the discomfort and fear caused by racial difference and, as such, renders whiteness invisible by evading whiteness's uncritical logic, ignoring whiteness's privileged vision, and relinquishing accountability. On the contrary, the alternate whiteness segment offers declarations, which attempt to explain away discomfort and fear resulting from racial difference, and, as such, renders whiteness visible by operating within whiteness's uncritical logic, revealing whiteness's privileged vision, and affording an opportunity for accountability.

The initial whiteness segment renders whiteness invisible by employing questions as a response to racial difference and discomfort. In this segment, a meeting of four friends, one white and three black, at a club compels the pixie to exclaim, "Oh my god — Three black guys!" The pixie suggests a course of action aimed at making the black characters "feel more *comfortable*" (my emphasis). Fear of racial difference and (dis)comfort overwhelm the segment. For instance, the fear of a curvaceous female also compels the pixie to ask: "Whatever happened to some good old fashioned pancake butt?"[51] Similarly, after the pixie notes that the white character looks "so *comfortable*" (my emphasis) when dancing to music with a beat, the pixie questions: "Whatever happened to some good old fashioned rock-n-roll?" Thus, although this segment presents viewers with a white pixie, viewers listen to the pixie articulating critical questions—critical questions that, according to Babb, are not coded white. By misrepresenting whiteness as inviting critique, this parodic treatment engages audience members not in a critique of whiteness, but instead in a critique of racial stereotypes. In effect, this segment shifts the parodic target to the racial stereotypes and, consequently, obscures considerations of accountability. This segment fails to ask questions of whiteness; instead, it allows whiteness to ask the questions. Thus, this segment fails to hold whiteness accountable for occupying a privileged position and exercising a discursive power. By portraying whiteness as an ideology that invites dialogue (at the very least, a response to the questions), this segment effaces whiteness's privileged power to control discourse.

Unlike the initial whiteness segment, the alternate whiteness segment operates within the uncritical logic of white ideology and, consequently, treats whiteness as its parodic target. Like the earlier whiteness segment, this segment also confronts fear of difference and discomfort; however, the pixie in this segment enunciates declarations which embrace the privileged power of whiteness and consequently enable accountability. The discourse in this segment, which occurs at a bank of urinals in a men's restroom, directly addresses a racially coded fear of difference and discomfort. The pixie — commanding "Don't let that scare you"— barks directives at the white character. These directives literally instruct the white character to employ a privileged vision, one in which a white (male) character can review his position in the world.

In particular, the pixie diverts the character's eyes away from the two black characters that use the urinals to either side of the white character by ordering the white character to "look straight ahead." The pixie also attempts to assuage the character's fears by reminding the white character of his privileged power. "[N]o matter how big his dick is," explains the pixie, "at least you run the Goddamn world."

Indeed, the alternate whiteness segment reveals whiteness through discourse as much as privileged vision, or perspective. Whereas the pixie in the initial whiteness segment invokes racial stereotypes through questions that begin: "Whatever happened to?"; the pixie in the alternate segment invokes stereotypes through declaratives that employ: "Must have." For instance, the pixie refers to a stench in the men's bathroom, looks at the black character played by Rawlings, and concludes that the character "Must have drank a forty ounce." Yet, this segment immediately questions these declaratives. Rawlings's character responds to the declarative, along with the uncritical logic and privileged vision of whiteness, which undergirds the declaration, by alarmingly looking at the pixie. Looking critically at whiteness begins dialogue; the pixie asks, "Can you see me?" and the black character replies, "Yeah, I can see you."

The alternate segment renders whiteness visible to the black character, the white pixie, and, potentially, the audience of *Chappelle's Show*. Whiteness can be seen, and, therefore, whiteness can be held accountable for its limited vision and uncritical logic. However, when the pixie addresses the black character, considerations of vision and acts of viewing collide with considerations of discourse and acts of listening. The pixie, directing "Well listen, this is an A and B conversation, so why don't you C [see] your way out of it," reveals how whiteness assumes the perspective of discursive authority. Although, whiteness attempts to dominate, to regulate, and to control conversation, the black character's reply, "Why don't you see these nuts?" not only dismisses the pixie's directive and questions the uncritical logic of whiteness, but it also forces the pixie to confront "that" which initially proved scary, as the character proceeds to urinate on the pixie. The act of urination counters the privileged vision of whiteness and holds whiteness accountable for viewing "that" which might be different or uncomfortable. Whiteness is forced to occupy a perspective from which it earlier escaped.

The closing lines of the segment further illustrate how the alternate whiteness segment reveals whiteness's ideological perspective through discourse. Just before he departs, the pixie addresses the black character and exclaims, "I don't know how you saw me. I'm going to take a look at your tax return. You must've made a lot of money, if you can see me." Once again, the pixie employs a "must've" declaration in order to rationalize whiteness's now visible status. Apparently, whiteness possesses the answers; the pixie connects visibility with privilege, specifically economic privilege. Nonetheless, the perspective of whiteness remains clear: Whiteness *authoritatively* assumes invisibility and privilege. Whiteness invokes authoritative discourse in order to regulate discourse; the pixie, we recall, invites the black character to "C [see]" his way out of conversation. The alternate segment treats whiteness as occupying a privileged perspective, and, subsequently, both characters and audience members can hold whiteness accountable. Just as Rawlings's character sees, hears, and questions the pixie, *Chappelle's Show* audience members can view whiteness, listen to whiteness, and question whiteness. Moreover, audience members can laugh whiteness and race through sketches like the "Pixies" sketch.

In sketches that target race, laughter escapes the confines of language and thereby creates an extra-linguistic space in which individuals can confront authority by maneuvering in, around, and/or about racial markings. In the case of the "Pixies" sketch, the white male audience member's maneuvering in, around, and/or about authoritative discourse proves problematic. His laughter, in Chappelle's estimation, seemed to belie complicity with authoritative discourse — his laughter seemed to sound an alarm. Indeed, other comics who target racial codes, comics like Margaret Cho, assert that the timbre of laughter sounding from an audience member reveals how that audience member has received a particular sketch.[52] But because laughter escapes the shared codes of language, laughter proves an impossible criterion with which to evaluate a sketch. As the difference between the two white segments of the "Pixies" sketch illustrates, an examination of the parodic target may potentially be a far more productive means by which to determine a sketch's particular effectiveness in subverting authoritative discourse. In particular, I'm reminded of a Roger Hailes stand-up routine, entitled "My Whiteness," that also aired on Comedy Central. In the routine, Hailes specifically targets a racial assumption. "I've realized exactly how white I look," says Hailes, "whenever I leave a clothing store and the alarm goes off."[53] Hailes continues, "They always assume something's wrong with the alarm."[54] While the logic targeted by Hailes's sketch should alarm us, the laughter produced by the sketch should not.

6

Impersonating Hollywood

The Conflicting Identity Discourses of Charlie Murphy's True Hollywood Stories

JULIA ROUND

Charlie Murphy's True Hollywood Stories are possibly the best known of all the sketches featured on *Chappelle's Show*.[1] Indeed, it might be too popular — at a stand-up performance in Sacramento Memorial Auditorium in 2004, Dave Chappelle stormed off the stage for nearly two minutes after the crowd wouldn't stop shouting "I'm Rick James, bitch!" at him. On his return the frustrated comedian blamed the audience, who wouldn't "shut up and listen — like you're supposed to." Chappelle declared, "The show is ruining my life" — by making him a "star." He continued, This [stand-up] is the most important thing I do, and because I'm on TV, you make it hard for me to do it. People can't distinguish between what's real and fake. This ain't a TV show. You're not watching Comedy Central. I'm real up here talking.[2] Although Chappelle's stand-up routine and his television sketches are both performances, the comedian draws a distinction between the two according to their performance context, naming one more "real" than the other. This article will address this notion by using the television broadcasts of Charlie Murphy's True Hollywood Stories to discuss the formation of identity and the veracity of the same in contemporary culture, with particular reference to notions of celebrity as discussed in the work of Richard Dyer.

This chapter will initially consider the effect of the multiple contexts used by the True Hollywood Stories (interview, monologue, sketches and so forth) on the production of identity. To do so, it establishes a working model of the discursive construction of the self and applies the same to the concept and workings of the True Hollywood Stories. It then proceeds to case studies of the broadcast material and examines the ways in which the True Hollywood Stories illustrate such philosophical notions as identity discourse and the parallax view of self. By situating this discussion within the wider context of celebrity culture, this article will conclude regarding the cultural relevance of these conceptions of identity to today's entertainment industry and contemporary society more generally.

Identity Discourse, Parallax and the Construction of the Self

The Socratic and Platonic notion of the soul as the incorporeal, eternal essence of a person is the basis for the notion of an inherent, constant self. This view may be categorized as a type of essentialism (a doctrine that says material objects have an essence distinguishable from their attributes and existence) and defines the self as unified and constant. However, contemporary and postmodern viewpoints deviate widely from essentialism and many now define the self as fluid and entirely changeable; no more than a performance that is chosen according to the situation. This view is common to multiple disciplines that include philosophy (David Hume denies the distinction between the self and constantly changing emotional responses), literary studies (Judith Butler's work on performative gender), cultural studies (Jean Baudrillard and simulacra), linguistic studies (discourse analysis) and religious studies (for example Buddhism), to name but a few. Cultural criticism also emphasizes the role of perception in identity construction; for example Stuart Hall comments, "If we feel that we have a unified identity from birth to death, it is only because we construct a comforting story or 'narrative of the self' about ourselves."[3]

Contemporary thought therefore struggles to reconcile the traditional understanding of the constant self with the variable nature of personality traits. However, these conflicting perspectives may be integrated to some degree by the theories of Slavoj Žižek. Žižek's seminal work *The Parallax View* relates the scientific notion of parallax to a variety of debates, including the ontological, the religious, and the political.[4] Parallax is defined as an apparent change in the position of an object that is actually caused by a change in the position of the observer. Our viewpoint of the moon, for example, is parallactic, as its changes of shape are also due to alterations in the position of the Earth with respect to the sun.

Žižek theorizes that this standard definition of parallax is applicable in a metaphorical sense as well as a purely physical one, stating that an awareness of one's self or position changes being itself; for example, as in politics, when the passive working class become the active revolutionaries.[5] He relates the concept to the notion of self, defining parallax as "this gap which separates the one from itself."[6] This enables him to argue that the self exists as both eternal and mutable, as "one and the same element in two different spaces," and the distinction between the two depends solely on the observational position.[7] Žižek also extends this theory to notions such as the real (as the opposite of semblance or appearance) and truth (which can then be defined as both an inherent quality and relative concept). He thereby "proves" their existence, not simply as inaccessible things but as having a dual status via this gap in perception.[8] In this way both the eternal and the mutable viewpoints are simultaneously validated.

Although this might appear to be the philosophical equivalent of having one's cake and eating it, it provides a rational basis for theories such as solipsism, according to which only the mind can definitively be said to exist. This is, of course, an extreme standpoint. However, the parallax view validates the notion of 'reality' as both produced by the mind (as all experience is necessarily mediated by our senses) and as having an objective existence (as even contradictory interpretations of events prove the external reality of the events themselves as source material). Both notions are one and the same thing, just approached from a different standpoint.

Less radical contemporary thought in this area uses the notion of discourse to argue that the construction of any reality is selective. Discourse here is defined as a system of options from which language users make their choice. Many contemporary theorists now view notions such as identity as discursively constructed: that is, our identity is formed through a series of choices we make every day. This process constitutes identity discourse, and theorists such as Ferdinand de Saussure, Jacques Derrida and Ludwig Wittgenstein have explored the notion of discursive thought and language.

In this way "philosophers and cultural studies writers have questioned the assumption that identity is a fixed 'thing' that we possess. Identity, it is argued, is not best understood as an entity but as an emotionally charged description of ourselves."[9] It is fluid, and constructed according to the specific context we find ourselves in. Nowhere is this more apparent than in the context of celebrity, where identity is both the symptom and product of the media.

Cultural discourse analysis therefore adopts a non-essentialist view of truth and meaning. It states that meaning in language is "generated through the relations of difference between signs and that, as a consequence, language cannot produce truth as a correspondence of the word-world relationship."[10] Essentially, it employs an anti-representationalist understanding of language, denying that language refers to an independent object. For Barker and Galasiński, "[l]anguage 'makes' rather than 'finds'; representation does not 'picture' the world but constitutes it."[11] Nowhere is this more apparent than in the context of an anecdote, where the layers of language that constitute the real are at their most opaque and apparent.

This article therefore proposes a model of discursive identity that uses the parallax terminology to posit a perceived coexistence of both types of self. It seems that the notion of an essential self may well be defined as a fiction constructed from a very selective narrative of one's life, where events that do not fit are ignored. However, this does not belie the essential self's perceived existence. This is because if one perceives oneself a certain way then this will color one's actions with reference to the changeable self. In this way, the essential self does effectively exist, albeit as a parallactic version of the changeable self, and vice versa.

The significant elements of this critical model are, therefore, self-perception and discursive production, which qualities bring into being the parallactic self: as both constant and mutable. A changing perspective creates the parallax gap (whether this is achieved through an awareness of self, the subsequent nature of events, or different audience positions). Identity is constructed through discourse, which is adapted according to context: including events, circumstances, relationships and so forth. Since celebrity anecdotes may constitute the most appropriate examples for cultural discourse analysis, as suggested above, this article will now apply this model to the structure and content of Charlie Murphy's True Hollywood Stories.

Charlie Murphy's True Hollywood Stories

The first of Charlie Murphy's True Hollywood Stories was broadcast in 2004 as part of Season Two of *Chappelle's Show* (Season Two; Episode 4). Following record sales of the Season One DVD,[12] the show was at the height of its fame at this time, and the segment was an instant hit. In fact it might have been too popular; Chappelle quit the show midway through production of the third series, despite the lure of vast amounts of cash and a contract that gave him the freedom to engage in as many side projects as he wanted. Although he cited artistic differences for this, the legacy of Charlie Murphy's True Hollywood Stories was certainly affecting his other work, as noted.

It is the production of the True Hollywood Stories that make them particularly interesting. The segments are collages made up of Charlie's monologue to camera, re-enactments of the events and (in the case of Rick James) interview footage with the star himself. In these dramatized skits, Chappelle impersonates Rick James and Prince, while Charlie Murphy plays himself and incidental characters are played by stock actors.[13] Multiple narrative forms such as dramatization, monologue, and interview are used, alongside a variety of techniques including impersonation, special effects, authenticity claims, and pastiche. These combinations produce plural — and often contradictory — subject positions for the characters involved. The segments also invoke multiple levels of audience as, although they were pre-recorded, they were played back in front of a studio audience, whose laughter is incorporated into the broadcast received by home viewers.

Each of the production styles used (such as monologue, interview, or sketch) has its own truth status and generic conventions and expectations. As such, the True Hollywood Stories may be defined as a discursive production, as discourse is a system of options from which language users make their choices. Both the events and the language used are key to their representation of reality. That they have been consciously scripted and selected to create a particular effect does not make analysis any less valid. This in fact might make them more relevant to the construction of celebrity, if this phenomenon is viewed as the deliberate manipulation of image — Dyer notes that the "real" identity of the star is just as produced as their various roles.[14] It should also be remembered that Chappelle apparently improvised many of the asides and catchphrases used.

The title initially sets up the truth claim of the entire story, although it is worth noting it is also somewhat paradoxical by combining the words "true," "Hollywood," and "stories." It opens with Charlie Murphy's monologue (although he is talking to a person behind camera their responses aren't heard), which, as a form of address, contains inherent truth-value. This is backed up by its content: Charlie frequently demands to be believed and makes comments such as "I'm not bullshitting, man," "Who the fuck could make up that shit?" and "Trust me." Rhetoric, repetition, and visual reinforcement are also used; at the climax of the Prince sketch, Charlie confronts the audience(s),[15] demanding, "You don't believe me? You think I'm making it up?" He then continues, "After it was all over he took us in the house and served us pancakes. [Pauses, nods, and reaffirms the line.] Pancakes." The pause, definitive nod of the head, and deadpan delivery stress the truth claim as Charlie stares down the camera, daring us to disbelieve him.

The interview format also has a high truth-value. Although the broadcast content of Rick James's interview has necessarily been selected in order to support the story, it is in fact largely representative of the uncut content. Although Rick disagrees on specifics and denies certain elements of the stories ("He may have smacked me, but there weren't no tears coming out of my eyes"), overall his version accords with Charlie's. Rick even verifies the Prince anecdote, saying, "There's a story that goes around in Hollywood to this day about this basketball game that went down. About this short androgynous skirt high-heeled fishnet-stocking going 'ooh ooh' wannabe-man type human being, and Charlie and him playing at basketball.... Do you know this little thing beat Charlie and them in high-heeled stilettos."[16]

The two formats of monologue and interview both have strong truth-claim status at multiple levels. This is present in both the speakers' tones (Charlie and Rick both raise their voices at various points) and content (such as Charlie's demands to be believed, Rick's concession that the two of them used to play-fight "a lot," and the overall corroboration of the two stories). The visual style used also supports such an interpretation as both appear in front of plain backgrounds and in close-up, giving the impression of letting the story speak for itself.

By contrast, the reenactment of the events is self-consciously comedic. It uses various tactics and genre conventions to defamiliarize and to exaggerate events for comedy effect. These include literality, juxtaposition, use of inappropriate genre conventions such as slow-motion replays or emotive music, exaggeration, and repetition.

The following case studies will consider specific examples of how the over-hyped fictional status of the dramatization contrasts with the truth-centered structure of the monologues and the ways in which this opposition informs a discursive view of constructed identity. This is obvious in the way in which minor contradictions are absorbed into the kind of "narrative of the self" that Stuart Hall identifies. For example, the full Rick James interview includes his statement that the ring he wore to punch Charlie was not his "Unity" ring (as Charlie claims), but another one. However, the broadcast clip only shows Rick pointing to his bedecked hand and saying "and this was imprinted in that black head of his for at least a week."

In this instance, we can see how the multiple subject position of the audience also affects the perception of the stories. At the widest level is the audience for the DVD sales, who have access to all the extras, interview footage, and so forth. There is also the at-home audience for the television broadcast as an event, and the studio audience for that evening, who provided the live laugh track as the pre-recorded segments were aired. There also exists an implicit audience for the filming of the segments, which includes the interviewers. Finally, there is also the implied audience of the original tales, which Chappelle states were told "at lunchtime" in a different, informal context. As noted in my theoretical discussion of parallax, it is achieved through a difference of perspective, and, therefore, these multiple positions are integral to the creation of differing versions. Different audiences have access to different levels of information, for example as illustrated by the ring anecdote, and, therefore, will perceive the truth value and personalities of the people involved in the story differently. In this way, the competing nature of these versions seems to inform a parallactic view of self. An identity discourse is thereby created through the coexistence of competing versions, and this article now considers some of the specific ways in which this is achieved.

Case Study: "I'm Rick James"

The sketches used in the True Hollywood Stories rely on various tactics to achieve comedy, and I will now analyze some of these and explore the other effects they have on identity discourse. Literality is used frequently: Charlie Murphy comments that, when he met Rick James, "I seen like an orange, his aura or whatever, I seen it. It was orange." We are then shown a clip of Chappelle dressed as Rick James (with long braided hair sporting silver beads and wearing an animal print top) in front of an orange glow (presumably created through lighting effects and a colored background), looking into the camera and beckoning us towards him.

The construction of this image, while adhering literally to Charlie's words, also undermines them by exaggerating his description and aping a divinity that is somewhat at odds with our understanding of Rick James as a funk singer. It may be this that produces the laugh with which the studio audience responds, although it may also be that their amusement stems from this first glimpse of Chappelle dressed in such an outrageous manner.

Chappelle's engagement with the camera has the effect of flattening all the various audiences into one, as he is directly addressing the camera-as-audience (while filming), the studio audience and the at-home audience (who are both watching the clip). However, the laugh included in the broadcast has the effect of separating the three audiences again, since only the at-home audience will experience it as part of the sketch. In this sense, the audience(s) exist in a parallactic relationship; simultaneously both merged into one through the experience of being directly addressed, and segregated due to the (non-)inclusion of the laugh.

Juxtaposition is also used for comedic effect, as the outrageous sits alongside the realistic. This is most obvious in the characterization; although Chappelle's impersonation of Rick James initially seems exaggerated for comedic effect, the evidence seems to state otherwise. Chappelle states that "most of the Rick stuff was ad-libbed," but, notwithstanding this, a lot of the phrases are accurate and on the DVD commentary Chappelle reveals that he had met Rick on a few occasions. At another point in the commentary, director Neal Brennan asks, "Did anyone tell you Rick used to say 'celebration'?" After Chappelle responds in the negative, Brennan continues: "Apparently Rick used to say 'celebration' all the time. I went to Rick's funeral with Charlie and on the front cover it said, 'A Celebration.'" Similarly, the now-infamous catchphrase "I'm Rick James, bitch" has an authentic basis although it was actually created only as an afterthought for the show's "To be continued" shot. Chappelle notes that "Rick actually used to say that ... it just became the thrust of my impression."[17]

Events in the skits have a similar status; the implausible is in fact correct. Near the beginning of the Studio 54 sketch, Chappelle (as Rick) licks a girl's face. Again, this seems excessive; but Charlie confirms he witnessed similar events. He is incredulous: "It was none of the things you would think would happen if a black man ... walks up to a white woman and licks the whole side of her face and calls her a bitch." Rick also confirms that "I did a lot of licking of girls' faces ... [but] I'd always pick out somebody I knew ... so I fooled his ass."[18]

Depending on perspective, then, both the linguistic and dramatic constructions of Rick's idiosyncrasies have a dual status as both true and false. On the one hand, the phrasing (such as "celebration") is improvised and based on no actual knowledge; on the other, however, it accords exactly with Rick's reputation and, uncannily, even aligns with certain quoted words of his. Similarly, unlikely events such as licking girls' faces, not only happened, but also are actually rationalized by Rick James's extra information. In this way the notion of truth also becomes parallactic.

Genre conventions are also used for comedic effect, for example, in Charlie's confrontation of Rick in his hotel room. After Charlie kicks Chappelle, a slow motion replay of the kung fu kick is shown from a side angle. Chappelle then summons security. At this point dramatic music is played and Chappelle declaims, "Now, Darkness, the tables have turned! [To security guards] Do with him whatever you like!" The use of inappropriate genre conventions adds comedic effect, for example by making Charlie's kick into one to rival Bruce Lee's. It also fictionalizes the events by invoking genre expectations, for example, that of a kung-fu movie and its associated excess in special effects.

This process is continued in the second Rick James sketch, in which Rick deliberately damages Eddie Murphy's expensive new couch. Chappelle's frantic grinding of his feet into the couch, along with his shouts of "Fuck yo' couch, nigger!" and "Buy a new one you rich motherfucker!" are clearly an exaggeration of the actual event. Similarly, after receiving a beating from the Murphy brothers, an apparently crippled Chappelle drags himself out of the room on his elbows. This also uses genre convention in a similar manner to the above, as emotive music is played as he crawls out while sobbing further insults.

However, in some senses the excess is in fact merely a literal representation of the truth claim of the story, as Charlie Murphy's voiceover states that after the beating Rick's legs were "like linguini." We are then shown Chappelle's battered, flattened legs as he drags himself out. As before, literality is used for comedic effect, which again results in a parallactic scene where literalized events can therefore be defined as both accurate and fictional.

The truth-value of the anecdote as a whole is treated similarly, as Rick's motivation was indeed that Eddie was a "rich motherfucker." Ridiculous though the story seems, Rick's interview again confirms the events as he concedes, "Yeah I remember grinding my feet into Eddie's couch" and, when asked "Do you remember why you did it?" he replies, "Because Eddie could buy another one." This explanation is also born out by external sources; for example, Rick's funeral instructions, which he had drawn up years before his death and given to his children with the emphatic statement: "And then call Eddie Murphy and tell that rich muther to pay for it."[19]

However, the Chappelle Show does not use this portion of the interview, preferring instead to show Rick contradicting himself for comedic effect. Of the following complete statement, the italicized words were the only ones broadcast:

> And I bet it was something like, uh, Eddie or Charlie or somebody did it to my couch. *See I never just did things just to do them. C'mon, I mean what am I going to do, just all of a sudden just jump up and grind my feet into someone's couch like it was something to do? C'mon, I got a little more sense than that. Yeah I remember grinding my feet in Eddie's couch,* you know. It was probably a dare from Charlie and I wouldn't do it.[20]

Truncated in this way, the broadcast section seems contradictory. However, despite the confused syntax it seems clear that what Rick is actually trying to say is that he would have had a reason for ruining the couch, rather than simply doing it on a whim.

The truncated statement is rewound and played back as part of the segment, which technique emphasizes its inconsistency. The same technique is used with Rick James's statement "Cocaine is a hell of a drug," which appears in this sketch four times. Brennan and Chappelle point to the role of the audience in these decisions, saying that when the rough cut of the sketch was shown to a test audience with the phrases only played once, people only "sort of thought they heard it."[21] Therefore, repetition is not just used for comedic effect but for emphasis. However, this creates a different effect: repeating the statement makes Rick's comment sound like an excuse rather than the aside it actually is. It also emphasizes the role of this drug and in so doing undermines the reliability of Rick's side of the story still further.

The monologues are edited for broadcast so that no such suspicion attaches to Charlie Murphy, despite the fact that his uncut interview contains similar content. As Charlie himself says, "Whatever was available for Eddie Murphy, on the dark side, I got all of it.... Millions of chicks, kilos of blow, bales of weed." Rick is less subtle in his assessment of Charlie's reliability, saying in his interview (also not broadcast): "Charlie, he has a very short-term memory bank. You know, all the cocaine we did in the eighties, and drinking, has got to him, it's got to him, he's got like two brain cells left. He's a liar, Charlie's lying like a Persian rug."[22] The point is somewhat moot since, not only do both men agree that the event took place, but there is also validation (albeit second-hand) from a sober source: Eddie Murphy, who "pointed out it was a red couch, and Rick was wearing Capezios." Again, we can see a simultaneous validation (of the events that took place) and denial (of the image offered to us), which illustrates the idea of truth as a parallax.

The third of the sketches suffers from none of these problems of verification, as it opens with Rick's statement: "I heard him [Charlie] tell a story that he came into the China Club one time and I was behind the bar. Now this is true." The tale continues as Rick slaps Charlie without provocation, and Charlie responds in kind. Again, the slow motion replay is used for laughs as Chappelle (as Rick) slaps Charlie. However, this time the humor also derives from the fact that the "replay" is in fact separate footage that is exaggerated for effect; in delivering the "replay" slap Chappelle spins round in a full circle, so fast his hat falls off. This use of replay has in fact also been the subject of other sketches on the show. The first episode of the second season includes a sketch called "Everything Looks Better in Slow Motion." In this, various scenarios are played out, before an alleged slow motion replay (actually a re-filmed version of the sketch in question) is shown.

After the replay, Charlie elaborates, "I came down on it like this, and his extensions was flying all over the place." We then cut to Rick, who sternly says, "That is absurd!" This response could again be considered contradictory (since he has previously validated the whole tale) — but, taken in its entirety, Rick's statement is, of course, a little less definitive:

> Now, Charlie tells it like, after I did that, that he tells me to come over and he smacked me and tears start coming out of my eyes. Now *that is absurd!* What, I'm gonna cry, now? He may have smacked me, but there weren't no tears coming out of my eyes...[23]

The sketch continues as Charlie explains that Rick "totally, really, forgot" that he had previously slapped him. In Charlie's uncut monologue, however, he expands on this notion, saying, "Rick would be so fucking high, when he was doing a lot of these things, that when he received these beatdowns, he probably don't even remember getting them.... An ass-whupping is kinda hard to accept, so he probably was in denial, y'know, and blacked it out." Although this statement accords with Rick's (uncut) comments above, it also implies that both men might be in denial as to some elements of the story. Rick undermines Charlie's description of the karate kick in the hotel room in a similar manner, pointing to Charlie's cocaine use, and also say-ing,

> He didn't even know nothing about karate in those days. Why you
> think Charlie Murphy is taking karate right now? Cos Charlie Murphy
> could not fight.... Don't you think Charlie's a little old to be taking
> karate? He's probably taking it with the little kids.[24]

This returns us to Stuart Hall's notion of the "comforting narrative" we construct for ourselves.

Discourse analysis

The above points illustrate some of the ways in which the True Holly-wood Stories offer conflicting truth claims, and the ways in which the result-ing multiplicity of the segments can be considered as parallax. In *Cultural Studies and Discourse Analysis*, Barker and Galasiński use discourse analysis techniques to deconstruct conversation and demonstrate how the discursive construction of cultural forms takes place.[25] Their thesis is that "[w]e cannot have an identity, rather we are a series of descriptions in language."[26] Although they note that discourse analysis is not appropriate for edited, constructed language, the ad-libbed nature of much of Chappelle's impression goes some way to circumnavigating this restriction. Furthermore, as long as we retain an awareness of the constructed nature of the rest of the dialogue used, it may be that we can nonetheless use discourse analysis to identify the effect of the language used, even if we must then acknowledge that this effect is artificially constructed.

Although space does not permit a full discussion, discourse analysis allows for statements to be deconstructed at various levels, including the lex-ico-grammatical,[27] vocabulary, and interpersonal function. This last includes such elements as mood, metalanguage, modality (that is, the speaker's atti-tude towards the propositions/utterance), and forms of address. Other ele-ments such as social interaction, control and textual function (cohesion between comments, theme/rheme structure, and information structure) should also be considered.

A good example of an improvised statement made by Chappelle (as Rick) might be his comment. "I wish I had four hands so I could give those titties four thumbs down."[28] The lexico-grammatical level of this state-ment delineates it as a mental clause, through use of the term "I wish." It is not, therefore, an obviously active or passive statement. Its vocabulary uses slang ("titties") and invokes excess ("four hands"). At the interpersonal level the statement's modality is disparaging, but also humorous— not only at a visual level but also because it debunks the listener's assumptions as to why the speaker might want four hands (not to grope, but instead to reject). The social interaction value of this statement revolves around a power play.

The overall lexico-grammatical effect of the True Hollywood Stories comes from material clauses. This reduces the truth-value of the stories and makes them more personal and anecdotal. It might also be said that this is backed up by the focus on naming: Chappelle (as Rick) acknowledges Charlie with a "Charlie Murphy!" as often as possible and also refers to him in this way in mid-conversation ("Bitches! Show Charlie Murphy your titties!") The over-used catchphrase "I'm Rick James, bitch!" again allows naming to dominate, and emphasizes this further through the addition of the word "bitch," which both derides the addressee and renders them anonymous.

At the lexico-grammatical level, "I'm Rick James, bitch!" is an existential statement. The vocabulary, again, is profane. The interpersonal level includes a modality that focuses on the speaker's superiority, and a disparaging mode of address. At the level of social interaction, again, the statement is all about control. Also, there is no textual function; it is an empty statement, devoid of content, which is only emphasized by its repetition. This also creates humor when the statement is reversed — as when we hear Chappelle relating a story that begins "So I said look, bitch, I'm Rick James."

The vocabulary used in the dialogue — and monologue — is also very visually descriptive. For example, when Rick summons security to his hotel room, Charlie narrates, "The one in the front he had crooked eyes. One eye was looking at me and the other one was looking at Rick." Neal Brennan confirms, "Charlie's obviously a great storyteller anyway, but they're the most cinematic, visual stories you've ever *seen*." Dave Chappelle backs this up, saying, "Charlie Murphy, what you *see* in this is what you get. If you ever meet Charlie Murphy, you're not gonna meet anybody different than what you *see* right here"[29] (my emphases).

Both these statements align the visual with veracity, a strategy common to postmodern narratives. Mark Currie's narratological model is relevant here; Currie proposes that narrative founds identity in that we construe our identity against that of others, via difference, and externalize our conception of it by using narrative methods; by telling our own story.[30] Further, he raises the question of view, of vision, commenting on the "tension between seeing and writing ... in contemporary narratology" since seeing overrules the authority of verbal narrative.[31] Although the reconstructions used in the True Hollywood Stories are patently false, the visuals of the language used in their dialogue and Charlie's narration supports this theory.

Case Study: "The Shirts Against the Blouses"

The final True Hollywood Story broadcast refers to an encounter in which the singer Prince and his fellow artists the Revolution beat the Murphys and their friends at a game of basketball, after which Prince made them all pancakes (Season Two; Episode 5). The juxtaposition of the banal and exotic is one of the major sources of humor in this sketch. However, it also comes from the contrast between the public and private persona of Prince, an opposition that again relates to parallax as regards the construction of celebrity.

Prince is a notoriously private artist and his ongoing attempts to control his own name and image have been directed not only at corporations but even at his fans. In 2007, he announced that he was going to sue the websites YouTube and eBay for unauthorized use of music and film content. Disputed instances included a home movie of a thirteen-month-old boy dancing in the family kitchen while "Let's Go Crazy" is played on a stereo in the background. Prince also demanded that fan sites and communities ceased reproducing any artwork with his likeness, including "photographs of their Prince inspired tattoos and their vehicles displaying Prince inspired license plates."[32]

As such, Prince's public image is heavily controlled while his private life is closely guarded. Chappelle's impersonation thereby relies heavily on public perception of the star's persona. He and the Revolution play basketball in the same clothes and high heels they wear on stage, and Chappelle dances his way through the recreated basketball game, even letting out the occasional high-pitched squeal in imitation of the artist's singing style. This contrasts with the serious, sporting comments he makes in baritone ("Good hustle"). Similarly, in response to Charlie's request for a towel halfway through the game, Chappelle responds, "Why don't you purify yourself in the waters of Lake Minnetonka?" Again, this is lifted from the public sphere as the line features in *Purple Rain*. Overall, Prince's public persona is incongruously transplanted in order to fill the gap of information that represents his private persona, and this results in comedy.

This is most obvious in the final scene, where Chappelle (as Prince) makes pancakes for everyone and gazes into the camera while holding a frying pan. Although Charlie Murphy's monologue states that "he made us all pancakes," it is not clear whether this means that Prince did the actual cooking. Certainly it seems unlikely that Prince would have stood and served them all in the subservient manner depicted onscreen, or that he would have done so in a manner so reminiscent of his stage presence, as when he lets out a moan while gazing at the camera. Again, the public is resituated in the private space and, like Rick James's orange aura, a literal visual interpretation of the narrative is used for comedy.

Unlike the Rick James segments, the Prince story doesn't contain an interview with the artist, but Prince has confirmed the story in an interview with MTV, saying, "the whupping is true" (although he denies the high heels).[33] As noted, the unbroadcasted section of the Rick James interview also confirms this story as public knowledge. There is also independent truth-value as Prince was a basketball player in high school; the *Star Tribune* published an article in 2004 that includes comments from his sophomore basketball coach and physical education teacher, Al Nuness, stating that "Prince was a darn good basketball player."[34]

In this sense, then, the public and private personas of Prince are parallactic — our view of the artist changes depending on how much information we have. Seemingly contradictory elements such as his basketball skills are incorporated in this way, and rationalized. In conclusion, this article will consider how this process informs our understanding of the construction of celebrity and star culture.

Celebrity Culture

The celebrity figure seems to most obviously represent the notion of self as performance that this article seeks to explore. At the start of this chapter, I noted Chappelle's use of the words "I'm real" to contrast his live stand-up with his Comedy Central shows. In the past, Hollywood has only promoted the screen personas of its stars: for example, Cary Grant as the virile, charismatic and debonair leading man, with little being known about the personality of Archibald Alexander Leach (his real name). However, the contemporary construction of the star persona has made the personal lives of celebrities more and more open to the public. The plethora of reality shows that have emerged since *The Osbornes* are the most obvious examples of this, and the "real" star, who had previously been untouchable and unknowable, has become more accessible via celebrity culture.

Richard Dyer has written extensively on the subject, exploring the connection between the audience and the constructed star image. He attributes this development to the notion that "people increasingly wanted to take pleasure in people like themselves, realities like their own" and continues that one index of this trend's development "is the demystification of stars, no longer seen as special people but just like you and me."[35] Dyer also notes that, although the audience is aware the star persona is an appearance, "the whole media construction of stars encourages us to think in terms of 'really.'"[36] Tabloid publicity relies on the notion that "in its apparent or actual escape from the image that Hollywood is trying to promote, it seems more 'authentic.'"[37] It is thus often taken to give a privileged access to the real person of the star. It is also the place where one can read tensions between the star-as-person and her/his image, tensions which at another level become themselves crucial to the image."[38] The nature of publicity means that, despite appearances, it follows that the notion of the "real" identity of a star is just as much produced as their characters and roles.[39]

Dyer continues to explore the analogy between life and drama, a notion used from Plato onwards, and which informs the discussion of identity with which this article began. Life is where people, like actors, play parts. Dyer therefore concludes that we

> have two distinct conceptions of what we are, of our "selves." On the one hand, we can believe in "the existence of a knowable and constant self," which is theoretically distinct from the social roles we have to play and the ways we have of presenting our "personality" to others. On the other hand, as [Elizabeth] Burns stresses [in *Theatricality*], there is increasing anxiety about the validity of this autonomous, separate identity — we may only be our "performance," the way in which we take on the various socially defined modes of behaviour that our culture makes available.[40]

In this sense the construction of the celebrity in contemporary culture most obviously epitomizes the struggle for reconciliation between the inherent self and the self-as-performance. As the audience now demands— and gets— to see the star in both their public and private spheres, this structure seems to imply that even the inherent, essential self (the 'private') is performative. As P.D. Marshall states, "The celebrity sign effectively contains this tension between authentic and false cultural value. In its simultaneous embodiment of media construction, audience construction, and the real, living and breathing human being, the celebrity sign negotiates the competing and contradictory definitions of its own significance.... The power of the celebrity, then, is to represent the active construction of identity in the social world."[41]

This echoes the viewpoint of cultural discourse analysis. Chris Barker and Dariusz Galasiński define this contrast as being "between an eternal metaphysical self and a contingent linguistic self."[42] The result is multiple narratives of self due to different relationships, contexts and sites of interaction. The multiple formats used by the True Hollywood Stories illustrate this process by offering conflicting and contradictory truth claims that nonetheless exist within a coherent whole.

Conclusion

This chapter has tried to show how the notion of parallax can reconcile conflicting interpretations of the construction of identity. The self, and particularly the celebrity self, can be viewed as parallactic as it includes an "an awareness of the split between self-image and its commodified dissemination." Although the notion of self presupposes a "synthetic unity," "this unity is also the irreducible gap that emerges between the production of the self and its consumption, between the apperception of the self and its representation in photographs and records."[43]

The fact that so many elements of Dave Chappelle's impersonation have been adopted and merged with the "real" Rick James supports this notion of simultaneous unity and gap between the real/authentic self, and performed/changeable self. For example, the online "Rick James Soundboard" shows a central picture of Rick alongside smaller pictures of Chappelle, but the soundbites it contains are all from *Chappelle's Show*. In fact, except for Rick's now infamous "Cocaine's a hell of a drug" quote, all are actually Chappelle's voice![44] A teaser trailer shown briefly online for the 2007 Rick James movie (entitled *I'm Rick James*—a title that again references *Chappelle's Show*) also cut together the show's sketch footage with real-life footage of Rick. In this sense, Chappelle's identity claim ("I'm Rick James, bitch!") has indeed been fulfilled, albeit to the detriment of his other work, as noted.

The Charlie Murphy sketches make the distinction between "real" and "inauthentic" self a literal one by providing representations of both Rick James and Prince that are obviously false in many respects. However, using strategies such as literality, juxtaposition, genre conventions, editing and replay, the absurdities of these depictions are simultaneously validated. Multiple audience positions also contribute to this process and expose the notion of an authenticity that distinguishes between the public and private persona as a false one, attributable instead to parallax.

By smoothing over minor contradictions between competing versions of events into a coherent narrative, the editing of the True Hollywood Stories demonstrates the mediating processes of the discursively constructed self. In so doing, Chappelle's show redefines not just the notion of self but also the notion of truth as parallactic. The current "access all areas" approach to celebrity culture allows the notion of a star persona to exemplify the perceived divide between private/essential self and public/performed self, as both are constructed. Identity discourse that seeks to explore and rationalize the coexistence of the essential and performed self is, therefore, aided by Žižek's parallax view, and the True Hollywood Stories epitomize this process.

7

The Artistry of Ethnography in *Dave Chappelle's Block Party*

C. RILEY SNORTON

Inspired by the 1972 documentary *Wattstax*, *Dave Chappelle's Block Party* provides a compelling glimpse into the relationships between and among music, urban life, and everyday politics.[1] In what Chappelle has described as "the best single day" of his career, the film follows the comedian from the streets of his hometown, Dayton, Ohio, to the neighborhood of Bedford Stuyvesant (Bed-Stuy) in Brooklyn, New York, as he plans and promotes the ultimate outdoor concert. Some film critics, expecting the film to be a longer version of Chappelle's successful Comedy Central program, *Chappelle's Show,* stated that *Block Party* (2006) would appeal only to "fans of the bands."[2] However, to suggest that the film is merely focused on showcasing a stellar lineup of hip-hop and "neo-soul" artists glosses over the significance of the documentary as a piece of semi-ethnographic[3] evidence on urban life, black political thought and cultural expression.

Chappelle's reflexive considerations on the practice of celebrity, black masculinity, and the politics of cultural production might also designate him as a "native ethnographer," a term often used to describe those who share cultural, personal, and social identifications with the group they study.[4] Native ethnographers are expected to give an insider's perspective on a particular cultural phenomena or practice. However, providing an insider or "native" account is only one part of the practice of ethnography. Generally this perspective is called "emic," and all ethnographers are expected to understand how their informants make sense of their own culture.[5] On the other hand, ethnography, as a social scientific practice, must also provide an "etic" perspective, an analytic framework that successfully or at least compellingly interprets the data "into a more general theory of trans-local factuality and objectivity."[6] Anthropologist John L. Jackson, Jr., distinguishing native anthropology from anthropology more generally, argues that producing native ethnography also requires "embracing a certain brand of 'native politics'" such that native ethnography is "not simply an epistemological or method- ological corrective ... but also a distinctively political intervention."[7] In this tradition, *Block Party* explicitly engages the omnipresent, always untidy, and irreducible notion of politics, thus, blurring the distinctions between "emic" and "etic" designations in ethnographic research.[8] As this chapter discusses later, the film embraces the messiness of ethnographic fieldwork, routinely showcasing contradictory interviews and visualizing Chappelle's meditation on his interactions with the wide range of informants that help tell *Block Party's* story.

As a form of cultural expression, *Block Party* also visualizes the tension between Paul Gilroy's notions of "the politics of transfiguration" and "the politics of fulfillment," which he argues, animate the stakes in reading the politics/aesthetics of black cultural expression. As Gilroy suggests, the poli- tics of transfiguration "strives in pursuit of the sublime, struggling to repeat the unrepeatable, to present the unpresentable ... [its] hermeneutic focus pushes towards the mimetic, dramatic and performative" while the politics of fulfillment "necessitates a hermeneutic orientation which can assimilate the semiotic, verbal and textual."[9] Gilroy's definitions of the politics of transfiguration and fulfillment seem to mirror "emic" and "etic" distinctions in ethnographic practice. Transfiguration, in its pursuit of the sublime, par- allels the ethnographic impetus to assume an emic perspective, while the pol- itics of fulfillment, in its reliance on the semiotic and textual, correlate to the premium placed in social scientific research to provide an etic analytic. How- ever, as Gilroy argues and *Block Party* demonstrates, transfigurative politics interrupt discursive explanations of cultural objects by conveying the emo- tional and performative excesses of culture at the site of an event.

This chapter, divided into four sections, works from the premise that a critical examination of *Block Party* can contribute to ongoing popular and scholarly debates on the politics of hip-hop and sharpen conversations within anthropology on the relationship between representation and urban space. The first section explores how *Block Party* addresses questions of commodification and authenticity in hip-hop by focusing on the music as an event rather than as object. The second part investigates the relationship between media, representation and urban space. The third part discusses the narrative mechanisms employed in *Block Party* to examine the link between postmodernism and "post soul" politics. The final section takes a critical look at popular representations of anthropology mirror contemporary debates on ethnographic practice.

Viewing the documentary as a semi-ethnographic text in which Chap- pelle is an artist, native-informant and participant-observer in a meditation on the politics of black performance, researchers may gather valuable insights into the form and artistry of ethnography, which must be understood both as a genre and research practice. While a critical evaluation of *Block Party* may seem perceptibly useful to "urban ethnographers," the film should also be considered an aspirational model for any contemporary ethnographer who grapples with the effects of neoliberal globalization, which economically and socially complicate any simple notions of "home" and "abroad." Furthermore as cultural anthropologist Michaela Di Leonardo argues, anthropology has always been at home in America with more than fifty years of academic practice.[10] Mindful of the double meaning of "urban" as a descriptor for the processes of urbanization in a geographical locale and a euphemism for a particular subset of black culture, Chappelle's approach, i.e. his improvisational style and comedic approach, is also constructive for ethnographers who examine the complex relationships between and among race, vernacularism, power and space.[11]

Erve Chambers argues that ethnography involves not only "social scientific ideas," but also "humor and ironic subversion ... that finds its voice in exceptionality, exaggeration, reversal, and practice, [and] can lead us to a new understanding of [ethnography's] reflexive and sometimes radical intent."[12] *Block Party* "finds its voice" through these modes, but also in improvisation or spontaneous composition, which characterizes both the musical and comedic moments in the film as well as the movie's narrative structure. While Chappelle does not resemble the traditional prototype of the anthropologist, traveling to "exotic" lands to find the data and artifacts (à la Indiana Jones), he successfully brings the viewer into the ethnographic scene even as the film resists notions of finding any simple truths from the "evidence" provided.

It's Bigger Than Hip-Hop

Block Party opens on Chappelle stumbling upon two senior black men as they attempt to jumpstart a car. While one man examines the problem under the hood, the other fidgets with the ignition. Realizing that they could not hear each other, Chappelle pulls out a megaphone to alleviate the miscommunication caused by the thick glass window, which separates them. A hilarious moment aimed to garner the first belly laugh of the film, Chappelle's megaphone also performatively demonstrates the act of translation. Even as the two men share multiple identities— age, race, and gender — as well as a common goal, the megaphone reveals a need for additional mediation. Moments later Chappelle, with megaphone still pressed tightly to his mouth and the low sound of a marching band playing in the distance, introduces the premise of the film, listing the numerous acts slated for his block party.[13] What first appears to be a silly prop becomes an instrument, which communicates *Block Party*'s ethnographic sensibilities, namely to use comedy to translate and highlight intraracial differences and performatively amplify the contradictions of everyday life. Similar to the work of the megaphone in the opening scene, this section examines how *Block Party* produces a narrative about hip-hop and performance that exceeds and critiques certain popular and scholarly framings of the genre.

Early in the film, Roots member Ahmir-Khalib Thompson, also known as ?uestlove, explains a similarity among the artists—a quality they share with Chappelle—of possessing a fan base that "does not look like them." Since David Samuel's 1991 *New Republic* article, "The Rap on Rap: The 'Black Music' That Isn't Either," entered public discourse, many hip-hop aficionados have accepted that hip-hop's audience "is primarily composed of white suburban males."[14] Hip-hop scholar Bakari Kitwana argues that upon a preponderance of the data, there is in fact little scientific evidence to support such claims. Pointing to problems in sampling among marketing companies in the early nineties, Kitwana contends that this widely accepted "fact" is the result of a "nationwide game of Telephone, where one whispered thought gets twisted and exaggerated beyond recognition."[15]

Notwithstanding, the question of audience persists in most popular and scholarly discourses on hip-hop, and *Block Party* addresses this issue directly. The film captures several moments of Chappelle in his hometown, asking presumably random passers-by if they listen to rap music. A memorable scene includes Chappelle stopping at a convenience store in his hometown of Dayton, Ohio, to invite Ms. Hall, the store clerk to attend his block party. The cameras later return to the middle-aged white woman's home while she is packing for her stay in New York. As the camera shows her surveying her chosen outfits, the woman suddenly turns to the camera in a fit of exasperation to reveal that she does not quite know what to wear to a "rap party," but believes she should wear a thong. The scenes with the store clerk emphasize a recurrent theme in the film, namely that race and age remain key determining factors in who imagines herself part of hip-hop's listenership. Because Chappelle interviews mostly young black men and middle-aged and senior white people, the film produces a sharp contrast in how these groups constitute themselves vis-à-vis the music. However, *Block Party* also seems to suggest that unlikely listeners are not simply disinterested, unaware, or hostile to hip-hop, but rather have other impediments to listening. A Dayton interview with a senior white man is emblematic. Hailing the man down on a rather quiet street, Chappelle asks whether he listens to rap music, the older man claims that he would but the artists speak too quickly for him to hear the lyrics.

A notable exception includes Chappelle's interview with a senior white couple that inhabit the exquisite shambles of a house called the Broken Angel, which serves as the backdrop to the concert. The film spends considerable time on this couple, perhaps because their "quirkiness" is cause for a number of big laughs (sometimes at the couple's expense). While on a tour of their house, the camera captures the older woman explaining that hip-hop is inappropriate for children and adults due to its use of foul and vulgar language. In total, *Block Party* tells three versions of this story; we hear her retell her concerns twice and also see Chappelle relate his story of meeting them to performers during a rehearsal. As he shares the story of how the couple has worked for numerous years rebuilding the house, Chappelle seems struck by the ways their story mirrors his vision for the block party and the film, namely to create a beautiful imperfection from the disparate elements of life. Chappelle's retelling, both as a moment of intentional repetition and in its ability to subvert an earlier humorous moment in the film, demonstrates to ethnographers that each informant is valuable and all opinions are useful. As an instance of what Chamber's describes as an ethnographic "reversal," Chappelle's story reveals the attentiveness by which ethnographers should approach the rendering of one's informants' accounts, as they simultaneously tell us something about our areas of study and about ourselves.

Considering *Block Party* as one film among numerous documentaries on hip-hop, the movie distinguishes itself in its attempt to capture the experiential fervor of attending a "good concert." Reminiscent of blues performances in the 1930s, several other notable musicians, including John Legend and Big Daddy Kane, show up unannounced to jam. *Block Party*'s stress on performance necessitates a discussion of what Jackson describes as the distinction between racial authenticity and sincerity. In contrast to authenticity, or the verifiable and indisputable truthiness of an object, sincerity, which is accessed through performance, requires different measures. Jackson writes, "sincerity presumes a liaison *between* subjects— not some external adjudicator and a lifeless scroll. Questions of sincerity imply social interlocutors who presume one another's humanity, interiority, and subjectivity."[16] Avoiding mimicking popular tropes of music video-making in hip-hop, the film's editing sensibility underscore Jackson's definition of sincerity as it places moments of performance with moments of interiority and reflection. Instead the musical performances are interrupted by interviews with the artists as well as audience members.

Questions of audience in hip-hop literature also relate directly to the problem of commodification, a term that describes the process of replacing social values with market ones. Discourses on commodification and authenticity often take hip-hop as an object constantly in crises of losing its original potency and meaning. Fred Moten's theory of sounding commodities is instructive here in delineating the stakes of hip-hop as commodity and black cultural expression. Moten writes,

> The history of blackness is testament to the fact that objects can and do resist. Blackness — the extended movement of a specific upheaval, an ongoing irruption that arranges every line — is a strain that preserves the assumption of the equivalence of personhood and subjectivity. While subjectivity is defined by the subject's possession of itself and its objects, it is troubled by a dispossessive force objects exert such that the subjects seems to be possessed — infused, deformed — by the object it possesses.[17]

Moten, interested in the phonic materiality of the processes of dispossession and subjectivity described above, looks to a number of examples in jazz to substantiate what he calls "sounding commodities," or rather objects that speak. Moten elaborates, "what is at stake is not what the commodity says but that the commodity says or, more properly, that the commodity, in its inability to say, must be made to say."[18] Moten's theory helps us reframe the stakes of hip-hop in *Block Party*, directing us away from deriving any particular meanings from the lyrics sung by the performers and forcing us to consider the transfigurative politics of black performance. In other words, it asks us to consider how *Block Party* produces hip-hop as a black performance that struggles to present the *unrepresentable* by giving voice to the resistant screams of black commodity. The theory of sounding commodity also structures a particular understanding of Dave Chappelle's impromptu spoken word act performed during the concert, "Five-thousand black people standing in the rain; white people peppered among the crowd. All are welcome."

Understood through Jackson's model of racial sincerity and Moten's notion of sounding commodity, Chappelle's humorous welcome presents an anti-essentialist mode for understanding black cultural expression, which may also help critics forego circular arguments on questions of authenticity. As Michael Eric Dyson has written on this issue in relation to Tupac, the very question of whether a person is "real" only makes sense when one presumes "to know true black identity when they see it."[19] *Block Party*'s narrative suggests that hip-hop and black cultural expression exceed the politics of who attends the concert or buys the record simply because it subsists. It exists, like blackness, in a realm somewhere between commodity and embodied performance in what Ralph Ellison might have described as "something subjective, willful, and complexly and compellingly human."[20]

Living Just Enough for the City

As the birthplace of many popular hip-hop artists, including Jay-Z, Mos Def, and Busta Rhymes, Brooklyn is a key site for hip-hop aficionados. In particular, Bed-Stuy, the stomping grounds of Junior M.A.F.I.A (Junior Masters At Finding Intelligent Attitudes), which included member Lil Kim, P. Diddy Combs, and the Notorious B.I.G., holds particular significance in hip-hop history. Chappelle describes the varied landscape as looking alternately like the set of *The Cosby Show* and the set of *Good Times* upon return from their respective commercial breaks. Chappelle's use of iconic television programs of the 1970s and 1980s as descriptors for the situation in Bed-Stuy cleverly indexes at least an eighty-year history of economic underdevelopment and migration patterns in Brooklyn. *Good Times,* which premiered in 1974 and ran for six seasons, centers on a working class family living in a housing project, loosely based on the Cabrini Green projects on the north side of Chicago, which historian Harold X. Connolly argues shares an important similarity with Brooklyn, in that both areas have among the highest density of black residents in the country.[21] In contrast to the bleak economic environment depicted in *Good Times*, *The Cosby Show,* which aired from 1984 to 1992, focused on the Huxtables, a black upper-middle-class family. The stately residence the Huxtables called home very well might have been a brownstone in Bedford Stuyvesant, a remnant of the pre-war buildings first occupied by middle class whites and later well off blacks following the implementation of Franklin Delano Roosevelt's New Deal policies.[22]

Craig S. Wilder explains in his historical account of race and social power in Brooklyn that New Deal policies, particularly the discriminatory lending policies implemented under the Home Owners' Loan Corporation, created a dividing line between black and white residents in Brooklyn, producing a concentration of black people in the North. By the 1940s, the *Times* declared Bedford-Stuyvesant "Brooklyn's Harlem."[23] And by 1957, nearly 90 percent of black Brooklynites lived in Bed-Stuy.[24] Wilder argues,

> In "The Box," as Bedford Stuyvesant was called, profiteering and abusive landlords, realtors, and banks were free to violate any and all laws. Men and women were kept from honest employment. Children were persecuted in an inferior, segregated and overcrowded, and "ethnomaniacal" school system. Gerrymandering left the borough's most populous district politically impotent. The government pursued an inhumane and destructive "policy of littering an already deprived community with low-income housing projects."[25]

S. Craig Watkins further explains the patterns of economic bifurcation at work in African American communities like Bed-Stuy. He argues, "At one end of this bifurcated class structure are poor and working class blacks in ghetto communities that experience social, economic, spatial, and demographic isolation. On the other end is a black middle and lower middle class buoyed by increased access to higher education and professional employment."[26]

Citing Mary Pattilo-McCoy, Charis Kurbin argues that the close proximity of black middle class and black working poor in most urban environments is an important feature in how "street codes" emerge from the socio-structural characteristics of a community.[27] It is perhaps then no surprise that this environment bred a vibrant hip-hop community, including many of the musicians, Big Daddy Kane, Talib Kweli, and Mos Def, who perform at Chappelle's block party. *Block Party* also spends considerable time tracing the footprints of the deceased Notorious B.I.G. (aka Biggie Smalls), featuring Chappelle visiting Smalls' day care and reminiscing with fellow Junior M.A.F.I.A. member Lil' Cease about the neighborhood. The practice of reminiscing, or nostalgia, figures largely in how urban space is conceptualized more generally throughout the film.

Block Party, by situating the concert in discourses on nostalgia, or the yearning for an idealized past, produces feelings of intimacy. Audiences experience the opportunity of having an all-access pass to the concert, its host, and the performers as they spend a few days side-by-side with Chappelle. Visual culture scholars Giuliana Bruno and Patricia Aufderheide theorize the complex relationships between space, aesthetics, and notions of public and private, which come together under the rubric of "public intimacy." Bruno argues that the merging of art, space and architecture create a screen of virtual cultural memory where art becomes a culture of recollection.[28] Aufderheide, who theorizes the emergence of first-person documentary, a genre marked by first person voice and a commitment to conveying the storyteller's experience and worldview, argues that such work blurs the boundaries between journalism, public affairs, art and culture.[29] Aufderheide suggests that, "As [first-person documentary] becomes a mini-genre of its own, it stands both as a symptom of and response to the challenge of social location in a postmodern society."[30]

While the following section attends to the relationship between *Block Party* and postmodernism more directly, it is important to note here how music and location work together to create a shared sense of memory. It is the very reason why Chappelle chooses Bed-Stuy, which he calls the birthplace of hip-hop, as the site for his block party. Chappelle and Gondry explain in the documentary on the making of *Block Party, September in Brooklyn,* that their initial idea was to host the party in Central Park, but in an effort to "bring it back to the people" decided on a block party in Bed-Stuy. ?uestlove, who also serves as the musical director for the film, adds, in *September,* that the "grittier and guttier the spot is, the better it is for our music to reach the actual people." Also, the film's choice to begin the story in Dayton produces a form of spatial nostalgia that denotes a history of hip-hop that exceeds the boundaries of place. As some ethnographers[31] have discussed, popular culture factors largely in how youth understand their environments. *Block Party* often intersperses scenes from the concert in Brooklyn with scenes from Dayton. These temporal and spatial disjunctures evidence a relationship steeped in nostalgia that simultaneously evokes distopic and utopic futurity. In many ways, *Block Party* seems to operate aurally in similar ways as Spike Lee's classic film set in Bed-Stuy, *Do The Right Thing*, which film critic Victoria Johnson describes as musically demonstrating "the interconnectedness of private lives and public space" through its reliance on historic-nostalgic themes.[32] According to Johnson, the "historic-nostalgic score" of *Do The Right Thing* "implies that an idyllic community is realizable."[33] *Block Party* also draws on this motif as it constructs a community by bringing various members from around the country and the world to participate in an event. However, the juncture of Downing and Quincy also visualizes a dismal future of both increased gentrification and continued dilapidation.

Post-Modern Aesthetics/Post–Soul Politics

Manohla Dargis, in her review of *Block Party,* points to two key differences between it and earlier film *Wattstax*. The first difference, Dargis explains, is that Gondry cuts away from musical performances, which according to Dargis "wreaks havoc on the documentary's rhythms and not in a good way."[34] The other difference for Dargis is "race." She writes, "*Wattstax* ends on a freeze frame of a black fist, an electrifying sign of the times. Outside of Dead Prez and a cameo by Fred Hampton, Jr., the son of the slain Black Panther activist, *Dave Chappelle's Block Party* appears fairly tame by comparison."[35] Both of the differences Dargis identifies are useful in an examination of the politics and aesthetics of the film, prompting this section to explore two interrelated questions. How does the film not quite seem satisfying in its depiction of the concert itself? And how might that connect to the difference in "race" she describes? Addressing these questions also maps the relationship between postmodern aesthetics and the practice of "post-soul" politics, which characterize the contemporary music landscape.

Dargis' use of the term "race" seems to be shorthand for "race politics," and more precisely black nationalist politics. While Dargis declares that race is "clearly never far from Mr. Chappelle's mind," she also seems ambivalent about the ways race is evoked and discussed on film. Part of that ambivalence might be due to her misrecognition of what Mark Anthony Neal calls a "post-soul" aesthetic. In contrast to the soul aesthetic, epitomized in James Brown's 1968 hit, "Say it Loud — I'm Black and I'm Proud," Neal describes the post-soul aesthetic as a meditation on contemporary issues such as "deindustrialization, desegregation, the corporate annexation of black popular expression, cybernization in the workforce, the globalization of finance and communication, the general commodification of black life and culture, and the proliferation of black "meta-identities," that continuously collapses on modernist ideologies of race and reanimates "premodern" (African?) concepts of blackness."[36] The combination of ideas, according to Neal, renders "traditional" (or modern) tropes of blackness meaningless.

Neal also explains that both soul and post-soul aesthetics rely on a commoditization of politics to become visible. *Block Party* humorously, if not ironically, presents this idea in its segment on Dead Prez, a group known for its socialist and pan–Africanist lyrics and an aesthetic orientation they describe as somewhere between N.W.A. (Niggaz With Attitude) and Public Enemy.[37] Following a serious discussion on black politics and performance with Dead Prez members M-1 and stic.man, Chappelle reveals to the camera an emblem of a black fist on the tongue of his gleaming white sneakers, which he announces is specifically in honor of the rap duo. In what seems like a riff on Dick Hebdige's *Subculture: The Meaning of Style*,[38] a canonic text in cultural studies that explores the political economy of personal style, Chappelle's sneakers demonstrate the ways in which commodification inform and implicate soul and post-soul movements. Related in the form of a punch line, Chappelle draws on the referential nature of humor with its reliance on a sense of shared history and meaning structures, to examine the commoditization of history, meaning, and milieu.

Stuart Hall has argued on the nature of "postmodernism" and its relationship to its antecedent that there is nothing "novel," "unified" or particularly distinct about the postmodern condition.[39] Similarly, post-soul aesthetic/politics rely heavily on codes reified during the civil rights and Black Power movements and produced during and directly after the period of U.S. Reconstruction. Literary critic Edward Pavlic compellingly argues for hip-hop performance's inclusion in the tradition of "diasporic modernism," which he describes as a negotiation of "the ever-present crossroads of horizontal (social) and vertical (psychological) spaces" that not only interrogate black American experiences in terms of their relationship to patterns of migration from South to North but also triangulate with conceptions of Africanness.[40] Throughout the film, Chappelle jokingly invokes his African heritage as an explanation for his ability and tastes. In the same breadth with which Chappelle welcomes the "mixed" audience to his block party, Chappelle asks the crowd "Do you know why I can play the drums? Because I'm black!" The mix of essentialist and anti-essentialist claims characterize in part what is meant by a post-modern aesthetic. *Block Party* is alternately contradictory, repetitious, and disruptive in its narrative modes. Drawing on Jean-François Lyotard's definition of postmodern art, *Block Party* never loses its ability to disturb (or "wreak havoc" on) the viewer's expectations, which is precisely what makes Chappelle a compelling storyteller. Lyotard contends that the postmodern artist is not "in principle governed by pre-established rules.... Such rules and categories are what the work or text is investigating."[41] For Lyotard, postmodern art occurs as an event that disrupts and challenges the rules of presentation. It becomes a means to question dominant genres and a site for exposing the "differend," or the existence of conflicting opinions inherent in the norm. Simon Malpas further explains that for Lyotard "it is not a question of resolving a differend according [to] some set of pre established rules. Instead, the existence of the conflict that engenders it must be brought to light and new means of bearing witness must be sought."[42]

An unsettling example of such occurs near *Block Party's* conclusion. The cameras show recording artist and Fugees member Wyclef Jean interacting with the Central State University's marching band, which has traveled to perform at Chappelle's block party. Jean asks the students what changes they would make if they were elected president. After hearing their answers, he provides an impromptu performance of his song "If I Was President," the lyrics of which narrowly straddle stark realities and fantasies of race and human experience. Both students and audience are drawn into the lyrics, which deftly portray the impossibility of anti-imperialist radical black thought in the current U.S. and global political climate. Directly following his song, however, Wyclef Jean launches into a familiar and conservative script about the necessity of personal responsibility. He states, "Don't blame the white man for nothing.... I came to this country — I didn't know how to speak English, I made something of myself. I went to the library.... They got libraries in the 'hood. And if they don't got libraries, tell your mayor, your governor, whoever in your county, put some more fuckin' libraries in the 'hood."

Jean's song and sentiments are iconic of the heterodoxy of what Melissa Victoria Lacewell-Harris[43] has described as the black public sphere, and, furthermore, they reflect a profound paradox in black racial imaginaries. The filmic inclusion of Jean's performance is also particularly instructive to ethnographers as it reflects a storytelling technique that researchers would do well to heed. Jean and the students' scene, as a moment of improvisation — both at the level of lyrics and musical performance, as well as an instance of unresolved contradiction — renders visible the untidiness of political thought and performs the ethnographic possibility of effectively capturing these moments. If ethnography is a particular form of bearing witness, *Block Party* invites different modes of spectatorship by insisting on contradictions in time, politics, and place.

Ethnography Remixed and Remastered

Among popular representations of anthropologists, Dr. Henry Walton Jones, Jr., better known as Indiana Jones, is the most widely recognizable. Known as one of director and screenwriter George Lucas' most beloved creations, Jones is a professor of history and archaeology (by day) and adventurer (by night). Film critics and media scholars often characterize Jones as marked by duality; he is cynical and romantic, fallible and superhuman, an intellectual and an action hero.[44] Jones also demonstrates the realities and fantasies of anthropological knowledge production. His action-packed adventures dramatize the colonial legacies of anthropology as Jones narrowly misses death in pursuit of some priceless, foreign indigenous artifact, leaving a trail of wreckage in his wake. In contrast, *Block Party* stages its intervention on U.S. soil, with no clear object of study. Throughout the film, Chappelle's adventures are experienced internally, as he meditates on his planning and participation in the block party. Positioning Jones and Chappelle as paradigmatic foils, this section reflects on contemporary debates in anthropology.

David Machin suggests that much of the debate on ethnographic practice within anthropology has centered on questions of transparency.[45] Given that ethnographers cannot reproduce the world transparently through text or film, researchers have attempted to offer a number of approaches to address this problem. Machin contends that ethnography produces knowledge about the everyday, which perhaps better equips ethnographers to deal with "the ambiguity and flux in social life."[46] While Machin acknowledges that ethnographers construct realities rather than reflect the social world, he is committed to fine tuning ethnographic practice in an effort to continue its viability as a research tool. *Block Party* provides a number of key reminders in an ongoing conversation about the utility and relevance of ethnographic practice.

On at least two levels *Block Party* is explicitly and self-consciously engaged in constructing a social world — both at the level of technology (e.g., editing and camera angles) and at the level of content as it focuses on the creation of the block party as an event. At each level the film provides invaluable insights for ethnographic practice. The filming sensibility and style of editing reflect a commitment to flexibility over perfection, which according to Gondry, allows for something to become more perfect. The temporal and spatial disjunctures, which characterize the film's narrative, resist the slick composition or polish of classic story-telling. Instead it mirrors the form of a joke, an off-the-cuff improvisation, which presents and subverts evidence through humorous slights-of-hand. The result is that *Block Party* visualizes the effort of ethnographic research; it demonstrates the irreducible excess in studying culture and acknowledges the moments of "thick" and "thin" description.

At the level of content, *Block Party* encourages ethnographers to embrace the constructedness of the social worlds we create by flaunting personal politics while also striving to create something that is bigger than one individual story, perspective or moment. Rather than mining for data, Dave Chappelle provides a model similar to participation action research as he works with musicians to construct an event, which perhaps above all, reminds them why they perform at all. And for the folks he encounters in Brooklyn and Dayton, he provides incentives reminiscent of the discourse on the practice of gift-giving as a means to address the power differential between informants and researchers. For ethnographers, Chappelle reminds us that part of the story we tell about a particular phenomena is about the interaction between researcher and informant. As the scene with the couple from the Broken Angel house suggests, it is from the disparate elements of living, through the exploration of the polyphonic and even cacophonic voices of life, that we might perform diligently and sincerely the task of rendering the messiness of social interaction ethnographically accessible.

8

Gramsci, Selling Out, and the Politics of Race Loyalty

Exploring Chappelle's No-Show

AMARNATH AMARASINGAM

In late April 2005, with *Chappelle's Show* at the height of its popularity and success, Dave Chappelle simply walked away. Rumors abounded about why he had left: some stated that he experienced a mental breakdown due to overwork while others in the media "reported" that he had checked himself into a drug rehabilitation facility. To the surprise of many, however, Chappelle resurfaced a few weeks later in Durban, South Africa, stating that he was on a spiritual retreat. By early June, he was back in the United States performing stand up. He started his sold-out Caesar's Palace gig by sarcastically saying, "Thank you very much for welcoming me back to America.... In case you haven't heard about me, I'm insane."[1] A darker theory, which thankfully has not gained much traction, also surfaced insisting that the public was being deceived. According to a popular conspiracy website supposedly created by a retired public relations executive, a secret cabal of African American "dark crusaders," ranging from Oprah Winfrey and Bill Cosby to Jesse Jackson and Al Sharpton, schemed to ensure that the third season of the *Chappelle's Show* would never happen. As the website notes, "Collectively, they felt *Chappelle's Show* reinforced negative stereotypes about African Americans, and that its content was, in the words of group leader Bill Cosby 'setting race relations back 50 years.'"[2] The dark crusaders made threatening phone calls to his house and apparently had the power to ensure that all of his credit card transactions were declined. The theory goes on to point out that in March 2004, Chappelle was awoken in the middle of the night by a man sitting on his stomach holding a gun to his head. Oprah, standing bedside, leaned in and told Chappelle that he better "watch his step" because the dark crusaders have "more money than God" and can keep the harassment up forever.[3] The theory has been disproven as a viral marketing campaign but is still making the rounds through email and various message boards.[4]

The speculations began to die down as Chappelle returned to the United States and began granting interviews to explain in his own words what caused him to abandon his show so abruptly. It turned out that his reasons were less extraordinary and much more human. This chapter attempts to contextualize some of these reasons. Specifically, I argue that Chappelle is a Gramscian "organic intellectual" who left his wildly popular show because he was trapped in an environment that he felt was leading him to betray members of his community, and the obligations he had towards them. In other words, he feared that he was becoming a sellout and was shirking his responsibilities to the black community. As Randall Kennedy has argued, "the specter of the 'sellout' haunts the African American imagination."[5] However, a theoretical exploration of what it means to be a sellout and the process by which an individual becomes one has yet to be adequately explored. In this chapter, I use Antonio Gramsci's writings on hegemony and the intellectual to reconceptualize the notion of the sellout. It is argued that as organic intellectuals gain popularity and become mainstream, they face the danger of being incorporated into the ruling class and are left with a decision to make. Chappelle's decision was to step back from the brink. After providing an overview of Gramsci's writings on hegemony and the intellectual, I show how the notion of the sellout can be better understood in light of them. Finally, using interviews that Chappelle gave upon his return, as well as a scene from the *Lost Tapes*, I argue that Chappelle left his show predominantly to refortify his role as an organic intellectual who, through comedy, can negotiate with the hegemonic power structure on behalf of the black community.

Gramsci and Hegemony

Antonio Gramsci's (1891–1937) writings on hegemony and organic intellectuals are based on earlier Marxist thought. Marxist notions of base/superstructure as well as ideology underwent a highly original and nuanced elaboration in Gramsci's hands, which provided a particularly illuminating discussion of the importance of culture. In putting Hegel and idealism "right side up," Marx argued that ideas are not what drive human history; they are "nothing more than the ideal expression of the dominant material relationships, the dominant material relationships grasped as ideas."[6] He argues that the arena in which economic activity takes place, which he terms the "base" or "structure," determines and influences everything that happens in the "superstructure" (the law, education, politics, etc). As Jones notes, for Marx the "economic base is the most powerful and crucial level of social life. It is the base that brings the superstructure into being and which gives it its character."[7] The superstructure, in turn, maintains the workings of the base and conceals its true exploitational nature. For Marx, if society is to change, it must begin at the structural level, which for him amounts to a worker's revolution. Changes in the superstructure, although they may be signs of progress, do not affect the exploitation of the working class and thus cannot be truly revolutionary.

Gramsci developed a more nuanced interpretation of the relationship between the base and the superstructure. He expanded the linear relationship of the two in Marxist thought and proposed that the base and superstructure have a dialectical relationship, constantly impacting "upon each other with no level assumed to be the primary level of determinacy."[8] Additionally, Gramsci divided the superstructure into two further categories: the state and the civil society. The state consists of coercive and state-funded bureaucratic enterprises such as the police force, the army, the civil service, educational institutions, etc. The civil society, for Gramsci, consists of other organizations, which are not part of the base (economic production) or the state, "but which are relatively long-lasting institutions supported and run by people outside of the other two major spheres."[9] These organizations range from religious institutions, women's groups, and media organizations to youth groups, sports clubs, and environmental protection groups. It is important to keep in mind that any particular collective may shift the category to which it belongs or may, in some way, belong to more than one at any given period. The interrelationship between these three categories has been widely debated. As Bocock has noted, "Either the economic element does operate in some determining and specifiable way to affect the activities of the state and the organizations of civil society, or the state, and/or the components of civil society, can produce changes in the economic area."[10]

For Gramsci, then, society is made up of three elements: the base, which is the arena of economic production; the state, consisting of coercive groups like the police and armed forces; and the civil society. Marxist thought was a form of "economism" in that it was believed that "the economic base determines the ideological superstructures of religion, politics, the arts, law or education."[11] It is Gramsci's emphasis on the other two aspects of society that distinguishes him from traditional Marxist thinkers. Traditional Marxism, according to Gramsci, over-emphasized the economic sphere and assumed that once "a change in the ownership of the main economic means of production, distribution and exchange has been accomplished there will be no major obstacles to a truly democratic, and free, society."[12] This contention, from Gramsci's point of view, was flawed because it ignored the influence of other elements in society. Gramsci did not argue that the economic sphere was now irrelevant; instead, he extended the analysis to explore the ways in which power was exercised in the state and the civil society. This exploration of the interaction between the three elements of society forms the basis for his writings on hegemony. Although an adequate definition of the term is elusive,[13] Renate Holub provides a superb attempt:

> Hegemony is a concept that helps to explain, on the one hand, how state apparatuses, or political society — supported by and supporting a specific economic group — can coerce, via its institutions of law, police, army and prisons, the various strata of society into consenting to the status quo. On the other hand, and more importantly, hegemony is a concept that helps us to understand ... how and where political society and, above all, civil society, with its institutions ranging from education, religion and the family to the microstructures of the practices of everyday life, contribute to the production of meaning and values which in turn produce, direct and maintain the "spontaneous" consent of the various strata of society to that same status quo.[14]

This is an important aspect of Gramsci's notion of hegemony — it is not maintained solely through institutions, beliefs and ideologies but through the "common sense" functioning of everyday life. As Raymond Williams has noted, "Hegemony is a lived system of meanings and values, not simply an ideology, a sense of reality beyond which it is, for most people, difficult to move, a lived dominance and subordination, internalized."[15] Thus, hegemony is diffused throughout society in a system of values, morals, and attitudes. As the maintenance of the status quo becomes intimately tied to the mere functioning of everyday life, the ruling values take on a "natural" or "common sense" quality and become more difficult to challenge. For Gramsci, common sense is not a unified set of values instituted by every new group that comes to power. As he noted, common sense consists of "stratified deposits" left from previous philosophies containing "Stone Age elements and principles of a more advanced science, prejudices from all past phases of history at the local level and intuitions of a future philosophy which will be that of a human race united the world over."[16]

One of the ways in which the fragmentary, yet powerful, nature of common sense can be challenged is by introducing counter-hegemonic ideas as "new sedimentations."[17] For example, a potential revolutionary in the United States would not have much success if he or she suggested outright that voting should be done away with, the constitution should be scrapped, and a totalitarian way of government should be embraced. However, if such ideas were siphoned into society's "common sense," the revolutionary *may* have greater success. For Gramsci, this logic would function even for issues such as race, abortion, stem-cell research and environmentalism. As Landy states,

"New meanings and new attitudes are in the process of being created alongside the old: change is constantly in the state of becoming just as dominant and traditional practices are constantly exerting their power."[18] If a group wishes to challenge the prevailing common sense, in other words, they need to form a counter-hegemony. Since the majority of society accepts the current hegemony as common sense and as "the way things are done," counter-hegemonic struggle is difficult. This leads us into the discussion of intellectuals, who, for Gramsci, were crucial for the creation of a counter-hegemony.

The Organic Intellectual

As Giuseppe Vacca and others have argued, the notion of the intellectual is fundamental to understanding Gramsci's project.[19] Gramsci's thoughts on the intellectual, however, are not uniform as they were developed throughout his life.[20] He begins by noting that "all men are intellectuals" but "not all men have in society the function of intellectuals."[21] He humorously states in a footnote that just because "everyone at some time fries a couple of eggs or sews up a tear in a jacket, we do not necessarily say that everyone is a cook or a tailor."[22] What is considered to be an intellectual venture also changes throughout history. For example, cooking was not historically seen as an intellectual endeavor. In today's society, however, cooking is at some level mediated through "collective intellectuals" such as TV chefs and nutritionists who express "expert" opinions about how ingredients ought to be used, and how to make something healthy and aesthetically appealing.[23] The seemingly mundane act of eating has also come to be largely mediated by intellectuals of etiquette, who convey "knowledge" about which forks ought to be used for particular dishes and how to place a napkin on one's lap. Such intellectual mediation eventually becomes part of society's "common sense" and dictates how things "ought to be done."

For Gramsci, there are two types of intellectuals: traditional and organic. Traditional intellectuals are those who are withdrawn from the mundane complexity of social life. They consider themselves to be independent of the dominant social group and believe themselves to be functioning outside of its influence. The clergy, professors and painters are good examples of traditional intellectuals. For Gramsci, although they wish to think of themselves as working outside of the dominant social group, traditional intellectuals are in fact always perpetuating their values. As Gramsci states, "The intellectuals are the dominant group's 'deputies' exercising the subaltern functions of social hegemony and political government."[24] Thus, for Gramsci, traditional intellectuals are not as independent from the ruling group as they would like to believe. It is important to note that traditional intellectuals were once organic to a particular group but "now appear to be autonomous of that class" and they may again become organic "to a class or cause if conditions threaten its autonomy."[25] In other words, new issues may arise in society with which traditional intellectuals may choose to become involved. In fact, Gramsci argues that one of the first tasks of a counter-hegemonic initiative should be to "win over" the traditional intellectuals.

Organic intellectuals, on the other hand, arise within a new group and provide this new class of individuals with "homogeneity and an awareness of its own function not only in the economic but in the social and political fields."[26] They must be equipped to convey the needs and desires of the community they represent and must recognize that they are products of this community, which has a vested interest in their representative ability. The *modus operandi* of these intellectuals must be to voice the interests of the group they stand for and "to inspire its self-confidence as an historical actor and to provide it with social, cultural, and political leadership."[27] The education of a new "human mass" depends on the ability and leadership of organic intellectuals. As the group begins to organize itself, it depends on its intellectuals for "conceptual and philosophical elaboration of ideas."[28] These individuals could be scholars and writers but, in contemporary society, could, as Adamson notes, be "journalists, publishers, television personnel, and everyone else associated with what is now sometimes called the 'culture industry.'"[29] Popular culture may at times be dismissed as "low culture" but the discourse that takes place within it often contributes to the marketplace of ideas. For example, as the American war in Iraq declines in popularity, antiwar groups do depend on scholars to articulate their viewpoints, but also turn to elements of popular television. In other words, Richard Clarke's *Against All Enemies* (2004) and *Your Government Failed You* (2008) may be important but equally significant are *The Daily Show, The Colbert Report*, and *Real Time with Bill Maher* for providing an "elaboration of ideas" with which to criticize the United States government.[30]

The comedian is particularly well positioned to serve as an organic intellectual, capable of satirically challenging the hegemonic common sense that exists around issues of race, gender, religion, etc.[31] Comedians like Chris Rock, Paul Mooney, Russell Peters, Margaret Cho, and Dean Obeidallah are a few examples of organic intellectuals who challenge the stereotypes and common sense beliefs held about their respective ethnic groups. At the same time, they communicate to their own communities the worldviews expressed by the ruling class in order to achieve, through parody and satire, a relational equilibrium between both sectors of influence.

For example, Chappelle in his controversial skit "Reparations 2003" (Season One; Episode 4) pokes fun at members of the black community who are "trying to get paid for the work of [their] forefathers." He states that if African Americans ever do receive reparations, they will need to get together and "come up with a plan for the money." The sketch explores what some members of the black community may do with the money if they receive it without understanding the historical and political context in which it is given. After Congress approves over a trillion dollars in reparations, the sketch reports that there are enormous line-ups in front of liquor stores, that Sprint stock has "skyrocketed after the news that 2 million delinquent phone bills have been paid just this morning," the price of chicken has risen to six hundred dollars a bucket, eight thousand record labels have been started in the last hour, and 3 million Cadillac Escalades were sold in one afternoon. These reports are quickly followed by a sharp critique when the white reporter states: "It's incredible, Chuck, these people just seem to be breaking their necks to get this money right back to us." In the sketch, Chappelle criticizes what he perceives to be the materialism of some members of the black community who would do little of substance with the reparations money. Aside from record labels, black businesses would not be formed and most of the money would be given right back to white-owned corporations.

Comedians like Chappelle can offer such powerful commentary particularly because they reside in a separate cultural sphere in which certain kinds of expression are expected and permitted. This does not mean, however, that these "jokes" lack social consequence. One would only need to watch the guerilla attacks of comedians like Bill Hicks to understand their social significance. In fact, it is particularly because comedians communicate through what Mintz calls a "publicly protected" mode of expression that they have the potential to say what the politician cannot.[32] The comedian, as organic intellectual, can use humor "to expose chauvinism, to expose ineptitude, to expose oppression, and to expose pretentiousness."[33] Majken Sorensen has even gone so far as to argue that comedy could be a "powerful strategy of nonviolent resistance to oppression ... in a different way than traditional resistance."[34]

An example of such nonviolent resistance can be seen in Chappelle's spoof of *Law & Order* (Season 2; Episode 5). Chappelle criticizes the "two legal systems" that exist in America, which allows CEOs of "major corporations [that] rip everybody off" to receive very little jail time. The sketch switches the situation around: a police officer phones a cocaine dealer, Tron, at home and informs him that a warrant is out for his arrest. Wanting to avoid being "embarrassed in front of his family," Tron offers to turn himself in "around Thursday" between 2 and 6 P.M. He testifies in front of the Senate committee and is given one month at "Club Fed." The CEO, on the other hand, is violently arrested after police break down his door and shoot his dog. He is then granted an overworked legal aid lawyer who states, "your like my fourteenth case this week" and is given life in prison by a jury of "his peers" consisting of seven African Americans wearing baggy jeans, jewelry, and sweat suits. This sketch keenly highlights the manner in which organic intellectuals like Chappelle challenge the hegemonic structure at work, pointing out that societal values like "everyone is equal before the law" and "justice is blind" are at times nothing more than facile self-congratulation masking the deep institutional racism that exists below the radar.

Having explored Gramsci's writings on hegemony and the intellectual, we may now examine the notion of the sellout in light of these theories. I argue that in their role as representatives of a particular community, organic intellectuals inevitably experience the specter of being branded a sellout. In effectively communicating the needs of their community to the ruling class, organic intellectuals like Chappelle must often times become part of the power structure. As Holub has noted, "Everything which influences or is able to influence public opinion, directly or indirectly, belongs to it."[35] For example, Viacom, whose board of directors is mostly a "bunch of rich white guys," owns all of the television networks that are commonly seen to be challenging the mainstream — Comedy Central, Music Television (MTV), and Black Entertainment Television (BET). Organic intellectuals must work within the mainstream but still maintain enough creative control to be effective and relevant. In other words, the avenues that an organic intellectual like Chappelle must follow are owned by the very forces that make the organic intellectual necessary. As some of the interviews with Chappelle discussed below make clear, such a balancing act can become very difficult and emotionally taxing.

The Sellout: Feared and Detested

The fear of the sellout is rampant among many ethnic groups in the United States. When members of these communities enter positions of privilege, they indeed become objects of pride and admiration, but these feelings are often accompanied by a nervous uncertainty as to whether they will eventually "forget where they came from." The sellout has been branded with several epithets in the majority-white North American context. Most of the derogatory terms have referred to being or "acting white," which has been one of the constant characteristics of the sellout. Black sellouts have been called "Uncle Toms" or "Oreos," while South Asians have been called "coconuts" and Asians have been labeled "twinkies" or "bananas."[36] These epithets point to a deep-seated animosity towards "race betrayers" who the host community regards as a traitor and an ungrateful free rider. In studying the fear of the sellout among black Americans, Randall Kennedy notes that a sellout is "a person who betrays something to which she is said to owe allegiance" and can refer to individuals whose actions "retard African American advancement."[37] A sellout is much worse than a generic enemy of the group. Since the community had invested in him/her and placed a certain amount of trust in their loyalty, the betrayal stings exponentially and produces equally virulent scorn and dismissal.

Some of the earliest members of the black community labeled as sellouts were those individuals who recaptured runaway slaves or forewarned white authorities of impending slave revolts.[38] Many black authors who wrote treatises against the community were also roundly hated. One example is William Hannibal Thomas, who throughout his early life championed the African American cause. Later in life, however, he underwent a radical about-face and published *The American Negro* in 1901. The black individual, he wrote, "has a mind that never thinks in complex terms; Negro intelligence is both superficial and delusive ... [and] represents an illiterate race, in which ignorance, cowardice, folly, and idleness are rife."[39] The African American response was swift and seething. Some threatened him with physical assault and told him to "go off and hang thyself," while others, like Booker T. Washington, remarked that, "It is sad to think of a man without a country. It is sadder to think of a man without a race."[40] Both Malcolm X and Martin Luther King, Jr., spoke with derision against racial betrayal. Malcolm X called sellouts "house Negros" and King stated that there are many blacks in America "who will seek profit for themselves alone from the struggle."[41] Malcolm X and Martin Luther King were, of course, powerful organic intellectuals who squarely challenged the hegemonic power structures of the ruling class. Others branded as sellouts were those individuals who, working as spies for the American government, infiltrated civil rights organizations and kept an eye on groups like the Black Panther Party.

The fear of the sellout is not confined to the past. It seems that almost without exception, every successful African American public figure in the United States— Oprah, Sean "Puffy" Combs, Clarence Thomas, Condoleezza Rice, and Colin Powell — has, at one time or another, faced the question of whether they were selling out. During Barack Obama's run for President, the "problem" of whether he was "black enough" was repeatedly discussed.[42] As journalist Peter Beinart pointed out, it seems that "the more whites love you, the more you must reassure your own community that you are still one of them."[43] In a sketch called "The Racial Draft" (Season 2; Episode 1), Chappelle himself accuses Colin Powell and Condoleezza Rice of having abandoned the black community. In a draft that will "state the racial standing of these Americans once and for all," the black delegation chooses Tiger Woods, who although of mixed ethnic heritage (Black, Caucasian, American-Indian, and Asian) is now "officially Black." The white delegation chooses Colin Powell and ignites much controversy. Since Colin Powell "is not even an eighth white," the decision must be accepted by the black representative, who states, "We the black delegation accept the white delegation's offer to draft Colin Powell on the condition that they also accept Condoleezza Rice as part of the deal." Rice is then shown on screen as having been "given away by blacks." In the sketch, Chappelle accuses Powell and Rice, who have attained positions of power, of working against the interests of the black community simply due to their collusion with the Bush administration. This early sketch provides some evidence that Chappelle's fear of being branded a sellout was only heightened by his increasing popularity.

Why Did Chappelle Leave?

Like the "Racial Draft" discussed above, the first episode of the Lost Tapes as well as some interviews he gave upon his return, highlight the fact that Chappelle walked away from his show predominantly because he felt he was shirking his responsibilities as an organic intellectual. As discussed, the organic intellectual must be capable of voicing the needs and concerns of the community he or she represents. The community has invested much into these individuals and should be confident that they will not violate their obligations. If, on the other hand, these individuals not only shirk their responsibilities but also begin to cast the community in a negative light, this is doubly insulting. For Chappelle, the comedic venue was allowing him to break down stereotypes, to challenge other misconceptions, and to ensure that discussions of race were never far from the earshot of the ruling class, who often reassured themselves that the problem of race was over.

The first episode of the Lost Tapes depicts Chappelle at a barbershop getting a trim. The television announces that Chappelle has just received $50 million dollars for the third season of his show. Everyone in the barbershop turns to stare, and the barber tells Chappelle that he owes him eleven thousand dollars for the haircut. The fact that this scene takes place in a barbershop is significant. As Alexander notes, the black barbershop creates an "imagined community" where African American strangers can meet under conditions of cooperation, equality and kinship. It is a cultural space where black men are "engaged in friendly exchanges" and where they go to "find sustenance."[44] It is a "black man's way station, point of contact, and universal home. Here he always finds a welcome."[45] Drawing on personal experience, Alexander recalls that as he traveled from state to state throughout his life, "the test of establishing community for me has often been grounded in locating a barbershop."[46] As seen in this sketch, Chappelle suspects that members of the black community will begin to see him differently and take advantage of him. He fears that his role as an organic representative will dissolve, and he will be seen as an outsider, even in the quintessential space of black kinship: the barbershop.

During the shooting of the third season, it seems that Chappelle was becoming increasingly aware of his role as an organic intellectual. He grew more careful about what sketches he wrote and which ones he allowed to be shown. As his former writing partner Neal Brennan told *Time*, Chappelle would rethink and rework his sketches so much that, if he had his way, the show would constantly miss deadlines. He recalls that either Chappelle or him would think of an idea for a sketch and eagerly start the writing process. However, Chappelle's enthusiasm would soon subside: "We'd shoot it, and then at some point he'd start saying, 'This sketch is racist, and I don't want this on the air.' And I was like, 'you like this sketch. What do you mean?' There was this confusing contradictory thing: he was calling his own writing racist."[47]

In his interview with Oprah, Chappelle recalls that he was getting so caught up in the *process* that he often did not stop and reflect about whether the sketches he was producing were positive. As he states, "I was doing sketches that were funny but socially irresponsible ... it's like you're getting flooded with things and you don't pay attention to things like your ethics."[48] Chappelle cited the sketch about "racial pixies" (which was aired against his wishes in Episode 2 of the *Lost Tapes*) as the one that led him to suspect that he "had gone from sending up stereotypes to merely reinforcing them."[49] As he tells Oprah, "the premise of the sketch was that every race had this pixie, this racial complex. But, the pixie was in blackface. Now, blackface is a very difficult image, but the reason I had chosen blackface at the time was because this was going to be the visual personification of the N-word."[50] He states that during the taping of the sketch, a white member of the crew laughed in such a way that made him uneasy. He tells Oprah: "I know the difference between people laughing with me and people laughing at me. And it was the first time I'd ever gotten a laugh that I was uncomfortable with."[51]

Chappelle believes that his sketches have a positive role to play and will be properly received and interpreted by most Americans. Others, however, may not truly understand the nuanced critique of racism that he puts forth. He notes that "the kinds of people that scream 'I'm Rick James, Bitch!' at my concerts ... are going to get something completely different." In other words, Chappelle's sketches are presented in such a way that if one misses the nuance, they actually have the potential to be offensive and hurtful to the African American community. As he tells Oprah, "I don't want black people to be disappointed in me for putting that out there."[52] As Kevin Powell notes in his *Esquire* article on Chappelle, black entertainers appropriately feel that they have the right to creatively express themselves as they choose, but many also feel a deep sense of responsibility to the black community. Black organic intellectuals must "think about the sights and sounds you put out there on television because you are not interested in being merely a source of enjoyment for white America at the expense of black America."[53] According to some black critics, part of this "enjoyment" has been Chappelle's frequent use of the N-word. In a 2004 interview with Bob Simon of *60 Minutes*, Chappelle responded to his critics by pointing out that his use of the N-word was "an act of freedom."[54] Two years later, however, he told James Lipton of *Inside the Actor's Studio* that he may use the word again in the future "but right now I just feel like people aren't responsible enough."[55] Once again, we see that Chappelle, over the years, was becoming more aware of his role as an organic intellectual and was more cautious about the type of sketches that he produced and the type of language that he used.

Chappelle's Show, it seems, not only provided viewers with a candid discussion of race in America but also provided Chappelle himself with a deeper understanding of his role within that discourse. In interviews given after his return, he notes that the economic interests of the culture industry largely mediate artistic endeavors as well as the agenda of organic intellectuals who practice their craft with a larger purpose in mind. He tells the student audience at *Inside the Actor's Studio*: "You guys are students now, so you're idealists but you don't know about where art and corporate interests meet yet ... get your Africa tickets ready, because it's coming."[56] For Chappelle, intellectuals from the ruling class do not have to experience such difficulties. Organic intellectuals, on the other hand, have "this greater struggle that we at least have to keep in mind somewhere."[57] In encouraging America to examine itself, to take an honest look at the systemic racism that exists in the country, organic intellectuals like Chappelle must intimately interact with the ruling class. From such a vantage point, critiques will be more incisive and will reach a wider audience. The balancing act continues, however, between being fully incorporated into the hegemonic structure and remaining a significant organic voice for the counter-hegemonic community. And, sometimes, you have to go to Africa to regain your footing.

9

"When 'Keeping It Real' Goes Wrong"

Subversions of Racial Authenticity

KATHERINE LEE

The recurring *Chappelle's Show* sketch from which this essay gets its title charts the life-altering misfortunes of people whose answer to their various dilemmas is to "keep it real" (Season Two; Episode 7). One installment features Chappelle in the role of Vernon Franklin, a successful corporate V.P. At their weekly meeting, the executives— all of whom except Vernon are white — commend themselves on the completion of another successful venture. One executive, in a celebratory mood, holds his hand up to Vernon and says, "You da man! Gimme some skin." The action then freezes, and a voiceover narrator informs us that Vernon, already troubled that he might be an "Uncle Tom," decides to "keep it real": when the action resumes, he launches into a furious rant. He asks the executives, "You want me to do a softshoe? Should I juggle watermelons?" threatens physical violence, and finally concludes the diatribe by forming a "W" with his hands and yelling, "Wu Tang!" signifying his allegiance to rap music and rejection of dominant culture. (Also, fans of the show know that the Wu Tang Clan is a Chappelle favorite and two members, RZA and GZA, appear periodically in guest spots). The sketch concludes by showing Vernon literally out in the cold, cleaning windshields at his new gas station job, for which he earns $6.45 an hour: this, the narrator intones, "is as real as it can be." The rather cynical lesson that Chappelle offers afterwards to the studio audience is that "it's good to be phony sometimes," that is, it's better to acquiesce to white corporate culture (which some might indeed view as "Uncle Tom"–ism) if it proves more lucrative than asserting racial pride.

Critics of *Chappelle's Show* view these mercenary messages (another example of which is the phrase that follows the end credits, "I'm rich, bitch!"), along with Chappelle's reliance on stereotypes and epithets, especially the "N-

127

word," as emblematic of a retrograde approach to racial issues, and characterize the show as doing little more than repackaging dominant ideologies with raunchy language and provocative sketch premises. Matt Feeney argues that "Chappelle doesn't 'subvert' [racism]—he exploits it," and instead of following the politically subversive comic tradition of Lenny Bruce and Dick Gregory, he relies upon the "gleeful, cruel slapstick of the Three Stooges—the jarring, unwarranted violence of poked eyes and conked heads."[1] Similarly, other critics focus on Chappelle's caricatures of African Americans whose behavior and views seemingly reinforce rather than undermine dominant racial ideology. Katrina Bell-Jordan cites a Season 1 sketch that hypothesizes about reparations for slavery actually materializing, with characters spending their remunerations on delinquent phone bills, jewelry, and chicken, as a vivid example of Chappelle's use of "gross characterization" to "'call out' some African Americans for attitudes and behaviours that do little to dispel ... myths and stereotypes."[2] Ironically, Bell-Jordan notes, Chappelle's detractors view these caricatures as a counterproductive confirmation of these stereotypes rather than an intraracial critique of them: "Chappelle's acts of calling out are what many black people point to as the reason for their embarrassment and disappointment with the show and with Chappelle specifically."[3] Chappelle himself recounts a friend's accusation that he's "setting black people back with [his] comedy," and alludes to other encounters with censure and disapproval throughout the Chappelle's Show's two seasons. According to these criticisms, then, Chappelle is guilty of gleefully perpetuating reductive images and exploiting racist ideologies. He may be funny, but is most definitely not "keeping it real."

While these views—founded on an earnest desire to utilize popular cultural representations to effect progressive social change—certainly seem compelling, they are nevertheless highly problematic. The implicit premise of this critical approach is that such representations should serve a corrective and emancipatory function, dismantling stereotypes and forwarding socially prescriptive messages. In this context, "keeping it real" requires explicit confrontation with and subversion of dominant ideologies about race. Yet this evaluation of racial representations as either "positive" or "negative," "real" or "fake," is both limited and limiting, and the idea that one can easily discern the line between "real" and "fake" racial representations belies race's fluid and constructed nature. Sander Gilman describes stereotyping, or the perpetuation of so-called "fake" images, as "dynamic in its ability to alter itself," an "inherently protean rather than rigid" process.[4] If the "fake" is constantly shifting in meaning, the "real" correspondingly shifts as well. Thus distinctions between "real" and "fake" are contingent upon definitions of race (and more broadly, of culture itself) as fixed, static.

In addition, as Cornel West argues, this critical view promotes compulsory racial and cultural sameness by assuming the existence of a "black perspective to which all black people should adhere."[5] The exclusion or dismissal of those who fail to conform to a certain perspective and/or political agenda ironically reproduces what Judith Butler calls the "domains of exclusion," the same "us versus them" structure that informs racial "Othering" and racial stereotypes themselves. In other words, in spite of its underlying emancipatory intentions, this critical approach, which Homi Bhabha calls "the inverted polarities of a counter-politics," merely reverses rather than subverts "us/them" binary configurations.[6]

Moreover, while this kind of Manichean framework can enable clearcut and authoritative-sounding evaluations of racial representations such as Chappelle's in the name of political exigency, it also compels scholars to avoid discussion of precisely those tropes that complicate assignations of "real" and "fake," such as ambivalence, ambiguity, and contradiction. According to Stuart Hall, cultural critics must acknowledge and engage with such tropes when dealing with both specific representations and more general assessments of culture itself:

> If you work on culture ... if culture happens to be what seizes hold of your soul, you have to recognize that you will always be working in an area of displacement. There's always something decentred about the medium of culture, about language, textuality, and signification, which always escapes and evades the attempt to link it, directly and immediately, with other structures.[7]

Like Gilman's description of race, Hall's view characterizes culture and representation as fluid rather than totalized and static, which problematizes definitive pronouncements about the messages that texts like *Chappelle's Show* produce. Hall's observation also implies that any critical aversion to the idea of "decentredness" can only result in reductive interpretations that foreclose the possibility that multiple meanings might circulate around racial representations such as those on *Chappelle's Show*, and belie the complexity and richness of representations that such sources can provide.

The notion of ambivalence particularly resonates with critics dealing with issues of race and racial identity, as it informs the very process of identification itself. Hall observes that "identification is always constructed through ambivalence. Always constructed through splitting ... between that which one is, and that which is the other.... This is the Other that belongs inside one. This is the Other that one can only know from the place from which one stands."[8] Psychoanalytic scholars maintain that this ambivalence results from the identification and maturation process and more specifically, the development of an internal self/Other split, in which a child's increasingly traumatic and anxious realization about the lack of control over his/her environment effects a compensatory bifurcation into a "good" (that is, in control) self and a "bad" (powerless) self. According to Gilman, this bifurcation eventually becomes projected onto models from the external world, thereby "sav[ing] the self from any confrontation with the contradictions present in the necessary integration of 'bad' and 'good' aspects of the self."[9] This projection onto an Other of the "'bad' aspects of the self" functions as a means of alleviating anxiety about identity.

Transposed onto a larger scale, this projection results in the construction of racial identity, which functions as a dominant culture's way of dealing with anxieties about itself by marking those who do not fit or conform as racial Others. While the objects of projection are taken from the material realm, the ideas that inform these projections are largely fantastic in nature; as Gilman argues, "Because there is no real line between self and the Other, an imaginary line must be drawn."[10] Racism's "us/them" opposition is a product of psychic fantasy, a projection of the self/Other split that resides within onto an external Other. Consequently, the boundary between self and Other must be vigilantly and consistently reinforced, hence the "protean" and fluid nature of racial stereotypes, which shift as necessary to preserve this boundary. Static distinctions such as "real" and "fake" thus seem overly simplistic and reductive in light of race's circuitous negotiation between internal fantasy and external reality.

Even those critics who dismiss Chappelle's work occasionally acknowledge race's complex nature; Feeney, who earlier deemed Chappelle's racial agenda as "cruel" and exploitative, describes racial discourse in America as much more complicated than the binary configuration of "real" and "fake." Race, he says, "function[s] like a hall of funhouse mirrors. Once we enter (and we can't not enter), we all end up as caricatures and distortions, not only in other people's eyes, but in our own as well."[11] While I disagree with Feeney's overall assessment of *Chappelle's Show*, I find his funhouse metaphor useful and think it ironically undermines his and other similar criticisms of *Chappelle's Show*: in the funhouse of the American racial imaginary, it is impossible to identify who's distorting whom or where the distortions begin and end because racial identity is always already — that is, constitutively — distorted. In this funhouse (which, as Feeney argues, we are compelled to enter), our views of racial identity are interpolated by cultural anxiety and fantasy so that the only recognizable reflections are, in fact, those distortions. Thus there is no original or pristine state of racial "realness" or "authenticity" that we can uncover, recover, or discover from dominant culture's clutches, however appealing such a prospect might seem. Put another way: when it comes to notions of "real" and "fake," *it's not that racial identity becomes distorted in dominant culture; it's that we perceive a certain distortion to be racially "authentic."*

Chappelle's Show consciously acknowledges race's distorted and constructed nature, and rather than merely perpetuating stereotypes, it serves as a meditation on the dynamics of these distortions and constructions. While all racial identities are informed by fantasy, they manifest themselves and are mapped onto our racial imaginary and material reality in different ways, corresponding to their relationship to dominant culture and power. Sketches such as "When 'Keeping It Real' Goes Wrong," the "Wayne Brady" episode, and "The Niggar Family," heighten these power dynamics in order to explore a number of issues: how the distortions work in relation to one another, the behaviors and attitudes that racial identities compel (both for whites and those marked as Other), the material and psychic toll that racial fantasy exacts, and ultimately, the inadequacy of categories such as "real" and "fake" as they pertain to issues of racial politics and identity.

Seen in this light, the plight of Vernon from "When 'Keeping It Real' Goes Wrong" shows much more than just a choice between material gain and racial pride: it undermines and critiques notions of authenticity. Vernon, plagued by concepts of "real" and "fake," sees himself as having only two choices: maintaining his "Uncle Tom" veneer or expressing his "true" feelings. That he doesn't consider alternatives suggests his view that any choice he makes will ultimately align with one of these two seemingly polar opposites, an implication that vividly highlights the ways in which adherence to categories such as "real" and "fake" narrowly circumscribes conceptions of racial identity.

In addition, the nature of Vernon's assumption of "realness" illustrates that "keeping it real" as is much a performance as being an "Uncle Tom," further underscoring the distorted nature of racial identities. His performance, parodic in its extremity, is an example of Butler's contention that parodic assumptions of so-called "natural" aspects of identity such as gender and race in fact reveal the constructed nature — the "unnaturalness" — of these categories. Recalling Gilman's view of the "imaginary line" between white and black established by dominant cultural anxiety, Butler argues that fantasy largely informs these identity categories. Adapting her characterization of gender to that of race, we see that the "original identity after which [race] fashions itself is an imitation without an origin"; in other words, since our conception of racial identity is itself based on fantasy, then parodic performances of racial identity — both "real" and "fake" — are basically imitations of imitations and call attention to themselves as such.[12] Rather than implying that Vernon makes the wrong choice between authenticity and inauthenticity, the sketch's emphasis on race-as-performance suggests that his mistake was to situate his racial identity as either "real" or "fake" in the first place.

Along with its subversion of notions of racial "realness," this installment of "When 'Keeping It Real' Goes Wrong" reflects the dynamics of white fear and containment of the racial Other. Vernon embodies the dominant anxiety that, underneath even the most benevolent and accommodating exteriors, black men are essentially angry, dangerous, and violent. As the personification of dominant culture's biggest nightmare, Vernon must be banished and rendered powerless. His demotion to a low-paying job and exile from corporate culture is indeed, as the narrator has informed us, "as real as it can be." Thus, Chappelle's comment that "it's good to be phony sometimes" could be a caution to folks to become more strategic negotiators of dominant culture, and while material and economic power cannot completely heal the damage wrought by racial abjection, it can serve as compensation — admittedly inadequate, but compensation nonetheless—for the psychic costs of being a racial Other in late capitalist America.

Chappelle revisits this issue of white anxiety about black masculinity, examining it in a more sustained fashion in the infamous "Wayne Brady" episode (Season Two; Episode 12). The episode departs from the show's typical format in a number of ways: first, it purports to reveal the "real" Wayne Brady and subsequently features a highly self-reflexive storyline centering on a power struggle over *Chappelle's Show*. The episode also directly responds to a recurring sketch from earlier in the season that recasts 16th-century prognosticator Nostradamus as "Negrodamus," played by comedian Paul Mooney (Season Two; Episode 5). Both the plot and self-reflexivity work to blur the lines between non-fiction and fiction, thus underscoring the notion that fantasy — including racial fantasy — informs reality and problematizes notions of authenticity.

The episode's catalyst, the Negrodamus sketch, satirizes the supposed profundity of Nostradamus's psychic pronouncements. Instead of making cryptic prophecies about major historical events, natural disasters, and our impending apocalypse, Negrodamus takes questions from a studio audience and restricts his predictions to modern-day celebrities and politicians. When asked why Brady has so many white fans, Negrodamus replies, "White people love Wayne Brady because he makes Bryant Gumbel look like Malcolm X." According to Chappelle's audio commentary on the season 2 DVD, after hearing that Brady — unsurprisingly —felt slighted by the sketch, Chappelle asked him to guest star on the show as a means of making amends.

The episode features the (ironically prophetic) premise in which a burntout Chappelle quits and Comedy Central executives replace him with Brady.

Chappelle eventually regrets his decision and attempts to regain control, storming the stage and trying to convince Brady that the show isn't the proper venue for him. Chappelle tells him, "you got your thing, I got my thing," to which Brady asks, "What's my thing, Dave?" The sketch then moves into a flashback of an incident from two months earlier, in which Brady and Chappelle are in a car on their way to dinner. Chappelle declares, "That's the thing with black actors; we need to unify." Brady agrees, but then makes a series of stops and shocks Chappelle with his vicious criminality: he commits a drive-by shooting, extorts money from prostitutes, forces Chappelle to smoke PCP, kills a police officer, and finally, takes Chappelle's sandwich. In between stops, Brady voices suspicions about Chappelle's loyalty, which a terrified Chappelle attempts to appease by alluding to his earlier statement about unity, repeating the phrase, "black actors." The flashback concludes with Brady shooting Chappelle in the foot during this final exchange:

> BRADY: I make Bryant Gumbel look like Malcolm X, huh, mother-
>   fucker?
> CHAPPELLE: Black actors, man.
> BRADY: Black actors. Hey, Dave! [*Shoots Chappelle.*] I'm Wayne Brady,
>   bitch!
> CHAPPELLE [*lying on the sidewalk*]: It was Mooney!

The action returns to the *Chappelle's Show* stage and order is restored, as Chappelle regains his show. The end credits provide the final self-reflexive gesture by showing a presumably unscripted moment between takes, in which Brady tells the studio audience about the circumstances around his guest appearance and thanks Chappelle for his graciousness.

The Brady episode clearly responds to the parameters of "real" and "fake" racial identities established by the Negrodamus sketch, particularly as they apply to Brady himself. Negrodamus unfavorably compares him to sports journalist and former *Today Show* host Bryant Gumbel, long perceived by some as a "sell-out" who has sought white rather than African American viewers. Brady has similar "mainstream" appeal, one of the few African Americans to star in his own variety show on a major broadcast network (since cancelled), and winner of numerous Daytime Emmy Awards for Best Talk Show Host. Negrodamus's comment disparages Brady as a race traitor who panders to white audiences by conscientiously cultivating "white-friendly"— that is, non-threatening— demeanors and on-air personas. The allusion to Gumbel functions as a kind of racial shorthand that casts him as an archetypal representative of a larger group of African American entertainers who conform to dominant cultural expectations. Negrodamus's comment makes clear that Brady is not just a member of this larger group, but has in fact supplanted Gumbel and become its new figurehead. For Negrodamus, the widespread nature of Brady's appeal is evidence that he must be one of the biggest "sell-outs" of all, the personification of not "keeping it real."

The episode's depiction of Brady beginning his stint as the new host initially seems to confirm Negrodamus's views on racial authenticity, particularly the criticism of Brady's investment in white approval over racial pride. Brady proudly tells the *Chappelle's Show* studio audience during his opening monologue that "there are only a few of us black actors that happen to be working, and nothing makes me happier than to be able to take another black actor's job," a statement that runs counter to Chappelle's comment about the need for unification amongst black actors. Backstage, the white Comedy Central executives and Chappelle's then-writing partner, Neal Brennan, all profess their preference for Brady, describing him as more appealing, better-looking, and more charismatic, reinforcing the notion that white people love him. The episode's opening thus sets up a striking contrast regarding racial self-definition: while Chappelle's and Negrodamus's observations support a configuration of "keeping it real" which prioritizes racial allegiance and collective opposition vis-à-vis hostile racial politics, Brady's monologue instead emphasizes individual success and dominant cultural appeal.

But while the episode might initially seem to endorse Negrodamus's take on authenticity, the flashback featuring the "real" Brady unmistakably undermines it. The encounter with the white police officer, for example, revises the thesis that Brady's white-friendly persona is a form of race treachery and reflection of a "false" consciousness by portraying it as a self-conscious and tactical performance. The policeman, who is initially hostile, immediately becomes apologetic and accommodating once he realizes who Brady is. After he professes his admiration, a spotlight hits Brady, who pulls a mike from his pocket and sings "I Say A Little Prayer," alluding to his appearance in a coffee creamer commercial (and further underscoring his "crossover" appeal). This mini-concert entrances the policeman, rendering him completely vulnerable and helpless to Brady's swiftly and mercilessly breaking his neck. What we see here is that Brady is well aware of the distortions about blackness that dominant culture commodifies and perpetuates, and unlike Vernon, has learned to capitalize on them accordingly. His public persona functions as a means for professional gain, and allows him to bypass white scrutiny and brazenly indulge his "real" self in a way that he could not without his celebrity. Far from being an "Uncle Tom" controlled by white consumers' and viewers' demands, then, the "real" Brady is a strategic manipulator whose actions manifestly reinforce Chappelle's comment that "it's good to be phony sometimes."

The flashback also evokes the previously discussed dominant anxiety of black men as dangerous and threatening through its depiction of Brady as a hyperviolent criminal. Anne Cheng contends that "if the ideal racial/social mirror reflects the image of idealized whiteness, then 'blackness' can only become an abhorrent, even obscene visual image," and the outlandish nature of the "real" Brady certainly calls attention to how dominant culture distorts blackness in relation to whiteness in precisely this fashion, in order to reinforce white normativity and justify racial Othering.[13] The fact that Chappelle himself is terrified of Brady underscores the fantastic nature of this anxiety and forecloses any potential criticisms of the sketch being guilty of implicitly collapsing "real" African American identity with transgression and criminality.

Indeed, Chappelle's role in the flashback subverts notions of racial authenticity that he himself endorsed, particularly the prioritization of race loyalty over other concerns. In spite of his pledges of loyalty to Brady, Chappelle repeatedly and unsuccessfully attempts to alert others: he tells a prostitute to run and get help, and mouths "help me" to the police officer Brady eventually murders. One can hardly blame Chappelle for violating his earlier avowals in this instance. However, as the final lines of dialogue indicate, Chappelle is in fact guilty of and subsequently punished for a different act of betrayal: his tacit endorsement of the Negrodamus sketch. The implication here is that, while the cultivation of racial unity might help secure a sense of identity, especially for those marked as Other, it also compels the reinscription and maintenance of exclusionary us/them configurations. In addition, such affiliations require the suppression of any identificatory divergences which, as the stark difference between Brady's and Chappelle's characters in the flashback demonstrates, can be an extremely problematic proposition.

Finally, the episode, while playfully self-reflexive in its so-called behind-the-scenes look at *Chappelle's Show*, is also a parody of the film *Training Day* (2001), further underscoring the impossibility of making definitive distinctions between "real" and "fake." *Training Day* focuses on two police officers: corrupt veteran Alonzo Harris, and idealistic rookie Jake Hoyt, played by Denzel Washington and Ethan Hawke, respectively. The scene in which Harris forces Hoyt to smoke PCP-laden marijuana is the one explicitly replicated in the episode, with Brady assuming Harris's role. This replication, like the original, reinforces the contrast between the experienced villain and the helpless novice and further subverts Brady's and Chappelle's public personas, with the supposedly straight-laced Brady serving as dealer, and Chappelle, an experienced marijuana smoker, playing the naïve dupe. The episode's oscillation between the "real" and "fake" here is dizzying: put as simply as possible, we are offered a representation of Brady's "real" identity as partially informed by a fictional character, in a fictional flashback framed by a fictional premise (Chappelle quitting the show) that purports to reveal the real-life machinations of an actual television show. This Mobius strip of the fictional and the real clearly upends notions of "keeping it real" and lends new meaning to the phrase "black actors"; in this episode, Brady and Chappelle are always black actors, regardless of whether or not their "roles" seem to subvert or concede to dominant culture. On a larger scale, these imbrications of real and fake that shape conceptions and representations of identity compel all of us to be actors, regardless of racial affiliation.

To further illuminate this point, Chappelle uses a sketch entitled "The Niggar Family" as a springboard to brazenly examine how race's distorted nature impacts those within dominant culture (Season 2; Episode 2). The sketch depicts the hi-jinks wrought by a white family with the last name "Niggar," who themselves are completely ignorant of their name's synonymous relation to the racialized epithet. The sketch begins in the Niggars' kitchen, where Mrs. Niggar is cooking breakfast for her husband. The couple's son, Timmy, enters the scene and informs his parents about an upcoming date that night with Jenny Halsted. He is followed by the "colored" milkman, Clifton, who addresses Mr. Niggar as "Mr. N-word" and reminds the family that they still haven't paid the previous week's bill, noting, "I know how forgetful you Niggars are when it comes to paying bills."

The action then moves to the Halsted household, where Jenny's father initially objects to the news that Jenny is dating "a Niggar boy from school," but is appeased hearing that her date is Timmy Niggar. Timmy takes Jenny to a restaurant, where Clifton and his wife take offense when the maitre d' calls, "Niggar, party of two." After the misunderstanding has been cleared up, Clifton tells Timmy, "I'll bet you get the finest table a Niggar's ever gotten in this restaurant," and while all the characters laugh heartily, he rather abruptly comments, "Oh, Lord. This racism is killing me inside." The sketch concludes back at the Niggar household, where Mr. and Mrs. Niggar meet their new neighbors, the Wetbacks, and allude to another family, the Jews.

The sketch, of course filmed in black and white, satirizes mid-century television images of the "ideal" American family as white, patriarchal, and affluent, the most well-known example being the Cleavers from *Leave It to Beaver*. Like the Cleavers, the Niggars are also blissfully unaware of racism, but with a key difference: the ignorance of the former seems reasonable enough, given their apparently all-white, race-free community, but the ignorance of the latter is patently disingenuous since race explicitly informs virtually all of the Niggars' interactions with others. While even a willful sort of obliviousness might be a luxury that whiteness affords, the Niggars' conspicuous lack of awareness in relation to everyone else illustrates Toni Morrison's contention in *Playing in the Dark* that the refusal to acknowledge race's omnipresence in fact requires vigilance. "It requires hard work not to see," claims Morrison, and necessitates an engagement with racial dynamics that is far more angst-ridden and circuitous than it might originally seem.[14] As with the Vernon Franklin piece, then, Chappelle works to expose the constructed nature of whiteness and its reliance upon racial "Othering": here we see that the Niggars' attempt to embody the ideal requires a kind of anxious elision of any points of divergence from it.

A large part of the sketch's humor is, of course, the incongruence that results as a wide spectrum of racially charged stereotypes and slang is imposed onto this seemingly oblivious family. This spectrum, which ranges from the benign to the hostile, includes physiological stereotypes and behavioral stereotypes, such as African Americans as lazy and irresponsible debtors (as evidenced by Clifton's remark about paying bills), and Mr. Halsted's seemingly more liberal but no less racist praise of Timmy as a "well-spoken" athlete. That this spectrum is constituted by such diverse — even at times contradictory — images is, as Slavoj Žižek notes, characteristic of racist discourse: "To the racist, the 'other' is either a workaholic stealing our jobs or an idler living on our labor, and it is quite amusing to notice the haste with which one passes from reproaching the other with a refusal to work to reproaching him for the theft of work."[15] Thus the sketch's allusions to such a wide range of stereotypes underscore the adaptability of racist fantasies, and Chappelle and Brennan utilize these stereotypes in a variety of ways. At times, they present racist images in their traditional incarnations, such as the family's delinquency on bills. In other instances, Chappelle and Brennan offer the inverse, as when Mr. Niggar describes his niece's "Niggar lips" as being "so thin," and the Halsteds use the term "nigger-rich" in reference to the Niggars to signify their actual wealth instead of debt-inducing and ostentatious displays of wealth.

Towards the end of the sketch, Chappelle and Brennan expand the scope to include racist discourse that originates in but departs from the black-white dyad. The appearance of a new family — the "Wetbacks" — and the Niggars' reference to another — the "Jews" — feels somewhat awkward, tacked on to provide some sort of conclusion, but it does reinforce the idea that no racial group is untouched by distortion. Those categorized as Other suffer the relentlessness of dominant disavowal, resulting in tortured relationships between racialized Others and dominant ideals. Cheng calls this psychic condition the "double malady ... of having to incorporate and encrypt both an impossible ideal and a denigrated self."[16]

We see this psychic toll that dominant culture exacts most strikingly with Chappelle's character, Clifton the milkman, who also alludes to characters from television's past, such as Jack Benny's sidekick, Rochester. These stock figures, always in secondary roles, often provided comic relief and implicitly normalized the white principal characters as "ideal." In this case, however, Clifton provides comic relief not by normalizing the Niggars, but by explicitly and knowingly highlighting their whiteness and the dynamics of racism (one example of which is his reference to Mr. Niggar as "Mr. N-word"). Phrases such as "You niggers cookin'?," usually spoken exclusively within African American communities, underscore the lack of affiliation or shared collective identity between Clifton and the family. He initially seems to enjoy directing racist discourse towards the family, but any pleasure he gleans from this reversal of dynamics is highly circumscribed and only a temporary amelioration at best, which is made abundantly clear when Clifton disrupts the sketch's tone and says, "This racism is killing me inside." Like Chappelle's take on economic power, the subtext here is that the assumption of the dominant point of view cannot fully compensate or repair the alienation resulting from racial Otherness. The interjection of pathos into this sketch shows us that the psychic fragmentation wrought by racial distortion might be the "realest" condition of all.

Ultimately, *Chappelle's Show*'s representations of racial identity have been too easily dismissed by detractors whose view of authenticity elides the nuances, contradictions, and sheer messiness of the American racial imaginary. Chappelle's provocative, profane, and funny explorations clearly reflect a deep investment in tackling race's complexity. Ironically, the very vehicle through which he explored these issues— his show — prompted his own professional and personal crisis about racial identity, thus further attesting to the impossibility of "keeping it real" in a society that simultaneously generates the promise of commensurability and inflicts the trauma of disavowal. Whether or not he manages to reconcile these conflicts remains to be seen, but his work should compel scholars to move beyond reductive conceptions of racial identity and undertake with equal thoughtfulness the same difficult inquiries and assessments as Chappelle himself.

10

When "Keeping It Real" Goes Right

KIMBERLEY A. YATES

If we smoked out, hip-hop is gonna be smoked out; if we doin' alright, hip-hop is gonna be doin' alright. People talk about hip-hop like it's some giant livin' in the hillside comin' out to visit the town people. We are hip-hop— me, you, everybody. We are hip-hop; hip-hop is goin' where we goin.' So, the next time you ask yourself where is hip-hop going, ask yourself, "Where am I going? How am I doing?" Then you get a clear idea. See, if hip-hop is about the people, and hip-hop won't get better until the people get better, then how do people get better?— Mos Def[1]

The accuracy of the assertion that hip-hop has multiracial and multicultural origins does not suggest that it is not black. Only a worldview that subjugates blackness marks the phrase "it's just black" as an offensive designation. Why can't something be black (read, black American) and be influenced by a number of cultures and styles at the same time? The idea that it cannot emerges from the absurd reality that blackness in the United States is constructed as a kind of pure existence, a purity, to most, of the negative kind, defined by a pure lack of sophistication and complexity and a pure membership in a group of undesirables.— Imani Perry[2]

On his 1999 debut CD, *Black on Both Sides*, multitalented hip-hop artist, Mos Def, speaks of a "we" that is first and foremost Black but also inclusive of all who consider themselves part of a hip-hop nation.[3] Five years later, hip-hop scholar Imani Perry theorizes this same fluidly complex hip-hop "we": specifically Black, yet simultaneously inclusive — as evidenced in its cross-racial, transnational appeal and influences. Hip-hop, as an art form receptive to external influences and dependent on voice, as well as both cooperation and conflict, is a truly democratic space. The "we" then is paradoxical — seemingly narrow but ultimately expansive.

A hip-hop nation, with transnational appeal, that is the cultural product of Black USA — itself a group within a nation — whose "core ideology" is black nationalism, according to political theorist and scholar Ronald Walters,[4] is either a revolutionary coup or an indication of just how convoluted the concepts of nationhood and nationalism are in today's world. Revolution, democracy, and freedom have historically been chief concerns of black people in this country. It is no surprise then that hip-hop reflects, responds to, and expresses, directly and indirectly, anxieties about the three and their relationship to each other. Indeed, it is relatively commonplace in current scholarship on hip-hop culture to identify the revolutionary influences of Black Power. One aim of this paper is to follow that thread of Black nationalism specifically from the Black Arts Movement through hip-hop.

Understanding hip-hop as the legacy and fruition of specific Black Arts Movement values opens pathways to think about the Movement's successes beyond what seems to be its rather infamous and unfortunate death so well documented and lamented, and to think about black nationalism's shaping of U.S. democratic ideals. My goal here is to position Dave Chappelle as a hip-hop artist himself (rather than as simply a comedian who likes rap music) in order to raise the stakes on the significance of his work, of hip-hop, and of the Black Arts Movement, in this society. The point is to historicize the social function of Chappelle's work and place him along a difficult continuum of black nationalism complicated by histories of black men and their performances in front of white audience members.

The argument is that Chappelle has used his *comic* artistry not to reinforce minstrel images but to move beyond a simplified minstrel vs. radical binary for Black male entertainers. Indeed, he moves in the tradition of Dick Gregory, explicitly involved in the Civil Rights and Black Power Movements, and Richard Pryor, who circulated within the Black Arts Movement with writers Ishmael Reed, Cecil Brown, and Claude Brown[5] — Gregory and Pryor being Black men who successfully confronted racial inequity boldly and uncompromisingly through humor. With laughter functioning as the primary basis of audiences' consent and the comic's success, these three comics demonstrate the ability of "revolutionary humor" to simultaneously challenge and re-shape mainstream thought, Chappelle having the widest impact. Focusing primarily on *Chappelle's Show* and *Block Party*, in the context of his early 2006 interview with James Lipton on *Inside the Actor's Studio*, I contend that ultimately Chappelle as a hip-hop artist has successfully continued in a black nationalist legacy to democratize the U.S. ideal of democracy (equal access, participation, and representation) ironically by deploying Black Arts Movement values: adhering to a sense of authenticity, Chappelle caters to a black standard while creating broader debate about racial inequity. He creates a sense of nation precisely by challenging this nation's mainstream to consider the ways in which it is not living up to its ideals of democracy, equality, and inclusiveness.

Hip-hop has had profound effects on U.S. culture and ideology — having black perspectives and voices (versus blackface mimicries) shape the mainstream, even as an "authentic Blackness" is "countercultural," perhaps even "antisocial." Some argue that mere contact with the mainstream waters down the "real," the "authentic." A Frontline documentary, *Merchants of Cool*, that first aired on PBS on February 27, 2001, makes the case that underground music groups/artists operating locally constitute a fringe and potentially subversive element in youth culture.[6] This ambition for financial success, however, leads them to MTV, a network continually on the search to uncover teenage desires and habits to further tailor their consumer habits. The documentary argues that these underground groups' mere appearance on MTV propels them into the mainstream: though they once challenged the status quo, they are now co-opted by it. While this certainly has its own convincing logic, it also simplifies people into predictably formulaic positions with inevitable outcomes by assuming a constant, unchanging, unaffected, omnipotent mainstream that unequivocally consumes, victimizes, and stamps out possibility in a way that makes any kind of change impossible. It also does not adequately apply to hip-hop, which shapes the mainstream and is shaped by it, while concurrently nurturing a vibrant underground. Nor does such a schema adequately explain groups such as The Roots, who as Grammy Award winners clearly have a mainstream visibility but whose prolific music is not in heavy rotation on major radio stations, particularly as compared to 50 Cent, so that they simultaneously maintain an iconic underground status. Thus there is slippage that affects and alters "the" mainstream because contact changes things; hip-hop is subcultural, protocultural, and countercultural. Hip-hop is Black American, American, and worldwide.

Some of its mainstreaming impact is obvious—airplay on a variety of radio stations, trendsetting "cool" in terms of fashion, language, and comportment, in ways that are pervasively received and perceived negatively.[7] Hip-hop scholar William Jelani Cobb gets it right when he asserts that the "hip-hop *industry* is largely responsible for the global re-dispersal of stereotypical visions of black sexuality, criminality, material-obsession, violence, and social detachment" (emphasis added).[8] While prevailing public discourse focuses almost exclusively on artists rather than the industry, my interest here is not to reinforce hip-hop as a "nihilistic, dysfunctional, and pathological"[9] social force spawning ills and dis-ease. Instead, I want to think about our debt to hip-hop and position it as a protocultural force: hip-hop—even, if not especially, that more elusive underground brand—has actually fertilized seemingly unforgiving cultural ground. Perhaps hip-hop has helped to make it possible for a viable black presidential candidate to finally have broad support, outside of black communities, across the nation. As Cobb asserts, "hip-hop is not fundamentally a political movement—no matter how many political implications the music and its mass marketing have,"[10] yet its aesthetics— deriving from a Black Arts Movement base — have proven to be quite powerful in affecting today's mainstream, including the national political scene.

The title of this essay is "When 'Keeping It Real' Goes Right." As indicated also by the previous essay in this collection, this is a well-known referent for any self-respecting Chappelle fan. In the introduction to the first of the three "When 'Keeping It Real' Goes Wrong" sketches (Season Two; Episode 6), Chappelle makes a generational identification rather than a racial one, noting that most of the members of the audience are more or less his age, "and our generation has a phrase we like to say. That phrase is 'keep it real.'" Though it is sound advice, he warns it is "not always as easy it seems," and it "sometimes works against you." "Keeping it real" is a staple principle of hip-hop that is about the struggle to be true and authentic. While Chappelle takes honesty and authenticity to the extremes, demonstrating the potential absurdity, he also indicates that there can really be great value in aiming to keep it real, and I am interested here in the effectiveness of his ability to do so and capture "the" mainstream versus being absorbed, or as Paul Mooney, in his responses to "Ask a Black Dude," would say, "taken" by it (Season One; Episode 10).

Black Nationalism and Black Arts

In his seminal 1967 work, *The Crisis of the Negro Intellectual*, Harold Cruse argues that "American Negro history is basically a history of the conflict between integrationist and nationalist forces in politics, economics, and culture, no matter what leaders are involved and what slogans are used."[11] Cruse concludes ultimately that the young nationalists of the day were actually interested in reform rather than the revolution they touted, for they intended to "change, not the White world outside, but the black world inside, by reforming it into something else politically and economically."[12] He criticizes them for not having any real understanding of politics or economics, as evidenced by their naïve and contradictory anti-bourgeois stance given that they were "prey to bourgeois aspirations" as Cruse saw it.[13] Indeed, the Black Panther Party's 1966 Ten-Point program is constructed within a U.S. discursive framework of "rights," lending credence to Cruse's comment that the Black Power theorists, despite "their vaunted anti–Americanism ... are more American than they think."[14] Even when a U.S. Black nationalist agenda has had an eye toward revolution, its ideology is still informed by a foundational national discourse of freedoms, rights, and access as framed within the Declaration of Independence and the Constitution.[15] Rod Bush in his study of black nationalism usefully identifies "revolution" as a profound *social transformation* that not only redistributes power but democratizes it; empowers ordinary people to participate in and help determine the affairs of state, economy, and society; challenges the law of value that impels all production to center ultimately on the profit motive; establishes a cooperative commonwealth in which production for human needs takes priority over production for exchange.[16]

The route to achieving this is the age-old question at issue for black nationalism — whether through cultural nationalism changing self-perception, through efforts aimed at altering white perceptions of blacks, through closing economic gaps between blacks and whites (either through communism or economic empowerment), or through pan–Africanism (itself a multi-layered possibility). The Black Arts Movement was principally concerned with transforming society and democratizing power both by redistribution, i.e., stripping whites of significant, unearned entitlements, and by empowering ordinary people, black people through art. Black nationalism has generally operated within an explicit U.S. paradigm of entitlement and access, driven by a desire to be integrated into democracy's freedoms without having to assimilate culturally. Black Power was not about creating a new nation but about creating a new aesthetic of blackness disassociated from the popular White imaginings of nation and about changing the circumstances characterizing black life, such as police surveillance and harassment, poverty, and unemployment.[17]

In *Playing in the Dark: Whiteness and the Literary Imagination*, Toni Morrison argues that the racialized slavery of this country functioned to position blackness as a signifier of the "not free" and hence "not me."[18] Blackness was the conceptual and supposedly visual counterpoint to Whiteness, freedom, Americanness. Very literally then, blackness has been positioned as countercultural by the demands of a white nationalism. But, also from a Black perspective, a Blackness that sees itself as embraced by mainstream American culture is at most Tommishly treacherous (to a sense of Black nationhood united in solidarity against the weight and terrorism of a White nationalism) and at least naïve, as is evident in Michael Eric Dyson's critique of Bill Cosby in *Is Bill Cosby Right? (Or Has the Black Middle Class Lost Its Mind?)*. Black Power nationalists explicitly positioned themselves as counter to U.S. hegemonic cultural practices, values, and standards. Thus, for all involved, an "authentic" Blackness is a Blackness that recognizes its distinction and exclusion from a White mainstream and functions quite literally as a marker of counterculture.

In his 1965 Black Arts Movement manifesto, Amiri Baraka defined revolutionary theatre as one of "assault" that must "Accuse and Attack anything that can be accused and attacked," primarily a white/Western mode of supremacy, synonymous with fascism and predicated on the victimization of black people. But, this is primarily an argument for black people's self-determination and self-actualization by their own standards. So, when Baraka asserts that "even if [the Revolutionary Theatre] is Western," it "must be anti–Western,"[19] this is clearly not a call to construct a separate nation and government but to establish a separate *sense* of selfhood and nationhood, distinct from a popular image mired in stereotype popularized and proliferated by minstrelsy and white America. When Larry Neal similarly opens his 1968 manifesto of the Black Arts Movement by positioning it as "radically opposed to any concept of the artist that alienates him from his community," he signals an understanding and acceptance of a black community that is unified in its distinction from a white community. He argues for controlling that separate space, where black people decide the value of the art, thereby establishing a black standard. He mirrors Baraka: the Black Arts Movement's desired "separate symbolism, mythology, critique, and iconology" that radically reorders "the Western cultural aesthetic" was not about secession from the United States but rather about actually democratizing U.S. democracy.[20] This, in part, involves understanding and practicing blackness as multiplicity not as monolith. Within the boundaries of any black community, this goes without saying. It is only in contact and interaction with "the mainstream" of whiteness that blackness floats as a reduced, flat, stereotyped state.

In practice, this multi-valence translated into a proliferation of discussion, debate, and ideas, as evidenced by the numerous Black Arts journals and conferences, as well as the multiple roles that the artists engaged. People like Baraka and Neal, as well as Carolyn Rodgers, were both essayists/theorists of the movement and poets. Baraka founded the Black Arts Repertory Theatre and School (BARTS), wrote *Blues People*, and just generally indulged a diversity of spirit and work. The Black Arts Movement fostered and nurtured a fierce individualism supposedly at the core of American identity but consistently denied to black people in U.S. popular culture, dominated by the imagination of Whiteness. We can look to the Black Arts Movement not merely as interested in democracy but as a model of democratic access and participation. There were values at the core of the Movement that reflect both its ideological imperatives and its practices, which have become hip-hop's inheritance: (1) authenticity; (2) black standards; (3); debate/conflict; and (4) improvisation and innovation as artistic technique. More important than these individual values, however, is the sum total effect on a U.S. mainstream: not surprisingly, a people in pursuit of democratic participation create democratic artistic spaces, characterized by debate and contradictions, as in both the Black Arts Movement and hip-hop. This marginalized space that enables open critique mirrors the comic's space.

Revolutionary Humor

In its entry on Richard Pryor, the Museum of Broadcast Communications refers to Pryor's work as "revolutionary humor" because the characters he created "from black folklore as well as ... from the streets of Anytown, U.S.A.," "ridicule[d] and comment[ed] upon the circumstances under which African Americans lived."[21] Seeing comics as having a potentially revolutionary role of profoundly transforming society resists a ready ghettoization of Black comedic performance as necessarily shameful due to an inherent minstrel-like shuckin' and jivin'.' For example, Robin R. Means Coleman argues that comedy *as a genre* has a lulling effect and does not require that African Americans be taken seriously in a way that drama does.[22] One could argue that this helps to explain a proliferation of opportunity in comedy for Blacks, but one would be hard pressed to argue convincingly that Dick Gregory, Richard Pryor and Dave Chappelle have had lulling effects on their audiences' consciousness. Lawrence E. Mintz argues that the comedian is granted social license to deviate from the norm, both in behavior and expression.[23] The comic, therefore, can function as an invaluable social commentator who both reflects and shapes community through jokes, "establish[ing] for the audience that the group is homogenous, a community, if the laughter is to come easily."[24] Having the social license to articulate that which is universally understood but taboo to speak, the comic democratizes discursive spaces, and the revolutionary humorist exercises freedom of speech — intersecting here with Black nationalism's social effect and goals. Revolutionary humor then can affect and sway social thought, especially when the comic insists on addressing race and stoking dialogue as does Chappelle:

> We could actually be the greatest country that ever existed if we were just honest about who we are, and what we are, and where we wanna go. And, if we learn how to have that discourse — things like racism are institutionalized; it's systemic. You might not know any bigots. You might feel like, "well I don't hate any Black people, so I'm not a racist." But, you benefit from racism just by the merit of the color of your skin. There's opportunities that you have; you're privileged in ways that you may not realize because you haven't been deprived of certain things. We need to talk about these things in order for them to change. I do the show; I walk down the street; Black people like it, White people, the generations, it doesn't matter because it needs to be talked about. It's like the elephant in the living room that nobody says anything about.... The only way you know where the line is is to cross it ... you just wanna try to be on the right side of history.[25]

The lines he crosses are the ones that silence honest public discussion of this country's deployment of race. In a social context where powerful Whites can easily accuse Blacks of playing "the race card," thereby suggesting that race is not an issue until Blacks vocalize and create it as an issue, Chappelle's comic voice is not to be underestimated. He is a comic whose racial critiques function as good satire, and he utilizes that comic social license to articulate racial taboos, effectively offering the "critique and iconology" that radically reorders "the Western cultural aesthetic," urged by Larry Neal some forty years ago. He thereby continues a longstanding Black nationalist legacy of committing to democratizing U.S. democracy, as evidenced by his opening declaration of his belief in this nation. His broad appeal and success are proof of this "reordering" apparently *because of* the open critiques he offers.

During this same interview, James Lipton tells Chappelle that Richard Pryor's wife had conveyed Pryor's feeling that he had passed the torch to Chappelle. Given the earlier association of Pryor with revolutionary humor, it is worth considering exactly how Pryor and Chappelle do this. Recognizing that there could be little else in the world more of an honor, Chappelle characterizes Pryor as "the highest evolution of comedy" because "the mark of greatness is when everything before you is obsolete, and everything after you bears your mark."[26] Some of what distinguished Pryor's comedy — storytelling, writing, improvisational ability, strong acting skills, poignant insight into issues of racial difference and inequity, and presentation of broad array of Black characters — is what also characterizes Chappelle's artistry. But, what really separated Pryor from the pack once he decided to stop imitating Bill Cosby was his ability to "keep it real" through the latter element of presenting a host of Black characters.[27] Pryor developed a character and narrative-driven comedy that was also brazenly and shamelessly autobiographical. Though perhaps less autobiographical, *Chappelle's Show* is clearly character and narrative-driven from his specific subject perspective, to which Chappelle strives to be true. Freeing themselves to enact a variety of types, Pryor's and Chappelle's brands of comedy resist easy or rigid "-typing." Indeed, Pryor passed the torch to a receptive Chappelle, much as the Black Arts Movement passed the torch to hip-hop.

Michael Eric Dyson provides a framework of types useful in analyzing the contributions of Pryor and Chappelle to comedy as distinct from the mass of Black comics who also rely on racial differences for their comic material. Particularly useful in identifying *how* Pryor and Chappelle have kept it real is the category beyond stereotypes and archetypes— antitypes. For Dyson, a stereotype is a "lazy assessment of the other" based on "prejudiced beliefs and bigoted intuitions ... dressed as objective observation and common sense."[28] Stereotypes endure because they codify within the popular, collective imagination; within the specific context of the United States, the minstrel codified Black people as the antithesis of "an ostensibly White American character,"[29] shoring up the boundaries of a white national body depending on blackness as counterpoint for its shape, as Toni Morrison argued. Further, the historical context of U.S. minstrelsy renders stereotypes particularly relevant to black male entertainers. Stereotypes become *Chappelle's Show* fodder, be it in the litany of stereotyped characteristics that give rise to Clayton Bigsby's stereotypical yet ironic ire on the first episode, Tyrone Biggums, or sketches on the *Lost Episodes*, such as Chappelle having to be self-conscious about ordering fried chicken in public, the likening of the Ying Yang twins to minstrels, and the apparently controversial sketch with the minstrel pixie.[30] He could ignore stereotypes, but that would be akin to protecting the elephant in the room, and when he deploys stereotyped images, he generally uses hilarity to unveil their absurdity. Against the damage of externally imposed stereotypes "tinged with paternalism and condescension," Dyson argues that archetypes, usually considered to be positive, are black projections of "the defining characteristics of black identity."[31] Stereotypes and archetypes then work as oppositions, the latter understood as organic rather than imposed, combating residual and persistent stains of the former. But because stereotypes often accommodate contradictory images, they can rather easily absorb and transform the good intentions of archetypes.

Most useful in thinking through a revolutionary humor though is Dyson's discussion of antitypes—black articulations of "the unsavory and politically incorrect" often excluded from the visible, archetypal representations. The antitypical is "unsavory" "because of class status, lack of power, [or] gender and sexual orientation," for example.[32] Richard Pryor's Mudbone character is perhaps an example of antitypical expression. Neither flatly stereotypical nor admirably archetypal, he is a foul-mouthed, straight shooting, wise old man who dipped snuff and whose only job apparently was to "sit in front of the barbecue pit and ... spit" but who offered funny stories and insightful advice, striking keyed-in audiences as real and familiar: "Every black town had someone like him. Some old geezer who talked shit about his life's experiences. Fancied himself a philosopher."[33] A character that Pryor liked, Mudbone also offers insight into Pryor:

> FASCINATIN'. That's what he is. Course the boy knew nothin' 'bout the shit he was talkin' 'bout, but knowin' shit ain't no prerequisite for achievin' great things. Lotta stupid people think they're smart and a lotta smart people know they're stupid. Everybody else, they just workst hard, try to get by, drink every now and then, and take a little pussy.[34]

If the goal is to put your best face forward in representations of black people, then Mudbone may prove to be "unsavory"—his most objectionable characteristic likely being his uncensored use of vulgar words. But unlike the "prejudiced beliefs and bigoted intuitions" of White stereotypes, antitypes are a Black expression. Antitypical representations diversify a binaried landscape of stereotype and archetype, allowing for a range of characters that may be "real" yet "unsavory." In a sense, his comic reliance on antitypes democratizes Blackness by presenting a range of individual characters that resist a monolithic Blackness that feeds stereotypes and that also resist easy categorization as either "good" or "bad." Their realness is determined by Black audiences, in line with the Black Arts Movement imperatives to be authentic and develop distinct standards.

One among many, Chappelle's character, Tron, is an exaggerated caricature perhaps leaning toward stereotype. The audience sees him repeatedly as "unsavory"—a self-interested, materialistic man whose main interests are money, women and laughing. He appears first as the world's richest man in "Reparations 2003" (Season One; Episode 4), then as a drug dealer on trial in a *Law & Order* parody (Season Two; Episode 5), and finally as one of the housemates in "Mad Real World" (Season One; Episode 6). With little depth to him, it is hard to argue he is a well-developed character, except that his caricature is precisely what positions him perfectly for Chappelle's exploration of a system that administers "justice" inequitably. The last sketch is premised in his argument that there are two justice systems—one for Whites and another for the rest. Defending Tron's right to plead the fifth as his only testimony for himself, Chappelle cleverly comments that one privilege of Whiteness is to exist above the law, being given the benefit of the doubt, and living beyond reproach. Furthermore, Whites really are treated as innocent until proven guilty in contrast to an all too common converse Black experience of being treated guilty until proven innocent. He is engaging Black Arts Movement ideals here by challenging status quo practice, using his social license as comedian to articulate that which is socially taboo: with access to a wide network of viewers, many of whom are White, Chappelle premises the sketch on an understood reality in many Black communities—that justice is often not blind and frequently sees race as a means for its inequitable administration. This particular deployment of Tron makes it more difficult to simply dismiss him as bad or stereotypical because he makes a good point. Further, Tron is merely one character among a broad array of many—some fictional, some real, including Rick James, Prince, and Chappelle himself. *Chappelle's Show* provides a plethora of representations.

Comedy theorist Joanne Gilbert agrees with Mintz that the comedian, the professional fool, creates humor by performing and mocking his own marginality. But, "[b]y performing marginality, comics perform power—which is to say, they depict for us how social relations could be transformed if their viewpoint were to prevail."[35] With Season One of *Chappelle's Show* being the highest selling DVD of a television show, it seems that Chappelle's viewpoints have prevailed to some extent with his audience, offering consensus both in their laughter and their dollars. Whether audiences fully understand the subtleties of his social critiques, his comedy disseminates Black nationalist ideals of democratizing U.S. democracy, and the success of his show, measured quantitatively in sales suggests a broad base of people being exposed to his viewpoint and liking it. Ultimately, the Black Arts Movement functioned as a model of democratic participation in its ability to create multiple spaces for multiple voices, much as hip-hop does.

Dave Chappelle as Hip-hop Artist

The deejay, the lyricist (aka the emcee or MC), break dancing, and graffiti have long been acknowledged as the foundational cornerstones of hip-hop by lyricists and theorists alike. Lyricist KRS-One consistently reminds the hip-hop community of this history in a variety of songs and in his concerts. Scholar Tricia Rose, in her seminal and still relevant work *Black Noise: Rap Music and Black Culture in Contemporary America*, examines the ways in which these cornerstones are premised on flow and rupture, or rather the ability to create flow from breaks:

> Interpreting these concepts [flow, layering, and rupture] theoretically, one can argue that they create and sustain rhythmic motion, continuity, and circularity via flow; accumulate, reinforce, and embellish this continuity through layering; and manage threats to these narratives by building in ruptures that highlight the continuity as it momentarily challenges it. These effects at the level of style and aesthetics suggest affirmative ways in which profound social dislocation and rupture can be managed and perhaps contested in the cultural arena. Let us imagine these hip-hop principles as a blueprint for social resistance and affirmation: create sustaining narratives, accumulate them, layer, embellish, and transform them. However, be also prepared for rupture, find pleasure in it, in fact, *plan* on social rupture. When these ruptures occur, use them in creative ways that will prepare you for a future in which survival will demand a sudden shift in ground tactics. [36]

As a "blueprint for social resistance and affirmation," for how to deal with social and economic instability, hip-hop is a means for youth who live these social ruptures to use them as a mode of flow. All of these forms— dj'ing, emcee'ing, breakdancing, and graf painting — depend on maneuvering through sometimes unexpected social ruptures and demonstrating artistic control over breaks. Ultimately, she concludes, "hip-hop style *is* black urban renewal." [37] In this way, though a new cultural force, this improvisational imperative is consistent not only with the history of Black music in the U.S. but also with the values of Black Arts Movement, and is equally central to the successful comedian as well. The broader hip-hop nation that has emerged is the direct result of the art form's ability to improvise and navigate social ruptures resulting from the larger nation's inattention to the Black, urban and financially struggling. And hip-hop, as Rose has defined it, is specifically these. Jeffrey O.G. Ogbar, in his more recent *Hip-hop Revolution*, follows this line of argument in relation to authenticity: "realness ... is inextricably tied to spatial notions that are represented by class and race assumptions as well as gender and generation."[38] Paul Gilroy also asserts in *The Black Atlantic: Modernity and Double Consciousness* that hip-hop culture as "the powerful expressive medium of America's urban black poor ... has created a global youth movement of considerable significance."[39] Thus when Dead Prez claim, "It's bigger than hip-hop," the implication is that what is at stake is far more than just music because hip-hop is a matter of culture and circumstance, of (in)justice and resistance.[40]

In *Laughing Mad*, Bambi Haggins lists Chappelle's affiliations with hip-hop — his theme music for the show, his showcasing of artists on the show who are not in heavy rotation on mainstream outlets like MTV's Total Request Live (TRL), and his appearance on the covers of hip-hop magazines *XXL* and *Blender*. But beyond this, she concludes that his relationship to hip-hop is more "endemic than strategic: the comic's persona is imbued with hip-hop sensibility — the aesthetic and the politics of musical genre are inextricably tied to his own."[41] What might seem to be surface connections are not irrelevant, and the list can be extended to include the variety of t-shirts he dons with Black iconic figures, usually men (Redd Foxx, Marvin Gaye, Richard Pryor, Muhammad Ali) and places such as Harlem, as well as a pair of Nikes with a Black Power fist on the tongue, reflecting hip-hop's characteristically nostalgic sampling of a recent past. It could also include the various insider allusions to hip-hop, particularly in the Chuck Taylor news anchor sketches — his name alluding to the popular Converse tennis shoe — the best examples of which, unfortunately, are on the *Lost Episodes*, remnants of what would have contributed to the third season, episodes compiled after and despite Chappelle's departure without his sanction. In a series of deleted scenes, Chuck Taylor's reports reference Nas, Dr. Dre, and Method Man (*Lost Episodes*; Episode 1). In yet another, his report is "Hello I'm Chuck Taylor. Today in the news, Bum stiggedy bum stiggedy bum, hon I'd like to rumpa-pum-a-pum-pum with your fee fi your fo diddly dum, here I come, with a one, two, unbuckle my um shoe yabba-do, hippity-hoo, skippity-scabble-skoo," a reference, of course to the quite recitable lyrics of DAS EFX's 1992 release, "They Want EFX."

Cataloguing the appearances of hip-hop on *Chappelle's Show* could conceivably go on infinitely. But, establishing Chappelle as a hip-hop artist requires thinking about the ways in which hip-hop and comedy as genres lend themselves to each other, the strands of Black nationalism, as well as his approach to his work, exploring that "hip-hop sensibility" Haggins identifies. There is a moment in *Block Party* when Chappelle begins playing the piano. ?uestlove of The Roots, the film's Musical Director, informs us that Dave, though not a trained musician, has dedicated his life to learning how to play Thelonius Monk's "Round Midnight" and "Misty," as we listen to Chappelle on the piano in the background. When the camera returns to Chappelle, he explains that Monk is one of his favorite musicians because "his timing was so ill. Every comedian is a stickler for timing, and Thelonious Monk was off time yet perfectly on time." Offering Mos Def and Jamie Foxx as prime examples, he goes on to argue that "every comic wants to be a musician. Every musician thinks they're funny. It's a very strange relationship that we have." In addition to timing, the comic and the MC — "Microphone Controller, Mic Checker, Master of Ceremonies" — are connected by their imperative to "move the crowd." [42] While comedy theorist Lawrence Mintz focuses primarily on the comic's role as social mediator, and while there is quite a bit of scholarly emphasis on the social implications of music in general and hip-hop in particular, it is critical to remember that first and foremost MCs and comics — at least the good ones — are artists, whose job is to move people. In an effort to move people, Chappelle indeed keeps it real.

Importantly though, in keeping it real, he intentionally resists a "preachy" approach by pulling his audience into his head and the way he sees the world. In his interview with James Lipton, talking about the joke series from *Killin' Them Softly* (2000) about a drug-dealing baby standing on the corner and selling weed, he articulates, "There's a little statement, but it's not preachy. I'm painting a picture, right?" Haggins identifies one of Chappelle's characteristic comic modes as storytelling. His goal is to have the world stop for a minute and see it through his eyes, which may be a perspective partially or largely foreign to them. Aaron McGruder, acknowledging the path opened for *The Boondocks* television show by *Chappelle's Show* "comedically hav[ing] virtually no barriers," explicitly states this as his goal with his series:

> If the comedy can bring you to a place where the audience can kind of feel what I feel, that's kind of my job as the artist — to put them in some kind of space where they can see the world a little bit from my point of view.... The goal is not to have people depressed by the end of the episode but just to maybe recognize what inspired the episode in the first place. That's, I think, the most you can hope for. [43]

Indeed, many of the skits on *Chappelle's Show* are literally about what runs through Chappelle's mind — "The Three Daves," (Season Two; Episode 3); what is going through his mind when people approach him to pitch ideas for new material (Season Two; Episode 9); what he would do if he got Oprah pregnant (Season Two; Episode 9); or what he would say on jury selection for Black celebrities on trial, like O.J. Simpson and R. Kelly (Season Two; Episode 9). What is perhaps the most salient example is in the show's very first episode, the relevance of which should not be underestimated. When Lipton asks about the appearance of Clayton Bigsby, the blind, Black White-supremacist on the premiere episode of the show as a "test" for the audience, Chappelle responds that it is "not a test, as much as a manifesto, a mission statement."[44]

Presumably then, this logic can also be applied to its introductory skit with the "pretty White girl" singing his thoughts because "America wouldn't wanna hear a young Black dude saying half of the things" he thinks about, for if he said everything he thought, "it would just freak America out," implying that the only way his ideas would be received by "people" (presumably all those who make up the various strands of the mainstream who would find his ideas utterly foreign) is for his words to be cloaked under a pretty, White, young female guise. There is logic to this in a racial economy with a long-standing history of valuing the White female body over the Black male body, indeed sacrificing Black male bodies for the supposed protection of White female bodies. Of course, a "pretty White girl" then comes on to sing a variety of his thoughts that he appears to be scribbling on note cards he passes to her, including commentary such as, "crack was invented and distributed to intentionally destroy the Black community"; "AIDS was too"; "Fuck the police," and a variety of sexually oriented commentary, like his insistence that although he finds gay sex gross, he likes lesbians. So, this show, though being co-written and co-produced by Neal Brennan, is under complete creative control of Dave Chappelle (hence the show's title), and much of what will be seen is unapologetically portrayed from the perspective of a hip-hop generation, (weed) smoking, heterosexual Black man who is a husband and a father. While not everything is autobiographical, as he explains on *Inside the Actor's Studio*, some of the events are true, but for him the value of the show was his creative *freedom* to express himself as he so chose, including sketches like "Ask a Black Dude" that rely on the uncensored, raw commentary of Paul Mooney who "wasn't likely to get an honest, open voice on another show."[45]

This brings us back to Chappelle's desire to offer subtle critiques and not be preachy. As much as the first show is a manifesto, his primary intention is not shock value. In positioning his audience to see through his eyes, he keeps it real and uses his comedy to say it straight. When he talks about race, then, he does first what he thinks is funny, and if it sparks dialogue, then that is a good thing. Black comedy scholar Bambi Haggins frequently argues that Chappelle's social commentary is often indirect. I would argue the opposite because as indicated earlier, his comedy consistently reaches across divides and stimulates discussion. In an earlier 2003 article, he is quoted as saying, "I'm more about promoting cultural dialogue than political dialogue.... I think more good things come out of cultural dialogue."[46] He is consistent in his position that his job and art as a comedian depend on his ability to work uncensored: he wants the space and social license to be specifically Black and broadly appealing by speaking the socially unspeakable.

What is clear from the scholarship is that hip-hop, as culture and as movement, emanating from social circumstances expressed via a music medium, over the years has grown to be far more than the four elements to include, for example, manner of dress and speech, body language, encounters with police and surveillance, prison, participation in the political process, and most encompassing as "sensibility and worldview," all manifesting as modes of resistance.[47] As KRS-One asserts on his 2007 CD, *Hip-hop Lives*, "Hip and hop is more than music; hip is the knowledge and hop is the movement."[48] Hip-hop, then, is an ideology — a set of attitudes developed in response to a quintessentially postmodern identity structured around rupture specific to living Black in the United States. In his second book, *Why White Kids Love Hip-hop: Wansktas, Wiggers, Wannabes, and The New Reality of Race in America*, journalist and former executive editor for *The Source*, Bakari Kitwana distinguishes between hip-hop consumers and hip-hop arts practitioners. Like Perry and Ogbar, he asserts, "To begin with, it must be stated unequivocally that hip-hop is a subculture of Black American youth culture — period."[49] Not that hip-hop cannot absorb or accommodate non–Black artists, but because hip-hop is produced and nurtured at the local level, the "street" level, hip-hop artists cannot "bypass that Black stamp of approval." It is not just a matter of artists; "[n]either has the hip-hop market yet circumvented Black gatekeepers."[50] In other words, as with Pryor and Chappelle, Black art and artists succeed at the say of Black audiences. The Black Arts Movement it seems has succeeded: "Even Eminem had to get past Black gatekeepers before White hip-hop consumers deemed him good enough. No matter how steeped in hip-hop or marketing finesse, no marketing machine exists that can bypass hip-hop's Black audience. *Are the streets feeling it?* is a constant refrain in the hip-hop industry."[51]

The point here is to see Dave Chappelle not only as an artist with hip-hop sensibilities but also as an active producer of hip-hop culture, using his celebrity to bring together not only artists who are friends of his, artists he wanted to see in concert together, artists who have something to say, but in

choosing to film *Block Party* in Brooklyn because he had heard that hip-hop
had started at block parties in Brooklyn, he wanted to recreate a "magic that
existed" among the "artists involved in the movie" who "kind of carry on that
core tradition as they push the music forward." Chappelle chose famed French
director, Michel Gondry, for the film precisely because he wanted something
different. Talib Kweli says of Gondry that he "brings a different eye" as
opposed to hip-hop directors who tend to shoot videos a particular way. It
was Gondry's idea to shoot the movie more like a documentary, as well as to
shoot in Brooklyn in order "to take it back to the people" — we, the people.[52]

And the people seem to approve, even as Chappelle forthrightly articulates his critiques of Hollywood, the mainstay of feeding America its sense
of status quo. He exercises his independence from that mainstream and effectively reshapes it precisely by his persistent and insistent specificity. Speaking from the local has a broad, universal appeal because the subject matter is
"real" and therefore authentic. In his study of the Black Arts Movement,
James Smethurst identifies a dynamic dialectic between local and national.
The mobility and wide circulation of cultural and political styles and activists
rendered the movement "always local" and "always national." Indeed, "the
growth of radical Black Arts groups and institutions in New Orleans, Hous-
ton, Miami, Memphis, Durham, Atlanta, and other cities in the South
confirmed to activists in centers more commonly the focus of accounts of the
movement (e.g., New York, Newark, Chicago, Detroit, San Francisco, Oak-
land, and Los Angeles) that it really was nation time."[53] With regard to hip-
hop, Kitwana argues that the "local level is slowly taking hip-hop back from
the corporate industry and is the real future of hip-hop."[54] I would argue that
hip-hop, like the Black Arts Movement, has always been local and always
national. It is this simultaneous circulation that allows hip-hop to also be
always international and always black. Indeed, hip-hop artists and fans often
speak of a hip-hop nation, created from its specific (Bronx) black American
roots and black nationalism. Chappelle seems motivated by an imperative to
maintain control of his work, guided by his father's advice that "if it ever gets
more expensive than the price you named, get out of there": he walked away
from the show at that moment when it could have been most financially lucra-
tive for him because it would have cost him his freedom.[55]

Indicating that he was on the verge of doing work that was potentially
socially irresponsible in its portrayal of blackness, the blackness he would
have betrayed was that which should have been properly countercultural and
specific. As much as the show demonstrated a Black Arts inheritance, his
walking away demonstrated his commitment to authenticity and black standards: if his work began to denigrate blackness, it would continue to be
profitable though for a different reason, not for its independence but for its

ability to feed enduring status quo stereotyped images. He has made it clear —
by walking away from *Chappelle's Show* when it began to cost him his artistic, and, therefore, ideological, freedom, and by making *Block Party*— that
his artistic production does not "center ultimately on the profit motive,"
achieving one of the aims of revolution as Rod Bush has defined it. He exemplifies Mos Def's theory of hip-hop — that it is going wherever "we" are going.
Without being preachy or intentionally political, Chappelle has found a way
of moving toward those ever elusive goals of freedom and democracy by simply focusing on his art and staying true to his hip-hop roots. Though not perfect, Chappelle's work demonstrates the ways in which hip-hop as a Black Arts
legacy contributes positively to society to powerfully transform "the" mainstream.

11

"White People, Run for Cover"

Dave Chappelle's Festival of Misrule

FRANCESCA GAMBER

There wasn't much about *Chappelle's Show* that could be called conventional. The sketch comedy series ran for only two seasons. It aired on the cable network Comedy Central, making the show potentially out of reach for audiences who could not afford cable. It made liberal use of profanity, including a jaw-droppingly casual employment of the historically and emotionally fraught word "nigger" to refer to both black and white characters on the show. Nonetheless, *Chappelle's Show* influenced—and continues to influence—popular culture in ways that are far out of proportion to the short span of time during which the program was actually on the air. From inner cities to college towns to suburbs, phrases from the show made their way into colloquial speech: "I'm rich, bitch!"; "I'm Rick James, bitch!"; and "Is Wayne Brady gonna have to choke a bitch?"

Perhaps the least conventional and, at the same time, most influential aspect of *Chappelle's Show* was its humor's head-on engagement with race. Americans, it is frequently said, have a hard time talking about race, but it was everywhere on *Chappelle's Show*. The observational humor made famous by Jerry Seinfeld in the 1990s—a brand of humor driven by the common experience, across race, gender, and class, of bad airline food or waiting in line at the bank—gave way in the new millennium to an edgier comedy that went looking for jokes in the very racial differences that have been the source of so much pain and violence in American history. Racial humor on *Chappelle's Show* was more complex than the humor to be found in the mere comparison of generalized racial traits—the variety of "white guys do this, but black guys do that" jokes. *Chappelle's Show* made race central to its humor, and it did so by challenging its audience to uncover and examine the stereotypes and other assumptions that have created conventional understandings of what "black" and "white" are.[1]

In academic terms, one could say that the racial humor of *Chappelle's Show* was supremely anti-essentialist and deconstructionist. "The Racial Draft" sketch (Season Two; Episode 1), for example, finds African American, White, Latino, Asian, and Jewish teams competing for the official racial designations both of racially-mixed celebrities (Tiger Woods, Lenny Kravitz) and celebrities who have been successful in fields that are not stereotypically associated with their race (Colin Powell, Eminem). The sketch establishes race as a shifting category that can be determined by setting and circumstance. Golf megastar Tiger Woods, who has black, white, and Asian ancestry and famously declared himself "Cablinasian" on the *Oprah* show, is deemed "officially black." The black delegation allows the white delegation to draft former Secretary of State Colin Powell, but only on the condition that they take Condoleezza Rice as well. Both are black officials who served in one or both of George W. Bush's administrations. When it comes time for the Asian delegation to make its choice, one of the Racial Draft's commentators warns that basketball player Yao Ming is in play because he "has been spending a lot of time with blacks learning slang and shit-talking." The delegation confers Asian status on the rap group Wu Tang Clan instead.

In one of the most memorable sketches from the first season, a spoof of the PBS news series *Frontline* profiles Clayton Bigsby, a blind black man who, unaware of his physical color, is a leading white supremacist (Season One; Episode 1). At one point in the sketch, Bigsby's car pulls alongside that of two young white men at a stoplight who are listening to loud rap music. Bigsby, assuming that they are black, calls them niggers and drives off. Rather than being offended, however, the young men are flattered to have been called as such. Another sketch in the second season, "I Know Black People," (Season Two; Episode 8) uses a game show spoof to prove Chappelle's assertion that some white people just "know" black people. The sketch quizzes a range of contestants, from a professor of African American studies to a New York City police officer to a social worker, on questions including "What is a badonkadonk?" and "Why do black people like menthols?" In Dave Chappelle's world, a black white supremacist is possible, and it's possible for a white person to win a game show called "I Know Black People."

In addition to questioning racial essentialism, the show's frequent play with the word "nigger" challenges our linkage of that word to African Americans and the whole package of pejorative associations that come with it. "The Niggar Family" sketch (Season Two; Episode 2), set in an idealized 1950s suburb, derives much of its humor from the application of stereotypical language about black people to a white family whose last name happens to be

Niggar. A new baby is said to have "Niggar lips"; a son who lingers in bed is said to be a "lazy Niggar." This is much to the amusement of the family's black milkman, played by Chappelle, who delights in referring to his white clients as Niggars/niggers. The world of *Chappelle's Show* is one in which all of the usual rules that govern racial categorization and interaction is suspended.

It is also a world in which those rules are occasionally turned upside-down. Several sketches on *Chappelle's Show* make use of role reversal and other forms of inversion that find African Americans suddenly at the top of the social, political, and economic order. In these sketches, this essay will argue, *Chappelle's Show* reaches back to the centuries-old humor of the folk carnival. As theorized by Mikhail Bakhtin, Natalie Zemon Davis, James Scott and others, carnivalesque humor — in history as well as in literature — often takes the form of a festival of misrule, in which a member of the lower social stratum is elected king for the day and other members of the group have the momentary freedom to laugh, eat, drink, and move around that they lack during the rest of the year. The folk carnival also allows its participants to poke fun at their so-called social betters.[2]

Nonetheless, the temporariness of the folk carnival and the unreal quality of the costumes and revels it employs permit a certain ambiguity to its humor. While its participants may read their festival as an opportunity to challenge the systems that sustain their subordination, elites may simply dismiss these events as politically meaningless fun. *Chappelle's Show* uses the medium of television and the relative racial liberalism of our time to push the carnivalesque tradition even further. During most folk carnivals in history, social elites have participated only tangentially in the festivities. Social inversion concentrated on the upward movement from subordinate to dominant, at least for a few days. But several role-reversal sketches on *Chappelle's Show* subject white characters to the unequal treatment experienced by African Americans on a daily basis. *Chappelle's Show* elaborates the political critique offered by carnivalesque humor in a way that is anything but ambiguous.

"Not Merely a Crowd": Carnivalesque Humor in History and Theory

Folk carnivals that feature social inversion or role-reversal elements date at least to the Saturnalia of ancient Rome. These carnivals were usually tied to religious or seasonal calendars, serving as celebrations of the spring, as a final bacchanalia before the Christian season of Lent (as in the Mardi Gras tradition), or as a Christmas festivity. In medieval Europe, the Christmas-time Feast of Fools poked fun at the rituals of the mass and the clergy during one of the Church's most important holy seasons. The church was only one of many structures to be skewered by the folk carnival in medieval and early modern Europe. Carnivals could also temporarily upend gender conventions that assigned different roles and value to men and women. During carnivals, men often wore women's clothing and designated one of their group as a queen or prominent figure. Christmas festivals in particular freed the folk from the etiquette mandated by their economic standing. The holiday tradition of wassailing sanctioned the temporary intrusion of the folk into the private homes of elites, where they demanded gifts of food and drink.[3]

When these European folk festivals arrived in the colonies of mainland North America and the Caribbean, not surprisingly, they reflected the new racial categories that were hardening under New World slave economies. Carnivalesque social inversions now involved the momentary suspension of the distinction between master and slave. Slaves in Jamaica, Belize, the Bahamas, and eastern North Carolina participated in John Canoe or Jonkonnu celebrations during the Christmas season. John Canoe, which may have been named for an African slave who was said to have noble ancestry, involved African music and dance, forms of dress that resembled the finery usually reserved for white people, and movement from house to house or farm to farm in search of tribute that resembled wassailing.[4] Slaves in other parts of the American South inherited the European tradition of relaxing social strictures at Christmastime. Slaveholders usually gave their bondsmen and women holiday presents, allowed them to come inside the master's residence, or even ventured into the slave quarters themselves. In fact, special privileges on Christmas were so routinely expected among slaves that they sometimes gathered under the master's window on the morning of the holiday shouting, "Christmas gift!"[5]

African Americans observed festivals that involved social inversion at other times of the year as well. In early national New York, the Dutch observance of Pentecost in the spring was modified by slaves into the Pinkster festival; the most detailed records of the festival describe its celebration in Albany. Pinkster, which lasted a few decades between the late eighteenth and early nineteenth centuries, saw African Americans erect a temporary encampment on Pinkster Hill that was presided over by one King Charles. In addition to music, dance, and games, Pinkster featured a wassail-like march through town and through the Pinkster Hill camp by King Charles. If a camp resident (who could occasionally be white) did not pay King Charles, his or her tent would be summarily demolished.[6] African Americans in early national Massachusetts, Connecticut, and Rhode Island staged Negro Election Days that, in addition to the usual assortment of amusements, food, and drink, culminated in the mock election of a black leader. It was one of few days of the year when African Americans could occupy public spaces like Boston Common without harassment.[7]

The political commentary involved in celebrations like Pinkster and Negro Election Day is readily apparent. The specter of slaves choosing their own leaders rather than acquiescing to the hegemony of slaveholders threatened the distribution of power that slavery needed to survive. In fact, white concerns about the ability of these festivals to cause insurrection contributed to their decline by the 1830s.[8] In the South, the loosening of the regulations that governed the lives of slaves during Christmas was both social and physical—the holiday was an occasion for many slaves to travel freely to other plantations to visit friends and family. These customary holiday latitude fueled many slave rebellion scares before the Civil War, with slaveholders fearing that slaves would take the momentary relaxation of rules during the holiday to mount an actual uprising. Fears were especially potent after the surrender of the Confederacy in the spring of 1865. Stories of insurrection plots assumed that the traditional topsy-turvy of Christmas made it a prime opportunity for former slaves to exercise their newfound freedom by murdering white people or claiming white-owned property for themselves.[9] Rumors of rebellion can sometimes be even more telling than actual rebellions, and Americans clearly detected a challenge to racial inequality in these seemingly innocuous slave festivals.

Festivals, agrees theorist Mikhail Bakhtin in one of the most influential interpretations of the carnivalesque, bring non-elites together in what "is not merely a crowd. It is the people as a whole, but organized *in their own way* ... to express their criticism, their deep distrust of official truth, and their highest hopes and aspirations." A slaveholder could perhaps congratulate himself for his display of planter paternalism in allowing his slaves a day off from work, a special meal, or a bottle of whiskey, but slaves had their own interpretations of these events. Other theorists of the carnivalesque caution against categorizing festivals that involve social critique and inversion as mere "safety valves" sanctioned by elites to control the resentment of the subordinated. Such an approach denies agency and authenticity to non-dominant groups. "It makes far greater sense to see carnival as the ritual site of various forms of social conflict and symbolic manipulation, none of which can be said, prima facie, to prevail," James Scott asserts. The carnivalesque, agree Peter Stallybrass and Allon White, is not a zero-sum game in which the dominant—by the very fact of their dominance—can point to a record of few uprisings as evidence of their success in manipulating the subordinate. Instead, carnivals deal with "the dialectics of social classification as such." The carnivalesque involves a contest between the dominant and the non-dominant because it is an instance in which non-elites possess a rare ability to voice their criticism, under the safe guise of festivity, of the distribution of social power. The meaning of the carnivalesque is not inherently on the side of either group, but I would venture that it is always political.[10]

"White People, Run for Cover": The Reparations Sketches

Theories of the carnivalesque, as we have seen, often deal with traditionally marginalized groups (peasants, slaves, women, etc.) and argue for their political agency in circumstances in which they are politically disfranchised. By the arrival of *Chappelle's Show* in the first years of the twenty-first century, African Americans no longer experienced the exact variety of disfranchisement faced by the social groups for whom the carnivalesque has been theorized. But inequalities remained, both in opportunity and expression. Entertainers of color continue to be underrepresented on major network television, and so does significant engagement with racism that can reach a broad national audience. Dave Chappelle used his platform on Comedy Central to give voice to a traditional form of folk humor that wields social inversion to question the persistence of racial inequality.

A carnival atmosphere is immediately apparent in two sketches from the first season of *Chappelle's Show* that deal with reparations—the proposal to pay African Americans monetary restitution for generations of slavery (Season One; Episode 4). Both sketches take the form of a newscast, in which white reporters conduct person-on-the-street interviews in black neighborhoods of New York City after they receive their share of one trillion dollars in reparations checks. With the distribution of the money, African Americans reverse the centuries-long trend of outnumbering other ethnic and racial groups among the ranks of the poor to become the nation's wealthiest citizens. Their wealth leaves no need to sustain the usual deference toward white people. "Hide the money, ya'll! There's poor people around!" shouts a black woman, waving a stack of bills, when a reporter approaches her. Another black man drives by with the spoils of his reparations money—a truck containing a lifetime supply of menthol cigarettes—and announces triumphantly to the reporter, "I'm rich, bitch!" In the second reparations sketch, software billionaire Bill Gates is displaced as the richest man in the world by a Harlemite named Tron, who amassed his fortune during a six-hour dice game. During his interview with another white female reporter, Tron gleefully announces to the white anchor, "Hold up, Chuck, I got your girl!" and challenges Chuck to "suck my n---." Tron's character deftly references the longstanding taboo around black male–white female relationships, once punishable by lynching and now a privilege of newfound wealth. Meanwhile, back at the television studio, reparations money allows the station's weatherman, "reliable, friendly, portly Big Al" to assume his usual manner of speaking (which he describes as "straight gangster") and end the pretense of being polite to Chuck. As further evidence of this bottom-on-top scenario, Al is even wearing a crown. Big Al's rant against Chuck is interrupted by the breaking news that then–Secretary of State Colin Powell had "bitch slapped" Vice President Dick Cheney. "White people, run for cover," Chuck declares.

Adding to the world-upside-down festivity in the reparations sketches are descriptions of the ways in which these newly prosperous African Americans are spending their money. The value of gold and diamonds soars, the newscast reports. Three million Cadillac Escalade SUVs are sold in a single day. Stock for the telephone company Sprint ascends with the resolution of millions of past-due accounts. A bucket of chicken now goes for $600, yet "watermelon is surprisingly flat." Certainly the reparations sketches find humor in lampooning stereotypical black behavior, prophesying that African Americans would spend their reparations checks on a truckload of cigarettes. But there is another social commentary at work. With the reparations checks, consumer goods and spending habits that were disparaged as the hallmarks of the ghetto now dictate what happens on Wall Street. A world with reparations money is a world in which the economic order is on its head. When Chuck asks another reporter about the paucity of banks in black neighborhoods, she replies, "[T]hat's because banks hate black people, but I think that's about to change."

Black Like Me: The "Mad Real World" and "Law & Order" Sketches

In 1803, one Absalom Aimwell of Albany, New York wrote a poem in the voice of the Pinkster festival's King Charles. His interpretation of the festival leaves out none of its high-spirited fun, but it infuses an unmistakable conservatism in King Charles's supposed message to the crowd of festivalgoers:

> What tho' for freedom we may sigh
> Many long years until we die,
> Yet nobly let us still endure
> The ills and wrongs we cannot cure.[11]

Aimwell's poem underscores the fact that there were many ways of looking at a festival like Pinkster. For Aimwell, the revelry and the celebration of a mock African American king were easily contained within the world of the festival. In voicing these words in the persona of King Charles, Aimwell is confident that Pinkster's attendees understand the immutability of their status and are resigned to "endure" it "nobly." One wonders what assessment actual Pinkster festivalgoers would have made of their celebration; it is likely that there would have been both radical and conservative strains of thought among them.

The practical, real-world meaning of festivals of misrule or social inversion is ambiguous and always the subject of competition between dominant and subordinate groups. I would argue that one reason for this ambiguity is the fact that almost all of the action during these festivals is performed by members of the subordinate group. As James Scott points out, even a festival is not a completely safe space for the expression of the full "hidden transcript" of resistance to domination. "So long as speech occurs in any social situation," he writes, "it is saturated with power relationships."[12] The extent to which elites participated in festivals of misrule was largely reserved to the donation of food, drink, and gifts during wassail or on a slave plantation. A slaveholder in the American South might go into the slave quarters himself or herself and assist in meal preparation, but this is not the same level of participation as donning a costume, joining the dance, or truly playing the part of the slave when social inversions are involved.[13] The sight of a member of the elite group enacting the servility reserved for the subordinate is a clear indictment of a society's inequalities. In societies like those of the slave South, the cost of forcing this kind of confrontation was far too high for slaves to risk. "Tactical prudence," Scott notes, "ensures that subordinate groups rarely blurt out their hidden transcript directly." Moreover, few elites were eager to participate in the unveiling of the farce upon which their domination was predicated. Festivals were one of many "arts of resistance" in which subordinate groups subtly expressed opposition to the status quo.[14]

With time, however, conditions were more amenable (comparatively speaking) to making a more explicit criticism of inequality through the use of social inversion. Several black writers and performers explored the commentary that could be produced by placing white characters in situations where they would be treated as African Americans normally are. In his 1931 novel *Black No More*, satirist George Schuyler centers his plot around the discovery of a chemical process that can turn black skin white. It is wildly popular among African Americans, and the forces of white supremacy — represented by the fictional Anglo-Saxon Association — become even more fanatical in their efforts to preserve white racial purity. The Association's president, Arthur Snobbcraft, hires Dr. Samuel Buggerie, a statistician, to research the presence of hidden black ancestry in the nation's populace. But when Buggerie's research uncovers black blood in both his and Snobbcraft's backgrounds, both men go on the run, heading for Mexico. After their plane crashes in Mississippi, they darken their faces, necks, and hands to blend into the black population. Unfortunately, they have stumbled into a town in the midst of a religious revival by a white supremacist minister. Seeking a miracle to prove himself to the townspeople, the minister begs God for "a nigger for his congregation to lynch." Snobbcraft and Buggerie unknowingly wander into a revival meeting, but even after removing their clothing to reveal their white skin, news of Buggerie's genealogical research had already reached the townspeople. "They're niggers just as I thought," the minister declares. The crowd mutilates and burns Snobbcraft and Buggerie in the sort of lynching usually reserved for black men accused of committing a sexual atrocity against a white woman.[15]

Lynching, perhaps the quintessential racially inflected form of punishment in American history, provided another opportunity for role reversal humor on *The Richard Pryor Show*. Comedian Richard Pryor's prime time sketch comedy show on NBC aired only four episodes in the fall of 1977. One sketch in the second episode uses the setting of a Southern courtroom in 1926 to ridicule the unequal treatment faced by African Americans in the justice system. In the sketch, a black man is being prosecuted for the rape of a white woman. The sketch uses several devices to underscore the uselessness of trial for that particular crime in this particular time and place: the judge cools himself with a fan from a local undertaker; a court official threatens the defendant with a gun whenever the judge invites him to defend himself. When testimony reveals that the accused was already in prison on the night of the attack (and that the alleged victim had a reputation for sexual looseness), the defendant is freed. Nonetheless, the crowd is so incensed at the acquittal that it leads the defense attorney (played by Robin Williams) away to be lynched. In this scenario, if a black man couldn't be hung for an alleged rape, a white man was an acceptable substitute.[16]

Both Schuyler and Pryor drew upon their audiences' familiarity with lynching and Southern summary justice to frame their racial inversion sketches. At the start of the twenty-first century, the shared lexicon to which Dave Chappelle turns is television. A set of four short sketches spoof the long-running MTV reality series *The Real World* (Season One; Episode 6). During the second season of *The Real World*, the majority-white housemates eject a black male roommate, claiming that they no longer "feel safe" with him in the house. When introducing the sketches, Chappelle questions what he believes is *The Real World*'s habit of making African Americans room with white housemates who are less than stable. His answer is "The Mad Real World," in which an innocent white man named Chad is sent to live in Hoboken with five unbalanced black roommates, including Tron, Chappelle's personification of the most extreme ghetto stereotypes. When he arrives at the house, his housemates are smoking marijuana and playing cards. When they are all sent to work at a juice bar, the pot-smoking continues, and hard-working Chad reprimands his roommates when he catches them playing dice behind the store. Chad is forced to room with the menacing Tyree, who introduces himself by saying, "My name is Tyree, and yeah, I went to prison." Chad's girlfriend Katie is happily seduced by Tyree and Tyree's ex-convict friend, Lysol, while Chad is forced to watch and masturbate. In later sketches, the other housemates put Chad in a sleeper hold, after which they rob and sodomize him and also stab his father. Finally, when Chad reaches his breaking point and screams at his roommates for having a loud party at 1:30 A.M., they call a house meeting and ask him to leave. "We just don't feel safe with you in the house anymore, Chad," a female housemate avers.[17] Like the reparations sketches, "The Mad Real World" sustains stereotypes about certain pathologies that are associated with African Americans. In this topsy-turvy world, however, it is Chad who is made an outcast and penalized for his sheer normalcy.

A popular television show provides the frame for what is probably the most effective racial inversion sketch from *Chappelle's Show*. In the second season, Chappelle muses about the handling of (white) white-collar criminals accused of financial misdeeds in scandals like Enron. "I got to get in on this being white thing," he jokes. "It's like there's two legal systems." The sketch that follows is Chappelle's vision of what it would look like if white corporate criminals were put through the same criminal justice system faced by black drug dealers (Season Two; Episode 5). Using the familiar format of the *Law & Order* series, the sketch follows two criminals through this world-upside-down. Charles Jefferies, the CEO of the fictional Fonecom, is at home with his wife when police break down his door and shoot his dog. By contrast, cocaine dealer Tron Carter is courteously notified by police that he should turn himself in. They allow him to set the time and apologize profusely for the "inconvenience." When Tron arrives, hours after the appointed time, he is greeted with a cheese tray and a promise of only two months in prison if he appears before a Senate subcommittee. Meanwhile, Charles Jefferies gets a harried public defender and a cigarette put out on his forehead. Tron pleads the fifth at his Senate hearing and walks away with a reduced sentence, while Jefferies is sentenced to life without parole. The judge also lectures Jefferies on his crimes at sentencing, calling him a "big-lipped beast" and promising him "plenty of [jail] time to lift weights and convert to Islam." If it initially makes little sense for the judge to be referring to Jefferies in such racialized terms, *Chappelle's Show* presses the question further, asking why it would be more acceptable for a judge to refer to a black defendant as a "big-lipped beast."

The traditional humor of the carnivalesque uses social inversion to show those at the bottom of the social order how the proverbial other half lives. But because folk carnivals have been employed as a means of resistance by people under intense forms of subordination like slavery and feudalism, the carnival is a necessary means of mediating their political critique. Festivals in which slaves dress up in the fancy clothing or military uniforms of the master class are easily dismissed as fun and games rather than a potent political suggestion. While racial inequality continues in the twenty-first century United States, African Americans are freer to critique their society than their slave ancestors ever were. Artists like George Schuyler, Richard Pryor, and Dave Chappelle took the traditional carnivalesque beyond putting bottom rail on top. They pushed the critique further, laying bare to elites the unequal conditions faced by black people by physically placing white people in these same unequal scenarios. It seems ridiculous to put an affable white man in a house full of socially maladjusted, even homicidal, roommates. It is laughable to plant heroin on the white CEO of a major corporation. But while we have our laugh, Chappelle, and others like him, ask us to consider why these scenarios, when black people are involved, go unchallenged and why they even assume a routine quality. This intensified form of social inversion humor tries to get at the root of why these sketches are funny. Plumbing the source of that reflexive laughter means uncovering some personal as well as institutional racisms that we might prefer to leave unexamined. *Chappelle's Show*, like the long history of folk carnivals, John Canoe, Pinkster, and Negro Election Day, exemplifies the old adage: many a true word is said in jest.

12

Haunted

Dave Chappelle's Radical Racial Politics in the Context of Co-opted Blackness

Chiwen Bao

There are few individuals within the current 18- to 35-year-old market-segmented population who are not familiar with *Chappelle's Show*. And there are even fewer who do not recognize one of the most popularized lines from the show, "I'm Rick James, bitch!" In the past several years, Dave Chappelle has gained undeniable popularity and influence through his work as a comedian, especially in his eponymous *Chappelle's Show*. First airing on the basic cable network Comedy Central in 2003, his sketch comedy show averaged 3.1 million viewers per episode.[1] Moreover, breaking records as the best-selling DVD ever for a television show, nearly 3 million copies of the DVD of the first season of *Chappelle's Show* were sold.[2] This 30-minute weekly program (minus commercial advertisements) facilitated Dave Chappelle's coronation as the "poster boy of black comedy."[3] What has arguably become even more well-known about Dave Chappelle is how he left the $50 million contract to continue his show. A tremendous amount of debate initially erupted as to why he left this cash cow, but he has since clarified what precipitated his unanticipated and abrupt departure. Chappelle has explained that he discontinued his show fearing that people were misinterpreting his humor and satire. This essay endeavors to lay bare some of the underlying dynamics of Chappelle's "racial paranoia" in the space of publicly staged humor.[4]

What animates this analysis of Dave Chappelle's comedy is a simple question: How do constituents of a widely diverse audience interpret and understand his humor? This query echoes Bambi Haggins' concern about how she doesn't know exactly what people are laughing at when they watch Dave Chappelle.[5] For instance, Haggins and others[6]—including myself—revel in Chappelle's sometimes liberating satire and side-splittingly hilarious and incisive social critiques, but not everyone reads Chappelle's humor as counter-hegemonic text and expressions of racial truths. In fact, it was this possibility — and probable reality — of people not interpreting Chappelle's satirical comedy as he intended that contributed to his "paranoia." However, my approach here is not to survey and speak definitively about how audience members situated at different social locations with varying vantage points read, interpret, and process Chappelle's humor. Instead, I venture to explore the ways in which the commercial space of race performance is both historically and currently haunted by literal and figurative enslavement and commodification. Occupying that space, Dave Chappelle is subject to the persisting specter of racism where his blackness marks him as a fungible commodity that exists in the service of others, namely whites. Thus, while various theories have examined the critical value of Dave Chappelle's comedy, the reasons for his popularity, and his unexpected exodus, my efforts here strive to expose how the hauntings of history, those that he attempted to and sometimes succeeded in unearthing, spoiled the power of his satire.

Although he radically articulated the persistence of racism(s) in contemporary forms, Chappelle could not deny his vulnerability to having his potentially resistant satire co-opted and, ultimately, serving a mainstream consumerist imagination of racial and racist objectification. His humor could not and cannot be extricated from a history that is laced with both spectacularized and quotidian dehumanization and abjection of blacks. Although neither Chappelle nor his comedy is predetermined by these hauntings, he and his audience inevitably must wrestle with them. This analysis does not aspire to claim determinism and fatalism but strives to speak about the haunted contexts of racial humor and how we reproduce the past when we fail to acknowledge how it lingers in our present moment. By doing so, we can further realize the liberating potential of this comedic mode of communicating critical social and political commentary that points shamefully at our complicity and hopefully at possibilities of racial justice and understanding.

Hauntings of Crossover Appeal

For Dave Chappelle, becoming a commercial sensation came with certain baggage. His abrupt departure from the show during the height of its popularity — and from the offer of tens of millions of dollars — demonstrates that success wasn't all fun and desirable. Chappelle's unannounced and unexpected disappearance from the set and from the entire show immediately followed this experience: when he was filming one skit, Chappelle put on blackface to probably demonstrate how he imagined people of color are constantly tormented by the fear and threat that they will unwittingly reenact and reaffirm denigrating racial stereotypes. Upon seeing how one white male crew member on the set was laughing, "Chappelle claims that he had a sinking suspicion that the person was laughing at him, laughing at black people, and relishing these racial stereotypes in a destructive way."[7] This incident seemed to validate Chappelle's growing suspicion that some individuals were not understanding his humor as he intended and were instead using his performances to fulfill racist pleasures, even as he worked to conjure stereotypes in order to show their absurdity and inhumanity. What John L. Jackson calls Chappelle's "racial paranoia" did not result merely from this singular incident but rather from his expanding recognition that the unprecedented success of his cable show clearly meant that he had "crossover appeal" where his comedic performances could and did attract a wide-ranging audience with innumerable vantage points and vastly differing politics. Moreover, crossing-over didn't simply mean appealing to a larger and dissimilar audience; it meant entering into a space that comes with baggage, that remains weighed down and haunted by its past.

Speaking about how the commercial space where race is performed is haunted is not about trivially talking about actors wearing white bed sheets and objects mysteriously moving across the stage; it is about seriously acknowledging how histories continue to be replayed in our present moment as long as they remain repressed and unchallenged. In the case of Dave Chappelle and his comedy, addressing how specters of a messy and burdened racial history hovered over his comedy and his own being allows us to recognize how his work did not exist in a vacuum but was to a degree possessed by the continuation of exploitative racial relations. Avery Gordon points out how our existence is encumbered by forces beyond and greater than ourselves. She wisely and concisely articulates that "to be haunted ... is to be tied to historical and social effects."[8] Through acknowledging these hauntings, we come to understand "a process that links an institution and an individual, a social structure and a subject, and history and a biography."[9] Examining this process, we can see that as much as Dave Chappelle is an individual artist embodying his own creative talents and producing his unique version of satirical humor, he is also part of a history located in a time and space that cannot be divorced from previous moments, especially ones that are burdened and loaded with patterns of racial exploitation.

To understand Dave Chappelle's swelling discomfort with his audience and the moment when he decided he needed to desert his show, I examine particular hauntings to enlighten us about how the unresolved past cleaves to the present moment. In doing so, we can begin to reexamine how the history of white dominance, racism, and even the construct of race in America haunt both our subjectivities and institutions, such as those involved in Chappelle's comedy. The legacies of slavery and racial performances are the "historical and social effects" that become particularly relevant to an analysis of Chappelle's work to the extent that unresolved dynamics of a problematic past cast a shadow over the current stage. Through employing this theoretical approach of hauntings, I venture to go beyond simply stating that Chappelle's humor was easily co-opted for a mainstream audience with diverse tastes and interests; I explore the processes by which appropriation is possible and the ways the space Chappelle occupied on commercial prime time network television was a place already inhabited by specters of racial cannibalism.

Chappelle's space of performance, a stage set before a racially mixed audience, is particularly haunted because of how the relevant past is unsettled, despite strongly and widely held beliefs that social progress from the post–Civil Rights era sufficiently countered societal racism.[10] According to Gordon, a haunting is the return of what has been previously, and unsuccessfully, repressed. She describes this situation as "one way in which abusive systems of power make themselves known and their impacts felt in everyday life, especially when they are supposedly over and done with (slavery, for instance) or when their oppressive nature is denied (as in free labor or national security)."[11] In other words, closeting explicitly violent and exploitative institutions, such as slavery and minstrelsy, and stifling collective memories of their existence ironically results in concretizing their presence as animated specters in our lives, including our spaces of entertainment.

Moreover, situated in a contemporary period where ideologies of colorblindness prevail, Dave Chappelle and his comedy are further disconnected from relevant yet obfuscated histories of minstrelsy and other forms of performance that dehumanize African Americans. Discourses of colorblindness and "political correctness" in our post–Civil Rights era silence constructive conversations of race and persistent racism and actually blind us to ongoing ugly realities of subtle, covert, and evolved forms of racism, the direct descendants of the parent lineage of explicit racial violence.[12] This ideological and discursive gag only adds strength and power to the specters and legacies of racist histories of racial exploitation, such as the physical and symbolic enslavement of blacks for the purposes of pleasuring and serving the white master class. Thus, borrowing the theoretical lens of hauntings, we can see more clearly how repressed memories and histories surfaced and shaped the exploitative context of Dave Chappelle's crossing-over to be consumed in mainstream venues.

Describing the Specters

Turning to specific qualities of the hauntings, I draw upon Saidiya Hartman's work to reveal how historical dynamics of enslavement and performance permeate contemporary spaces, such as *Chappelle's Show*.[13] In particular, reflecting back on a troubled past to understand the present uncovers how racial terror previously occurred in everyday spaces and through objectifying black individuals via their blackness. Coming back to the current moment and the commercial space where both Chappelle and his comedy are sold for profit, specters of this past cast a shadow on the stage and orchestrate processes that allow for racial and racist commodification.

First of all, Hartman shows how racial terrorizing did not occur only in "the shocking spectacle" but also in "the mundane and quotidian."[14] There is an exigency to examine the non-explicit violence perpetrated in everyday spaces precisely because of the difficulty in discerning insidious brutality in those locations. Moreover, as in the contemporary spaces of comedy, entertainment and television, there is a "diffusion of terror" and "violence perpetrated under the rubric of pleasure, paternalism, and property."[15] The seemingly lightheartedness of these venues conveyed through qualities such as the catchy sing-along jingles and colorful graphics of *Chappelle's Show* conceals the racial subjugation and subjection committed under the guise of pleasure and enjoyment. Thus, with *Chappelle's Show*, teasing apart the embedded dynamics of viewers' consumption potentially unveils terror, a violence that is insidious because of its inherent surreptitious nature. In the show's very first episode, Chappelle directly points out a materialization of this haunting when he jokes seriously and critically about how the cartoon frog on the cable network HBO is basically a cutesy animated version of racist fantasies of blacks' "shucking and jiving" (Season One; Episode One). In this moment, he is criticizing the racist ideologies that show up in seemingly neutral and exceedingly normalized contexts, like a cartoon character on TV. Ironically, as *Chappelle's Show* continues, the jingle of his show (with the two older black men at the beginning of each segment singing "Chappelle's show" and playing a guitar and harmonica) and other widely disseminated and marketed hallmarks of his show (like the exclamation "I'm rich, beeeotch!") become a "rubric of pleasure" through which racial violence takes place and Chappelle devolves into merely an entertainer.

Further unraveling the seams of "routinized terror" to reveal its inner workings, Saidiya Hartman articulates how black bodies were objectified and commodified to serve a white master class during slavery and through minstrelsy:

> Blacks were envisioned fundamentally as vehicles for white enjoyment, in all of its sundry and unspeakable expressions; this was as much the consequence of the chattel status of the captive as it was of the excess enjoyment imputed to the other, for those forced to dance on the decks of slave ships crossing the Middle Passage, step it up lively on the auc-

tion block, and amuse the master and his friends were seen as the purveyors of pleasure.[16]

A ghostly appearance of this dynamic, where blacks were simply regarded as
means of pleasure, turns up each time strangers call upon Dave Chappelle to
enact their fantasies off stage. Carpio recounts how "people repeat funny but
obscene lines from his show ('I'm Rick James, bitch!') in front of [Dave Chappelle's] children and expect him to act out his characters on request."[17] In
those moments, Chappelle becomes what Hartman terms "purveyors of pleasure."[18] Strangers disregard his personhood, forgetting that he is an individual (i.e., a father) with a life outside of his work as a comedian, and simply
desire, if not demand, that he perform, entertain and delight.

Importantly, blackness[19] provided the necessary mode through which
individuals could be literally and then figuratively enslaved. The instrumen-
tal function of blackness for commodification draws upon what Frantz Fanon
defines as the "racial epidermal schema."[20] Occurring within a white supremacist society, this "schema" dictates that a nonwhite person's skin color is a way
of seemingly knowing the individual by simply assigning her to a racial collective and reducing her existence to a host of stereotypes, thereby robbing
the individual of her personhood. In the case of race performances, the process
whereby the individual is obscured and only race is seen allows audience
members to use blackness as a means of consuming the performer and performance as mere stereotypes and nothing more complex or critical than that.
Moreover, the blackness of the performers and attached racial stereotypes are
employed as a conduit for spectators of the master class' self-discovery and
self-fulfillment. By engaging in that process, those audience members can
delight in the amblings and expressions of racist caricatures and experience
that they are more than what the stereotypes (and their beholders) are. Hartman explains how "the value of blackness resided in its metaphorical apti-
tude, whether literally understood as the fungibility of the commodity or
understood as the imaginative surface upon which the master and the nation
came to understand themselves."[21]

Chappelle conjured blackness through two mediums in his show: his
own blackness and his black characters. As such, spectators could enlist the
"racial epidermal schema" to objectify him and his characters, thereby degrading his artistry and satire to a simple commodity consumable for the master
class' self-actualization. Additionally, although Dave Chappelle is obviously
a person distinct from his characters, the shared blackness (his own and that
of his characters) promoted the interchangeability of him and his characters,
thus further viciously displacing his personhood. (The example above involving the infamous Rick James line demonstrates this process.) Furthermore,

the conflation of Chappelle's own racial ascription with his racial perform-ance serves to problematically validate stereotypes that he strives to disrupt. Thus, while he brings to life stereotypes to present their meaninglessness and vacuity, especially as ways of knowing racialized individuals, Chappelle's own epidermal blackness actually comes to validate the supposed reality and truth of the racist descriptors. In those moments, he and his work are haunted by historical constructions of blackness that enact the "brutal corporealization of the body and the fixation of its constituent parts as indexes of truth and racial meaning."[22] Illustrating this haunting, crossover audiences, likely transfixed by unacknowledged specters of a racist history, not surprisingly and probably very uncritically popularized the most absurd black caricatures from *Chappelle's Show* (such as Tyrone the Crackhead, Chappelle's impersonation of music icon Rick James and the rapper Lil Jon). Consequently, Dave Chap-pelle became very well known for these characters, not necessarily for sati-rizing them but for his embodiment and enactment of black stereotypes.

Returning to Hartman's description of how captive black bodies, such as those of performers, facilitated self-augmentation for viewers and specta-tors endowed with racial privileges, Chappelle's work can be contextualized within this legacy to reveal dynamics that animated his "racial paranoia." Resonating with Saidiya Hartman's analysis of black individuals' employment in a political economy of slavery, servitude and entertainment, Frantz Fanon pointedly states, "The Negro is a toy in the white man's hands."[23] Karen Sotiropoulos illustrates how black performers at the turn of the twentieth century experienced being commodified and co-opted in ways that substan-tiate Fanon's conclusion.[24] For instance, Sotiropoulos discusses how "by the 1910s, whites understood their status as modern through their ability to buy the blackness that the new culture of consumption produced. For the most part, however, whites did this without interacting with black artists or even acknowledging African Americans' contributions."[25] At that historical moment, white identities and constitutions of their selfhood relied upon can-nibalizing black culture and disregarding any complexity of blacks' human-ity. With this sort of history repressed from public acknowledgement and discourse, it inevitably resurfaces in the same space — the stage on which race is performed.

Haunted by this legacy of racial cannibalism, Dave Chappelle grappled with "what it can mean for a black man when he makes white people laugh."[26] As he occupied a space where he consciously performed race for a racially diverse audience, Chappelle stood where race, particularly blackness, had been previously used to facilitate "prohibited explorations, tabooed associa-tions, immodest acts, and bawdy pleasures" for the pleasure and self-aggran-dizement — through a sense of racial superiority — of whites.[27] The specter of past racial exploitation cast a shadow on how Chappelle's satire had the potential and high probability of being co-opted, as it had been done to many others before him. In short, the growing popularity of *Chappelle's Show* intensified the hauntings of past racist exploitation and invigorated specters on stage.

Telling Ghost Stories and Speaking Racial Truths

While ghosts of racism's past, present, and future eventually stole the scene, Dave Chappelle didn't simply leave without putting up a fight or addressing the specters. In confronting hauntings, Avery Gordon contends, "It is sometimes about writing ghost stories, stories that not only repair representational mistakes, but also strive to understand the conditions under which a memory was produced in the first place, toward a countermemory, for the future."[28] Chappelle attempted to do just that with his humor — write ghost stories in the form of sketch comedy and tell racial truths to offer possibilities for a more racially just future. Even though his comedy did not always seemingly aim to articulate problems of racial denigration and was even epistemologically and politically backwards sometimes, Chappelle frequently brought our attention to the destructive legacies of racial hierarchies, myths of racial inferiority, and misrepresentations of personhood and culture through the sketch comedy show.[29] In these ways, he wrestled with ghosts that would otherwise dehumanize certain racialized individuals and misconstrue their situations to fortify systems of racial injustices and inequalities.

Within a repressive discursive field of ideological colorblindness and "political correctness," Chappelle moves beyond the simple genre conventions of comedy of "pushing the envelope" to naming and pointing out the persistent, complicated, and messy issues of racial domination and subjugation. Derrick Bell contends, "For some of us who bear the burdens of racial subordination, any truth — no matter how dire — is uplifting."[30] Dave Chappelle's work communicates those racial truths that are — especially for some of us — relieving, encouraging, and necessary for survival. Furthermore, through his widely broadcasted sketch comedy, Chappelle courageously radicalizes public racial discourse by speaking truth to power in this commercial space and by holding a mirror up to the face of white political and cultural supremacy and all of those who participate in upholding this racist regime. In this way, he continues a tradition of Black American humor that "began as a wrested freedom, the freedom to laugh at that which was unjust and cruel in order to create distance from what would otherwise obliterate a sense of self and community."[31] By participating in this practice of racial humor, Dave Chappelle tells ghost stories of past and present racist realities in order to liberate those of us who comprise the underbelly of racist regimes from that which could annihilate us.

Carrying on the liberating legacy of African American comedy and providing that "wrested freedom," Chappelle gestures at the hauntings of minstrelsy and shows how people of color are misrepresented by ironically and hilariously representing white people. By "flipping the script" on blackface and donning "whiteface," Dave Chappelle does not simply co-opt whiteness and poke fun at white people, but astutely demonstrates both the often performative nature of race and the ridiculousness of essentializing race. For instance, Chappelle enacts whiteness not just through full make-up and hair, but by changing the timbre of his voice, grammar and speech patterns. But what is perhaps most politically and socially significant in his performance of whiteness is the way his white characters express thinly cloaked sentiments and judgments of racial superiority and condescension. In this way, he exemplifies DuBoisian "double consciousness" by revealing his keen awareness of a racist belief system that underlies constructions of whiteness. For instance, Chappelle's character Chuck Taylor, a white news anchor, reveals his horror in response to the distribution of slavery reparations when he states in a restrained and severe tone that it is a "wild day that none of us will forget no matter how hard we try" (Season One; Episode Four). With this comment, Dave Chappelle both verbalizes the often unspoken resentment many whites may harbor in light of seeing non-whites achieve limited degrees of power and demonstrates his recognition of these racist beliefs. In doing so, he reveals his awareness of how whiteness, like before, has a "coherence and illusory integrity dependent upon the relations of mastery and servitude and the possession of a figurative body of blackness."[32]

In the same episode, Chappelle displays his "double consciousness" of how the racially privileged master class can harbor racial prejudices that lie beneath outward façades of "political correctness" and outside of public spaces. Chuck Taylor jokes about how the way crime rates went to zero must indicate that Mexicans received money as well. Chuck Taylor then realizes he is still on air and momentarily puts on a serious face and ostensibly apologetically says, "I shouldn't have said that." Once he goes off camera, his insincerity is immediately revealed as his face instantly changes from seriousness to amusement. He erupts into laughter, first somewhat controlled then into full out belly laughter as he continues with racist comments. Not only does Chappelle show how people of color are homogenized and misrepresented in the eyes of some whites (where Chuck Taylor believes that Mexicans are all criminals who watch the cable network Telemundo) but the way these beliefs continue to powerfully haunt and reinforce racial hierarchies and, therefore, maintain racial superiority because of the way they lay hidden in private spaces, off-camera and within their own communities. This extremely clever sketch exemplifies Bambi Haggins' assessment of how Chappelle and his writing partner for the sketch comedy show "model comedic social discourse where the unspoken is spoken — and the absurdities and hypocrisies that often inform 'polite' conversations about race relations are laid bare."[33]

Additionally, Chappelle simultaneously puts stereotypes "in motion"[34] and "has slapped race back onto the discursive table of sketch comedy" when he demonstrates the absurdity of racialized and racist imagery, such as those of glamorized depravity, and offers an alternative narration and explanation of certain scenarios.[35] For example, in the reparations sketch, white television news correspondents comment on how Blacks spend their reparations money in stereotypical ways: on Menthol cigarettes and "expensive clothes, fancy cars, and gaudy jewelry." While this scene might be read simply as a reenactment of racist stereotypes (images to be co-opted and consumed), the skit allows for another story that includes a partial contextualization of Blacks' "ghettofabulous" consuming behaviors to reveal their sources in the predatory nature of consumerism and a political and economic environment that systematically and systemically disadvantages low-income people of color. An instantiation of this point is the exchange concerning why there are no banks in "the ghetto" where the news correspondent's bluntly stated response that "banks hate black people" captures the essence of the context where there are few institutional resources which facilitate sustainable financial stability and economic mobility.

In his continuation of telling this ghost story of the racialized space of "the ghetto," Dave Chappelle cleverly critiques the grave racial implications of contemporary capitalism in his skit about the fictive fast food chain WacArnold's (Season Two; Episode Two). Through the skit, Chappelle mocks weak, limited, and disingenuous efforts to bring sustainable and meaningful employment into impoverished communities. His character strives to provide for his family and gains self-respect in becoming employed, but his aspirations are stunted by characteristics of demoralizing and dead-end low-wage jobs in the growing service industry. Moreover, the skit ridicules the fast food corporation's claims to improve and contribute to low-income communities of color by showing a depressing reality of epidemics of poor health and continuous impoverishment. By staging this skit, Chappelle shows the insidiousness of economic and political ghettoization where aspirations are met with despair and despondency. He tells a racial truth about dislocation and poverty, about how some communities of color are placed at the demoralizing margins of society, devoid of educational, political and economic opportunities available to those who are located safely within the margins. In doing so, Chappelle crafts a ghost story of "the ghetto" and builds a "countermemory" of how some lives are haunted by systemic poverty and structural constraints.

Not only did Dave Chappelle point out the way specters of racism and capitalism haunt society, but also how they lingered in his own particular space of comedic performance. Demonstrating his awareness and fear of racial cannibalism in "show business," Dave Chappelle self-consciously and presciently satirized how "blacks were envisioned fundamentally as vehicles for white enjoyment" in one of the *Lost Episodes*.[36] In this skit, Chappelle, playing himself, approaches the balding white male incarnation of "Show Business," who, in turn, explains that the comedian needs "merchandising" (*Lost Episodes*; Episode 3). As Chappelle imagines what that would be like, he envisions a cereal product where he becomes a caricature of himself as a cartoon figure slapped on a cereal box to promote "Dave Chappelle Cereal." Chappelle's comedy becomes literally and metaphorically boxed into a cereal consisting of a colorful reduction of *Chappelle's Show*'s most popular content: "purple crackpipes," "yellow titty jokes," "brown musicians," and "black and white observations." Thus, to promote the successful evolution of Dave Chappelle in the market economy of entertainment (a.k.a. "Show Business"), his personhood as an individual and an artist simply devolves into a racialized commodity where he symbolically becomes packaged for mere consumption. Dislocated from his creative work and his own body, Chappelle is replaced with a cartoon rendition of himself while his work gets shrunken into edible morsels. Completing the process of cannibalism, a typical couple of quaint and charming white kids and their mom eat Chappelle and his comedy via the cereal in order to shake up the boring routine of their lives, experience "bawdy pleasures," and even momentarily transform themselves (as shown by the young white girl suddenly and strangely adopting the deep voice of a black man as she exclaims, "I'm rich, beeotch!").

As shown through the skit detailed above, Dave Chappelle grappled with the hauntings of gaining crossover appeal, experiencing burgeoning commercial success, and inevitably becoming objectified, packaged and sold as a commodity for the delights and gratifications of a master class of spectators and consumers. Moreover, the ingenious sketch of "Dave Chappelle Cereal" reveals how racial terror takes place in commonplace and mundane moments (such as during breakfast) as Chappelle decomposes into a mere "purveyor of pleasure," even as he points out radical racial truths and wrestles with ghosts through his comedic work. However, that terror could be deflected if audiences took his humor seriously and recognized how Chappelle does not merely broach controversial topics of race and racial stereotypes, but narrates alternative ghost stories, which expose persistent specters in society. As illustrated through the skits discussed above, such specters include minstrelsy, people's private prejudices, a racist capitalist system that ghettoizes and impoverishes communities, and racial co-optation. Through using sketch comedy to unveil the workings of these specters, Chappelle shows how systems of racial signification and misrepresentations, like the "racial epidermal schema," promote and uphold racist domination. However, as he wrestles with some ghosts, specters remain as some people fail to appreciate his racial politics and grasp the meanings of his alternative ghost stories.

Lingering Specters and the Demise of Chappelle's Show

Although Dave Chappelle exposed some hauntings, there were others that loitered without his acknowledgment or, more importantly, without the audience's recognition.[37] The specters attached to a wide crossover audience were beyond his reach; their deconstruction required awareness and responsibility on the part of the viewers. These were the ghosts of crossover appeal that enabled people to misinterpret his satire, to turn his political critique into simply a validation of degrading stereotypes, and to reinforce their own racist beliefs. Ironically, yet also predictably, it was the power of these specters that facilitated his immense success, but also eventually helped bring about the demise of his show when Chappelle realized that his alternative ghost stories were not as mighty as the ghosts themselves.

While Chappelle and his collaborators can be held accountable for the way in which they perhaps intensified some hauntings, the arguably greater problem lies in the specters that were out of his control and that had to deal with a mainstream audience. Gaining crossover appeal, Chappelle found himself and his satirical comedy in a place where a widely diverse audience embodied both the potential to understand his humor and to completely miss the metaphorical boat. In discussing implications of the sketch comedy show, William Jelani Cobb argues, "the problem was not so much the work as it was who was viewing it."[38] Cobb goes on by describing how Chappelle's crossover into appealing to a mainstream audience occurred after the end of the first two seasons: "By season three ... Chappelle's Show had officially crossed over, meaning he was virtually assured of an audience too big to really dig what exactly he was laughing at."[39] In short, the very nature of entertaining and charming an expansive audience meant presenting material, which in this case contained coded and controversial content, to viewers coming from varying social, cultural and political positions and endowed with differing sensibilities and political acuity. Consequently, as Chappelle strove to tell some ghost stories, they were neither heard nor understood by some of the audience. Even though he gained the respect and praise of those who found liberation in his expression and representation of their racial disenfranchisement and dislocation, his wide ranging popularity was also necessarily willed by those who enjoy the bounties of racial privilege. For *Chappelle's Show,* where racial stereotypes were regularly conjured for both comedic effect and profound social criticism, the effects of this sketch comedy in front of a diverse audience could be either "uplifting" or tragically destructive.

This process of sharing insider humor (especially of the racially marginalized) with outsiders (such as the racially privileged) not only posed problems because outsiders often didn't and couldn't understand what was going on but also because there was a tremendous potential of being misinterpreted and co-opted.[40] As he transformed from a comedian who was unfamiliar with and also intimidated by "show business" to a pop culture icon, Chappelle and his comedy became subject to superficial readings and distortions. Cultural theorists, scholars and Chappelle himself suggest that entering the mainstream threatened the integrity of Chappelle's work which consisted of shining a light on and poking fun at the dysfunctions and pathologies of society. In the commercial space of race performance, specters haunted him and his humor with the threat and likelihood of exploitation and cannibalism. For those who didn't comprehend the message behind the satire, they at best just missed the point and at worst hijacked Chappelle's comedy to reinforce racial hierarchies and reify racist stereotypes. Reflecting on Chappelle's success through his sketch comedy show, Carpio ponders, "What kind of success is this for stereotype-derived humor? Surely the success depends on Chappelle's numerous gifts as a performer. But, as Chappelle himself suspects, it could signal the co-optation of his power to conjure stereotypes."[41] While Carpio suggests that appropriation of Chappelle's racial humor may be fueling his success, William Jelani Cobb states more bluntly that misreadings will necessarily result when the audience to the jokes is not equipped with the prerequisite political and cultural lexicon.

> In the case of Chappelle, you confront the one question at the heart of his dilemma: what happens to an inside joke once the whole world is in on it? An inside joke is inside for a reason — usually because only a select few people share the references necessary to decipher it, or the background to appreciate where the actual comedy is. In the wrong hands the joke will inevitably be misinterpreted.[42]

Dave Chappelle also suspected that his jokes were in the wrong hands and possibly sorely and dangerously misunderstood.

Without gauging the exact interpretations of every individual viewer in order to verify that Chappelle's satire was misinterpreted and misused, we can draw upon history to intuit the present and consider how an unresolved past of audiences consuming blackness for their own amusements lingers as a specter on stage. For instance, the sketch on "Keeping it Real" (Season Two; Episode Eight) with Vernon Franklin offers various readings, including a counter-hegemonic ghost story and also a haunted tale of co-optation. In this skit, Chappelle plays Franklin, a highly successful and upwardly mobile black man who exemplifies the rags-to-riches story. However, during one ill-fated board meeting, his mentor, a white man, offends Franklin by trying to relate to him in stereotypically "black" terms, such as through street slang and hand gestures. Franklin then blows up at his mentor because he is fed up with being an "Uncle Tom" and starts to enact all of the racial stereotypes the mentor probably could only begin to imagine. The "countermemory" that Chappelle creates through this skit involves recognizing how the information conveyed through the "racial epidermal schema," i.e., stereotypes, is largely about performance and not truth. Also, in his tirade, Franklin offers profound insight into how tiresome and demeaning it is for people of color to always have to entertain others' racist fantasies of their stereotyped and essentialized nature. While those readings acknowledge Chappelle's wrestling with certain ghosts, other interpretations might prevail given the specters that remain on stage involving spectators' objectification and dehumanization of black performers via their epidermal blackness. For those who do not perceive and grasp the alternative ghost story crafted by Chappelle in this skit, Franklin's stereotypical behaviors do not disrupt racist narratives of black inferiority, but affirm them. And just like how the white mentor's enactment of racial stereotypes to attempt to relate to Franklin reveals both his own bigotry and his desire to be "down," members of a crossover audience could consume Chappelle's performance in a way that reifies their destructive ideas of black Americans and also augments their sense of themselves as "hip." With specters of racial co-optation and cannibalism hovering over the audience, the possibility of these problematic interpretations and misappropriations of Chappelle and his satire is great.

Thus, given the hauntings in commercial spaces of racial humor, including those he may have inadvertently reinforced, not only was Chappelle's liberating message probably lost on much of the audience, but his comedy was likely also co-opted to re-calcify racist reasoning.[43] Even though Chappelle's comedy harbors the potential to offer critically important lessons about racial politics, the venue of his delivery (prime time network television) and exploding success via crossover appeal confounded the transgressive possibilities of his humor. Comedic satire embedded in the skits perhaps became turned on its head to simply reinforce racist perceptions of black Americans and essentialist ideas of blackness. This may have constituted Chappelle's experience of being haunted, which "draws us affectively, sometimes against our will and always a bit magically, into the structure of feeling of a reality we come to experience, not as cold knowledge, but as a transformative recognition."[44] With his performances, Chappelle may have felt in a very palpable, yet perhaps still indescribable, way how he was haunted by a still relevant and unresolved history of literal and figurative racial enslavement and commodification.

Then, when he saw the white male crew member laughing during the last scene he performed for *Chappelle's Show*, perhaps Chappelle actually sensed the lingering specter of historical racism before him. It was as if the apparition signaled that what was being repressed, racist consumption of his blackness, could no longer be repressed for Chappelle. Gordon suggests that "haunting and the appearance of ghosts is one way ... we are notified that what's been concealed is very much alive and present, interfering precisely with those always incomplete forms of containment and repression ceaselessly directed toward us."[45] Chappelle responded to his suspicions that he was becoming another victim of historical patterns or racial cannibalism and literally fled the scene of these racial crimes. The past could no longer be obscured; Chappelle saw the metaphorical writing on the wall as the inscriptions of literally and symbolically enslaved black bodies before him.

Confronting the Ghosts, Seeking Racial Justice

While Dave Chappelle's satirical humor struck a chord with mainstream America, his success was likely predicated on both genius and exploitation. His brilliantly funny and insightful evocations of racial realities and truths in his sketch comedy exhibited tremendous potential for social and political commentary and criticism. For some of us, his articulations were "uplifting" and liberating because he wrestled with ghosts of historical racial cannibalism and exploitation. However, a darker side to his success existed. Chappelle himself sensed the darkness and the perverse consumption of his work and reacted in kind — by leaving. In this analysis, I have ventured to explore how and why co-optation of Dave Chappelle's humor was possible and likely. To do so, recognizing how unresolved histories haunt the present facilitate an understanding of how Dave Chappelle's work was encumbered by historical dynamics of racial exploitation.

Chappelle's sketch comedy show occurred in a distinctly haunted space. He delivered his satire from a place where blacks' humanity and agency were contested for hundreds of years. Like in the institutions of slavery and other moments when blacks were enslaved, objectified and commodified, terror revealed itself in mundane practices where captive black bodies were used as vehicles for the white master class' self-actualization and identity formation. Blackness was critical and central to the processes of commodifying bodies since it translated into the fungibility of individuals. Through this process, individuals' blackness became the mode through which he or she became objectified for the consumptive pleasures of those who privilege from the power to displace others with their own desires, pleasures and enjoyment. These were the historical legacies Chappelle inescapably became a part of, had to reckon with and wrestle to the ground in order to win over his agency.

Speaking about black performers during the turn of the twentieth century, Sotiropoulos contends that "at every turn black artists and critics tried to shape black theater in ways that would earn black Americans equal status, but they did not count on the depths of white determination to buy and own black culture."[46] This dynamic of non-blacks' (especially whites') compulsion to perform racial cannibalism constituted the hauntings Chappelle probably experienced. In the same vein, so-called fans with a paucity of critical awareness probably recite "I'm Rick James, bitch!" to Dave Chappelle, their own friends and themselves for the sake of enhancing their own social status. In the moment when they evoke that line, they are riding off the coattails of Chappelle's popularity and racialized hipness to promote their own sense of being part of the new direction of cool. Playing into and strengthening hauntings of when "the fungibility of the commodity ... enabled the black body or blackface mask to serve as the vehicle of white self-exploration, renunciation, and enjoyment,"[47] those who regurgitate the infamous line without any awareness of its satirical meaning make Chappelle a racial caricature out of his own parody of degrading representations of blackness in order to co-opt the stereotypes for self-serving purposes. Through each exclamation of the abused phrase, they exploit that distorted imagery of black buffoonery by putting it on display to signal to others their familiarity with the show and to amuse themselves and others. Moreover, since the younger half of the 18- to 35-year-old targeted population for the show probably has little firsthand familiarity with Rick James other than through *Chappelle's Show*, they probably have little to no awareness of Chappelle's criticism of Rick James and a celebrity culture of consumerist excess and massive egos implied in the satirical line. As a result, they miss the punch line and read Chappelle's impersonation of Rick James as validation of blacks' essential foolishness, a misrepresentation that supports unfounded racial hierarchies and erroneous beliefs in whites' superiority. This, in short, illustrates how Dave Chappelle and his comedic satire became co-opted in a haunted context of racial commodification and exploitation. With a specter of racist history looming over his work, Dave Chappelle's satire may have simply reproduced the "abject status of blackness"[48] that he strove to dismantle.

To realize the potential of Chappelle's humor and that of black artists who will come after him, we must recognize the powerful ghost stories that

Chappelle tells in his humor that offer liberating potential and collectively exorcise the ghosts that continue to haunt us. As Avery Gordon suggests, "[T]he task then remains to follow the ghosts and spells of power in order to tame this sorcerer and conjure otherwise."[49] Through his satirical skits, Chappelle follows apparitions, such as racial misrepresentations, racist belief systems, and structural conditions of racism and poverty, in order to "conjure otherwise" and evoke alternative realities of racial justice. While he brings the ghosts out of private spaces to importantly narrate "countermemories" publicly, the space he enters is haunted. Unchallenged and uninterrogated, these ghosts aspire to perpetuate the co-optation and commodification of blackness, thus violently displacing blacks' personhood. Therefore, we need to examine the specters of anti-black racism that continue to linger in our current institutions and subjectivities (especially as audiences), prompting and promoting dynamics of racial exploitation. Black humor remains a space with tremendous promise, as exemplified by Dave Chappelle, but the haunted nature of commercial spaces where race is performed can continue to undermine possible freedoms if we fail to acknowledge how the unresolved past of racial co-optation lingers in our present moment and contest its power. Discussing a continuing legacy of slavery, Dave Chappelle reminds us: "You can't recover from a problem that you aren't willing to acknowledge you have it."[50] We can't tell ghost stories until we acknowledge the ghosts.

Conclusion
Legacy and Dave Chappelle

K. A. WISNIEWSKI

"Please, Mr. Taylor, buy me, too," pleads Lucy. Lucy is a pregnant slave and is on her knees, crying, begging, tugging on the trousers of the White man who stands above her, who ignores her, shaking his leg as if he's dismissing a whining dog from the dinner table. They are on the outskirts of a small mob — a couple of dozen — waiting outside a tavern on the side of the Duke of Gloucester Street down from the courthouse for the next slave to be auctioned. There are three other slaves, tied or shackled, scared, waiting for their new masters — the highest bidders — to emerge from the crowd. Lucy is crying, her face lowering down into the dirt road. This White man just bought her husband; the year is 1994. A crowd of tourists looks onto the scene, some horrified, others deeply touched. The auction is part of a three-day program called "Publick Times" and is sponsored by the African American Department of Colonial Williamsburg in Virginia. Despite the presentation's efforts to bring balance to the historical narrative constructed at the site, officials were concerned about the potential for such an event to be trivialized into entertainment, while the public was largely outraged by even the idea of it.[1]

The mock slave auction raises a number of questions surrounding not only the museum as a social arena in which people of different backgrounds interact with another to consume, produce, and exchange meanings but also questions of what stories are being told, who these stories belong to, and what stories are being forgotten. It is now largely agreed that public memory is a modern construct that mediates national consciousness, often building myths and displacing what is best forgotten. As Pierre Nora explains, "Memory has been wholly absorbed by its meticulous reconstruction. Its new vocation is to record: delegating to the *lieu de mémoire* the responsibility of remembering, it sheds its signs upon depositing them there, as a snake sheds its skin."[2]

Because of technology and industry and rise of a culture reliant on memo-rialization, cultural memory has taken a new shape: it is distant and artificial. It is now displaced from individual's scope. Moreover, what Nora defines as the "acceleration of history" reveals the disconnection or gaps between con-temporary definitions of memory and history.

Similarly, Michel-Rolph Trouillot examines these gaps, or as he sug-gests "the silences," of historical production in his book *Silencing the Past*, in which he examines ambiguity and tracks the exercise of power within the nar-rative of the Haitian Revolution.[3] To some degree, that is also the attempt of this concluding essay. The comedy of Dave Chappelle is largely built around the grand narratives of American history, but it is also based around the idea that the audience is aware of the untruths built inside these narratives. There-fore, the comedian works not only to deconstruct these narratives but also reconstruct some of the voices forgotten (or at least less heard) at present. This essay examines three specific elements of Chappelle's work. First, it examines how Chappelle finds and celebrates points of a shared American culture. As theorists of comedy suggest, there needs to be some common ground established before punch line. But the punch line arrives from the deviance of this established norm or expectation, in the "sanctioned" viola-tion of taboos. Within his community, Chappelle is able to expose gaps, the breaks from the system to which we are all socially linked. The punch line or rather the cultural anxiety that he stresses in his comedy is the second point of interest here. Finally, this essay hypothesizes how Chappelle's canon to date reflects a shift in public culture and how Chappelle has, in fact, shaped public culture.

Returning from a commercial break, the sketch fades in slowly with a camera panning left and following an aisle in the first class section of an air-plane where each row is occupied by a pair belonging to a particular race or ethnicity (or species) who is criticized and culturally labeled by the subse-quent couple behind them (Season One; Episode 5). *The American Idol–* obsessed Middle Eastern men are viewed as al–Qaida terrorists by African Americans sitting behind them; meanwhile the Caucasian man behind them cautiously clutches his daughter's hand and wonders how these "Negroes" in front of him earned their first class tickets, quickly deducing that they must be rappers. Behind the Caucasian family, two Native Americans, in full stereo-typical headdress, grip their seats in fear of losing them with the "white man's" proclamation of Manifest Destiny. Still more bizarrely two buffaloes retort, "At least you Indians got casinos." Beyond the buffaloes, the camera freezes on *Chappelle's Show* creators Dave Chappelle and Neil Brennan, an African American and a Caucasian, peacefully slumbering side by side with Chap-pelle holding an open newspaper entitled *The Daily Truth* with the headline

"America United." Several things are of note here. First, Chappelle highlights the absurdity of labels and demonstrates that fear is often what drives such thinking. Secondly, the White couple is de-centered in the hierarchy here, merely part of this chain of fearing and being feared. Most interestingly, though, is the final shot of Chappelle and Brennan asleep, comfortable beside one another and as part of this longer procession: they may perhaps be seen as a pair who have come to terms with their pasts.

Chappelle connects to this sense of community (even the conflicted one in which he finds himself) to dissension. In one episode, taking a series of drags of a cigarette, the comedian jabs at mayor Bloomberg and New York City's new ban on smoking indoors and proudly reflects on his "rebellious" lineage (Season Two; Episode 2). The sketch bounces through several generations of the Chappelle clan beginning with Dave himself shivering outside, smoking, and complaining, "Bloomberg is fucking up!" The scene quickly cuts to 1978, Washington, D.C., where Chappelle shakes his head at the traffic outside a gas station and repeats the aforesaid line substituting Carter for Bloomberg. The scene again repeats itself as the audience is taken to 1945 and the disaster of Truman's bombing of Hiroshima and yet again to the Civil War where two slaves blame conditions on first Lincoln and then "White people in general." The two smile innocently as white supervisors pass by. The final scene, the punch line, shows a seventeenth century Chappelle in African garb complaining about the chief and preparing, excitedly, to greet some "White people on a boat." Two weeks later, Chappelle and fellow tribesmen are shackled somewhere in the belly of that boat in the Atlantic. The character again shakes his head, confessing, "I fucked up." In taking the blame for his slavery, Chappelle shifts the status quo from having power as a dissenter, an outsider, into having none. What is disturbing about this punch line is how the blame of slavery gets placed onto the laps of African peoples. Although it is true that there were free black American colonists in the eighteenth century who owned slaves and that African tribes traded other Africans to European traders, there is a myth growing that these African tribes had dominant or even exclusive control over the supply of slaves and over the Atlantic slave trade in general. Anne C. Bailey takes a special interest in how such African oral traditions developed and how these stories of shame and guilt shaped into a truth understood but rarely discussed. She explains that this myth "assumes wrongly that no slave was ever kidnapped by European nationals, when in fact kidnapping played a major role in the early stages of the slave trade in the fifteenth century and then again in the last phase of its operation in the nineteenth century."[4] So Chappelle is perhaps, here, inadvertently spreading a harmful myth within this seemingly harmless joke about dissension. On the other hand, the punch line could also serve as critique of the extent paradigm or lesson to the masses: power, in negative terms, limits, obstructs, and prohibits.

Interestingly enough, unless the audience considers a single expletive spoken in private as dissension, the only public act of rebellion is delivered before the sketch as Chappelle smokes in front of the audience. In the age of post-political correctness and green initiatives, one might consider smoking to be a social taboo. In this reading, the cigarette then becomes a cultural artifact, "linked to the multiplicity of meanings and intentions that cigarettes bespeak and betray; they speak in volumes, rather than in brief emblematic legends. The cigarette is itself a volume, a book or scroll ... [that conveys] worlds of meaning that no thesis could begin to unpack, that require armies of novelists, moviemakers, songwriters, and poets to evoke."[5] While it may connote different meanings in other sketches, here, it is meant to provoke. Like the beginning of most sketches, Chappelle establishes his community, defines his terms, sets boundaries, and creates some commonality that is understood, if not generally accepted. Then he breaks these circumstances' rules. In his introduction of Tyrone Bigguns, for example, Chappelle sets the tone by reminiscing with his studio audience — generally speaking, a similarly aged group of people (for whom race is not seen as important here) from what Chappelle refers to as "Generation X," "the Pepsi Generation," and "Reagan babies" — of the 1980s' War against Drugs campaign and the school program that invited recovering addicts to discuss the dangers of drugs and alcohol with school children (Season One; Episode 2). In this context, the idea of Tyrone is familiar to most of the viewers. The chalky, grotesque figure who is introduced, however, is not what viewers have in mind. The dissension, the contrast from what is imagined or expected is the point where the comedy and critique begins. Maintaining a Victorian sensibility of the children's innocence and naïveté, the audience is shocked by Tyrone, who not only specifically explains where and how to find and to use drugs but also describes the experience of being on drugs. Tripping on acid, for example, is simply an enticing invitation to ignore parents and household chores and instead spend time with "Bugs Bunny and Scooby Doo and my favorite cartoon heroes [who] came to my room and ate cookies with me and sang songs." Tyrone continues his anti-drug talk by describing what dog food tastes like, by defecating in front of the class in a garbage bin, and explaining the first time he performed oral sex for crack. As symbols of purity and simplicity, children are a reliable contrast to Chappelle's unabashed performance of social taboos, whether it's related to violence, explicit language, sex, drugs, or public defecation. This formula is seen throughout *Chappelle's Show*, especially in the sketch "Kneehigh Park," in which puppets parodying a *Sesame Street* or some Saturday morning children's show attempt to justify drug use, explain apathy towards work and material wealth, and describe venereal diseases to children (Season Two; Episode 10), and is further highlighted during commercial breaks as Chappelle runs onto camera in front of the two tinkering musicians and shouts, "Better not bring your kids!"

Children of the Victorian Age, we are people who fear contagion and who are obsessed by purity and by the dangers of corruption. The rise of the modern nation-state in the eighteenth and nineteenth centuries brought forth new systems, new structures of scientific discourses to discipline and maintain order. Foucault specifically illustrates that "in order to see perfect disciplines functioning, rulers dreamt of a state of plague.... The image of plague stands for all forms of confusion and disorder."[6] While Foucault reads the plague as an attempt to control the masses, in a slightly different context, Mary Douglas discusses the way "pollution" ideas aid the support of social structures when political or moral authority is weak.[7] Similarly, Julia Kristeva has argued that when paternal structures of social authority are in crisis, a focus upon "abjection" and defilement occurs in a kind of return of fundamental cultural anxieties.[8] It can be said then that the topic of contagion offers the possibility of a resolution of difficult questions on law, morality, and social order, and some revelation to larger universal concepts of authority, power, and knowledge.[9] Indeed, this is also the claim of Lawrence E. Mintz in his article on comedy as social mediation. Building on both Mary Douglas and Victor Turner and their readings of the joke as part of a larger cultural rite and social activity, Mintz asserts that the joke is "an opportunity for society to explore, affirm, deny and ultimately to change its structure and its values.... [H]e [the comic] serves as a *shaman*, leading us in a celebration of a community of shared culture, of homogenous understanding and expectation."[10] While much of Chappelle's comedy does address race and conflict in America, as Chappelle himself often reminds us, his work is meant to be "a celebration, bitches," a reminder of cultural similarities and unity.

In his exaggerated emphasis on racial binaries of black and white or colonized and colonizer, Chappelle actually highlights the interconnectedness of races, classes, genders, and subcultures and demonstrates how cultural mixing, or emerging hybridity, enables further dialogue and reconsideration of identity. Sketches like "The Racial Draft" (Season Two; Episode 1) or "Trading Spouses" (Season One; Episode 12) realize Homi Bhabha's "third space," that permits new avenues for resistance and negotiation. Moreover, Chappelle's parodies can be read as an act of mimicry that translates and subverts inscriptions of power.[11] Nevertheless, from this perspective, identities are still contested, and race is still encoded. This is also largely seen in the "Blind White Supremacist" (Season One; Episode 1) and "I Know Black People" (Season Two; Episode 8). What creates the possibility for racial transgression, what reconfigures nationhood and offers the masses a common ground, and what gives Chappelle crossover appeal is the shared positions as consumers. The global market transcends time and space and, one could also argue, race, age, and gender. It potentially creates what Mary Louise Pratt refers to as the "contact zone," a liminal space that allows the "co-presence of subjects previously separated geographic and historical disjunctures, and whose trajectories now intersect."[12] While this space doesn't invoke neutrality, it serves as an arena in which dialogue may occur and similarities may be more clearly viewed. Each of these sketches parodies of mass media, to which all sub-cultures are in some fashion products. While the "Blind White Supremacist" models a broadcast news program, the subsequent sketches mock a reality television show, a sports draft, and a game show, respectively, all products that the masses passively consume.

It all leads to the issue of money. In his comedy special at San Francisco's Fillmore *For What It's Worth* (2004), Chappelle discusses September 11th and the Iraqi War. Despite his dismay at the Iraqi conflict, Chappelle does admit to getting "choked up" after viewing the press conference acknowledging the removal of Saddam Hussein's image from Iraqi currency. The comedian says, "I was proud to be an American because that's a very subtle psychological nuance of oppression to have dictator on your money, and it's thoughtful to take that motherfucker off for the goodwill of another person." But the conversation quickly diverts into another direction, U.S. currency, which resembles "baseball cards with slave owners on them." Chappelle quickly skates in the "mythologized" images of the Founding Fathers and commits what may be referred to as blasphemy by referring to George Washington as "the worst of the worst." In a scenario that is reminiscent of the Playa Hater's time traveling journey to the Old South (Season Two; Episode 11), Chappelle envisions going back in time with a white friend, where the impulses to shake the first president's hand and run away for one's life are "both right." The joke continues with Chappelle playing Washington and pausing during the writing of the lines "all men are created equal" in "The Declaration of Independence" to threaten a slave to make him a sandwich before returning the lines "liberty and justice for all." Interestingly, it is one of the few lines of the night that receives a modest reply. Chappelle is quick to defend his comments: "Am I wrong? Did he not own slaves?" While he is combining roles of Jefferson and Washington here as writer of the Declaration and as "father of the country" as well as bringing in the final lines of the "Pledge of Allegiance," Chappelle's efforts show the need to question our history and to face our memory. Unfortunately, despite high market sales of biographies of such founders and the public's awareness of early republican debates surrounding slavery and controversies concerning both men fathering children with slaves, Chappelle is quick to adapt to his audience's quiet response.[13]

He returns to Iraq and begins to criticize the United States' involvement in the region until he publicly remembers the backlash of recent comments made by the country music act the Dixie Chicks. He notes, "If they'll do that to three white women, they will tear my black ass to pieces." After a moment of self-deprecation, a higher volume of laughter from the audience allows him to plunge into the problems of celebrity culture. He asks why celebrities' opinions are so highly regarded in our culture, why the media often focuses on the political views of entertainers like Ja Rule and the Dixie Chicks more than scholars and political scientists. Chappelle's point during the comedy special is much more to the point than *Chappelle's Show* sketches: "Stop worshipping celebrities." The comedian wonders why people even listen to him, explaining that he promotes both Coke and Pepsi, can't really taste the difference between the products, but prefers Pepsi that day because they paid him most recently. While his larger-than-life impersonations of Samuel L. Jackson, P. Diddy, and Lil' Jon exhibit the same silliness or artificiality of these figures' public images, *Chappelle's Show* scenes of celebrity-endorsed products such as Rocka Pads and Redman toilet cleaner (Season One; Episode 5) further unearth Chappelle's larger conceptualization of the system of consumer culture and the power of the image.

In his work *The Fall of Public Man*, Richard Sennett blames the traumas created by capitalism for the masses' retreat from civic life. He worries that society's private and narcissistic lives ultimately lead to a fear of true personality exposure — what Chappelle dissects in his comedy's sentiments on keeping it real — and the blurring of the self.[14] As mass media infringes into the personal and part of the self can no longer be kept hidden, everyone's personal identity, once it becomes part of a new collectivity, is called into question. Sennett explains, "We are a community; we are being real; the outside world is not responding to us in terms of who we are; therefore something is wrong with it; it has failed us; therefore we will have nothing to do with it. These processes are in fact the same rhythm of discourse, disappointment, and isolation."[15] Chappelle acknowledges these sentiments throughout his canon. He witnesses the social problems resulting from the Internet and video games and the global village, and he sees the racist and chauvinistic ideologies in practice. But he also envisions an optimistic future.

Like Fukuyama and Baudrillard, Chappelle's work engages in the analysis of sociological forms of late capitalism. All conclude that the development of global capitalist development have changed modes of understanding history. While Fukuyama predicts the end of history and alternate ideologies, Baudrillard sees the displacement of reality due to the power of simulation.

He explains, "The illusion of our history opens on to *the greatly more radical illusion of the world.*"[16] Whether speaking of ideas or media, for both thinkers global access and the power to reproduce events mean "history ceases to exist as such." Still, both theories assume that alternative theories are invalid. Chappelle, however, already positioned within this market, is able to realize a new route, a way back to history through the ineliminability of difference, be it economic, cultural, political, or spiritual.

In 1994, Colonial Williamsburg's efforts to re-enact a slave auction resulted in large public backlash. Recreating such a horrific memory in U.S. history seemed too much to handle. But one decade later, Dave Chappelle was able to re-address this very subject (and other silenced memories and contemporary taboos) time and again in his stand-up and his sketches and to a much larger audience on national television. Again, Chappelle's work belongs to a new emergent class that is simultaneously separate and connected to the past he critiques. It is a group displaced by their engagement — infatuation and reliance — with technology, cyberspace and mass media especially, and their knowingness of world events, both high and low brow — that is their skepticism, their self-consciousness, their selfishness, and their sense for irony. This new class to which Chappelle belongs is less nostalgic that previous generations, no longer looking to preserve and savor the past but, in fact, reclaim and re-contextualize it. And from that blurred position as comic, Chappelle does just this. William Gibson, author of the futuristic and dystopian novel *Neuromancer*, who coined the word "cyberspace," captures the sensibility of this new class in the title of his 1996 *New York Times Magazine* piece entitled "The [Inter]Net is a Waste of Time and that's Exactly What's Right about it."[17] In the *Chappelle's Show* sketch that examines the Internet as a "real" place (Season Two; Episode 6), Chappelle shows the sleaziness of the world realized from looting to pornography. But he also sees these actions (at least in the virtual world) as commonplace and justified within that space. This in-between realm is a place where such social norms and civic restrictions are bent, unclear.

This realm is one in which Chappelle's comedy flourishes. Sketches including the "Home Stenographer" (Season One; Episode 1), the "Wrap it up" box (Season One; Episode 2), and the "Love Contract" (Season Two; Episode 4) illustrate a people who have become disengaged with listening (and even feeling) and yet are held accountable for everything they say or do. Other sketches like "Things Look Better in Slow Motion" (Season Two; Episode 1) reflect on the "cool" places mentioned in the introduction as actually uncool (at least without graphic manipulation). And, finally, sketches like "Third World Girls Gone Wild" (Season One; Episode 6) blends the images of *National Geographic* magazine that has served as a porthole to exotic peoples and places with the dodgy, yet perhaps as equally popular video series *Girls Gone Wild*, depicting young college-aged girls in lewd or scandalous positions. In drawing from and juxtaposing both well-established texts, or grand narratives, and contemporary pop culture stories and events, Chappelle creates a comfortable crossroads, an intersection on which viewers may confront the often contradictory, awkward, and painful questions that have troubled our past and continue to haunt our present. Chappelle is able to escape ridicule from the masses as he mocks the flogging of Kunta Kinte in a re-enactment of the classic miniseries *Roots* (1977) because he is seemingly so far removed from it. The scenes don't set out to imitate or reconstruct a moment in the institution of slavery but rather mocks the idea of DVD bloopers extras. In its depiction of *Roots*, it is twice removed from any actual event, while still chipping away at an American icon.

Raymond Williams correctly classified culture as "one of the two or three most complicated words in the English language."[18] If culture tells us "what makes sense," Chappelle's largest contribution is questioning this and offering alternative perspectives to those cultural myths and the assumptions and fallacies embedded in them. Concerned with the inconsistencies and absurdities of society, how we communicate, the comedian must be praised for this fearlessness to address these difficult subjects. As "removed" as these subjects may be, the curse of the class is that they are still equally close and meaningful. Impersonating Prince or Rick James has affected our lives. We see this as we impersonate the impersonation. But we often forget how we, the audience, have changed Chappelle's life. He has gained fortune and fame, but he has also traded in, sacrificed, much of his private life. These sketches, this comedy, do mean something. While Chappelle shows that race, place, and communities are, at best, imaginary, discourses around them are porous and open-ended and necessary.

In his first appearance on *Inside the Actor's Studio* with James Lipton, Chappelle reflected, "I don't know how this Dave Chappelle thing is gonna end, but I feel like I'm gonna be some kind of parable by either what you're supposed to do or what you're not supposed.... I'm gonna be something; I'm either gonna be a legend or just that tragic fucking story, but I'm going full throttle; I'm going all the way. I'm eager to find out how story will resolve itself."[19] In typical Chappelle fashion, the comedian turned the tables on the show by re-appearing for the show's 200th episode and serving as host and interviewer of James Lipton.[20] In a tête-a-tête for the final questions, Chappelle interestingly, and perhaps unsurprisingly, named "reality" both his favorite and least favorite word. In answering the comedian's questions — questions that are fun and funny, as well as mischievous and unsettling — the audience potentially finds themselves on a transformative journey to explore this very topic.

One of Chappelle's most common jokes revolves around "the division of our foods."[21] Despite often playing with stereotypes of African Americans' love for fried chicken and watermelon, in the stand-up special *For What It's Worth*, Chappelle proclaims that "if you don't like chicken and watermelon, there's something wrong with you!" He goes on to suggest that such cultural differences can be funny but "they're no reason to hate." Such an idea is reminiscent of Lisa M. Heldke's thesis in "Food Politics, Political Food" in which she claims that food, if we take what she defines as the Coresponsibile Option, evokes "the fact that acting in the world is a communal, relational activity — that we are in correspondence with, and are also responsive and responsible to, others in the world."[22] This is what Dave Chappelle has offered to the world. He has given us a chance to laugh at our differences and, more importantly, to look at our similarities. Louise Bogan's poem "Song for the Last Act" best reflects the comedian's impact on the world: "Now that I have your face by heart, I look." Chappelle's comedy proves that he's looking. And so we look.

Filmography

Blue Streak. DVD. Directed by Les Mayfield. Sony, 1999.

Buddies. ABC, 1996.

Chappelle's Show: Season 1. DVD. Comedy Central, 2004.

Chappelle's Show: Season 2. DVD. Comedy Central, 2005.

Chappelle's Show: The Lost Episodes. DVD. Comedy Central, 2006.

Con Air. DVD. Directed by Simon West. Touchstone, 1997.

Dave Chappelle: For What It's Worth. Live! At the Fillmore. DVD. Directed by Stan Lathan. Sony Pictures, 2004.

Dave Chappelle, interview by Jay Leno, *The Tonight Show with Jay Leno*, NBC, August 20, 2004.

_____, interview by Bob Simon, *60 Minutes*, CBS, October 20, 2004.

_____, interview with Oprah Winfrey, *The Oprah Winfrey Show*, NBC, February 3, 2006.

_____, interview with James Lipton, *Inside the Actors Studio*, Bravo, February 12, 2006.

_____, interview with James Lipton, *Inside the Actors Studio*, Bravo, November 10, 2008.

_____. interview with Terry Gross. *Fresh Air*, NPR, Sep. 2, 2004.

Dave Chappelle and Maya Angelou, "Dave Chappelle + Maya Angelou," *Iconoclasts*, Season Two. Directed by Joe Berlinger. Sundance Channel and Grey Goose Entertainment, 2006.

Dave Chappelle: Killin' Them Softly. DVD. Directed by *Stan Lathan. Urban Works,* 2000.

Dave Chappelle's Block Party. DVD. Directed by Michel Gondry. Universal, 2006.

Half Baked. DVD. Directed by Tamra Davis. Universal, 1998.

Joe's Apartment. DVD. Directed by John Payson. Geffen, 1996.

Nutty Professor. DVD. Directed by Tom Shadyac. Universal, 1996.

Robin Hood: Men in Tights. DVD. Directed by Mel Brooks. 20th Century–Fox, 2006.

Screwed. DVD. Directed by Scott Alexander and Larry Karaszewski. Universal, 2000.

200 Cigarettes. DVD. Directed by Risa Bramon Garcia. Dogstar, 1999.

Undercover Blues. DVD. Directed by Herbert Ross. MGM, 2003.

Undercover Brother. DVD. Directed by Malcolm D. Lee. Universal, 2002.

You've Got Mail. DVD. Directed by Nora Ephron. Warner Brothers, 1998.

Chapter Notes

Introduction

1. In her study of Dave Chappelle, Bambi Haggins positions the comedian's show beside *The Richard Pryor Show* and *In Living Color*. Bambi Haggins, "Dave Chappelle: Provocateur in the Promised Land," in *Laughing Mad: The Black Persona in Post-Soul America* (New Brunswick: Rutgers University Press), 178–236. Elvis Mitchell makes a similar comparison between *Chappelle's Show* and the Wayans' brothers' comedy in "Chappelle's 'Show': A Successor to 'In Living Color'?" *New York Times*, 23 March 2003, C24.

2. The "ecstasy of communication" refers to the title of Jean Baudrillard's essay of the same name.

3. Dave Chappelle, interview with James Lipton, *Inside the Actors Studio*, Bravo, February 12, 2006.

4. Manohla Dargis, "A Comedian's Ultimate Goal: Rock the Block," *New York Times*, March 3, 2006, E1.

5. Following the quote, still in the interview chair, he sings the film's theme song forms the movie's famous Crane pose. It is especially telling that amidst the seriousness and deep-felt sentiment here Chappelle maintains his sense of humor and light-hearted sense of narrative. Moreover, his reference to a 1980s "white" film is equally telling about his influences. Dave Chappelle, interview with James Lipton, *Inside the Actors Studio*, Bravo, February 12, 2006. DVD.

6. J. Fred MacDonald, *Blacks and White TV: African Americans in Television Since 1948*, 2nd ed. (Chicago: Nelson-Hall, 1992), 14.

7. Other noteworthy works centering on this topic include Ed Guerrero, *Framing Blackness: The African American Image in Film* (Philadelphia: Temple University Press, 1993); Darnell M. Hunt, ed., *Channeling Blackness: Studies on Television and Race in America* (New York: Oxford University Press, 2004); and Alan Nadel, *Television in Black-and-White America:* *Race and National Identity* (Lawrence, KS: University Press of Kansas, 2005). Also, it should be mentioned that comedian Bill Cosby's 1960s series *I Spy* was revolutionary in its depiction of interracial relations and, consequently, led to *The Nat King Cole Show* (which, in fact, was quickly cancelled), *Julia*, *The Bill Cosby Show*, and *The Flip Wilson Show*, all programs with black stars headlining.

8. Haggins, *Laughing Mad*, 183.

9. Several examples of this play appear in each role Chappelle undertakes. In his first major cinematic role, for example, the African exchange student Ahchoo tries to convince Robin against fighting Little John over the Sherwood river. In leaping from one side of the bank to the other, he performs a small dance that one could read as reminiscent of blackface/minstrel performers. Also of note, during this period, Chappelle was cast in the 1996 ABC sitcom *Buddies*, which was cancelled after only five aired episodes. Chappelle himself has shown little pride or satisfaction in the project in interviews.

10. Andy Bennet, "Subcultures or Neo-Tribes?: Rethinking the Relationship Between Youth, Style, and Musical Taste," *Sociology* 3, no. 3: 600.

11. Often Chappelle will refer to his generation — Generation X or the Pepsi Generation — in his stand-up or when introducing a sketch. Before the debut of his crack addict character Tyrone Biggums, for example, Chappelle recalls drug education week during his school days and labels his generation the "Reagan babies."

12. See Paulina Borsook, *Cyberselfish: A Critical Romp Through the Terribly Libertarian Culture of High Tech* (New York: Public Affairs, 2000) and David Brooks, *Bobos in Paradise: The New Upper Class and How They Got There* (New York: Simon & Schuster, 2001).

13. Bill Carter, "The Laughter is Fading in Sitcomland," *New York Times*, May 24, 2004, E5.

14. The Mitsubishi commercial parody serves as an even stronger postmodern vehicle when Chappelle plays a blooper from filming the sketch — again, this is the first sketch of the show — and mocks the video, laughing at the Janet Jackson-like wardrobe malfunction of the actress in the sketch and his own reaction to it.

15. Karl Marx, *Capital: A Critique of Political Economy*, trans. Samuel Moore and Edward Aveling (London: Lawrence and Wishart, 1996).

16. "Cool places" here is a reference to the anthology on youth culture studies, Tracey Skelton and Gill Valentine, eds., *Cool Places: Geographies of Youth Cultures* (London: Routledge, 1998).

17. Lawrence H. Fuchs, *The American Kaleidoscope: Race, Ethnicity, and the Civic Culture* (Hanover, NH: Wesleyan University Press, 1990), 276.

18. Haggins, *Laughing Mad*, 222–224.

19. It is interesting to note that on *Chappelle's Show* white characters are addressed as "niggers" almost as often as black ones.

20. Leon E. Wynter, *American Skin: Popular Culture, Big Business, & the End of White America* (New York: Crown, 2002), 10.

21. Edmund S. Morgan, *American Slavery, American Freedom: The Ordeal of Colonial Virginia* (New York: Norton, 1975), 5.

22. For a review of the Imus controversy see, James Poniewozik, "Who Can Say What?," *Time*, April 23, 2007, 32–37.

23. Chappelle, *The Oprah Winfrey Show*.

24. Dave Chappelle, *Inside the Actors Studio*.

25. The amount of literature on comedy is too much to include in this study, but worthwhile explorations on the topic may begin with the following: Sigmund Freud, *The Joke and Its Relation to the Unconscious* (New York: Penguin, 2003); Maurice Charney, *Comedy High and Low* (New York: Oxford University Press, 1978); Robert W. Corrigan, ed., *Comedy: Meaning and Form*, 2nd ed. (New York: Harper & Row, 1981); and Morton Gurewitch, *Comedy: The Irrational Vision* (Ithaca, NY: Cornell University Press, 1975). Other works will be cited throughout this collection and in the bibliography.

26. Christopher P. Wilson, *Jokes: Form, Content, Use and Function* (London: Academic Press, 1979), 13.

27. Jerry Aline Flieger, *The Purloined Punch Line: Freud's Comic Theory and the Postmodern Text* (Baltimore: Johns Hopkins University Press, 1991), 256.

Chapter 1

1. This definition is taken from http://www.urbandictionary.com/. For more information on the concept of *Niggerdom*, see R.A.T. Judy's "On the Question of Nigga Authenticity," in *That's the Joint: The Hip-Hop Studies Reader*, ed. Murray Forman and Mark Anthony Neal (New York: Routledge 2004), 105–117.

2. The three sketches in this study were co-written with Neal Brennan, Dave Chappelle's long-time friend and associate, who is, incidentally, white. Brennan appears as a contestant in the sketch "I Know Black People."

3. Evan Cooper, "Is It Something He Said: The Mass Consumption of Richard Pryor's Culturally Intimate Humor," *The Communication Review* 10, no. 3 (1997): 223.

4. As Kyle Pope states in "How Dave Spent his Summer (and Fall, Winter and Spring) Vacation," *Blender* 5, no. 3 (2006): 74–5, "Chappelle is politically astute and keenly aware of the potential contradictions in performing race through racialized poses and stereotypes in his comedic routines. He says he too thought some of the routines might have "morphed from satire to race-baiting." With increasing concern that his audience was growing more and more mainstream, Chappelle contemplated whether some of his newer fans were laughing with him, or at him — especially at his character Clayton Bigsby, a blind white supremacist who doesn't know he's actually black, and the Niggar family he introduced on the show in season two. Yet, this possibility does not disregard the show's ability to reinforce the major point that race still matters."

5. Sut Jhally and Justin Lewis, *Enlightened Racism: The Cosby Show, Audiences, and the Myth of the American Dream* (Boulder, CO: West-view Press, 1992).

6. For more information on Dave Chappelle's adolescence, see Lola Ogunnaike, "A Comic Who Won't Hold Back; Nothing Is Out of Bounds For Dave *Chappelle's Show*," *New York Times*, February 18, 2004, E1, E5.

7. In her article "Speaking Fluent 'Joke': Pushing the racial envelope through comedic performance on *Chappelle's Show*," *Performance Research* 12, no. 3 (2007): 74–90, Katrina Bell-Jordan alludes to this fact by stating that, "Although his entire audience might not be perceptive to the particular nuances of his humour, he challenges black and white audiences by situating them in tension with a critical, compelling and often incredibly funny text" (74).

8. Cooper, "Is It Something He Said," 246.

9. Mikhail Bakhtin, *Rabelais and His World*

(Bloomington: Indiana University Press, 1994),
12. Further, "All Comedy aspires to laughter,"
says R.B. Gill in his article "Why Comedy
Laughs: The Shape of Laughter and Comedy,"
Literary Imagination 8.2 (2006): 233–250, in
reference to Erich Segal's work entitled *The
Death of Comedy* (Cambridge: Harvard University Press, 2001). "This is explained," continues Gill, "by the simple fact that laughter
and comedy are complementary expressions of
a basic form of the human spirit — the carnivalesque, the élan vitale, the pure sense of life,
the komos, as it has been variously called" (234).
See also Susanne K. Langer, *Feeling and Form:
A Theory of Art* (New York: Scribner, 1953),
and Robert Provine, *Laughter: A Scientific Investigation* (New York: Viking 2000), 18.

10. Bahktin, *Rabelais and His World*, 47.

11. Ibid., 66.

12. Diran John Sohigian maintains that
"laughter is a symptom of man's inability to
have the last word, to lay down the law once
and for all, to end the discussion, to simply
shut up. Eruptions of chance, desire, laughter,
and playfulness unend the game" (158). See his
article entitled "Contagion of Laughter: The
Rise of the Humor Phenomenon in Shanghai in
the 1930s," *Positions: East Asia Cultures Critique* 15, no.1 (2007): 137–163.

13. Henri Bergson, *Le Rire: Essai sur la
Signification du Comique* (Paris: Presses Universitaires de France, 1964), 16.

14. Original: "Notre excuse, pour aborder
le problème à notre tour, est que nous ne vise-
rons pas à enfermer la fantaisie comique dans
une définition. Nous voyons en elle, avant tout,
quelque chose de vivant. Nous la traiterons, si
légère soit-elle, avec le respect qu'on doit à la
vie. Nous nous bornerons à la regarder grandir
et s'épanouir. De forme en forme, par gradations insensibles, elle accomplira sous nos yeux
de bien singulières métamorphoses" (9). All
translations presented in this article are those
of the authors.

15. Original: "se présente à nous comme
une certaine évolution dans le temps, et comme
une certaine complication dans l'espace" (42).

16. Original: "Est comique tout arrangement d'actes et d'événements qui nous donne,
insérées l'une dans l'autre, l'illusion de la vie
et la sensation nette d'un agencement mé-
canique" (35).

17. Bahktin, *Rabelais and His World*, 44.

18. We can certainly consider the "dis-
course" to which I am referring within the
Structuralist sense of the term. See, Jonathan
Culler's *Structuralist Poetics* (Ithaca: Cornell
University Press, 1975), 197–200 and Terence
Hawkes, *Structuralism and Semiotics* (London:
Routledge, 2003).

19. Bambi Haggins, *Laughing Mad: The
Black Comic Persona in Post-Soul America* (New
Brunswick: Rutgers University Press, 2007),
178.

20. Randall Kennedy, *Nigger: The Strange
Career of a Troublesome Word* (New York: Pantheon Books, 2002), 3.

21. Randall Kennedy, "Allen and the N-
Word. White Lie," *The New Republic*, October
16, 2006, 10.

22. Keith Allan and Kate Burridge, *Forbidden Words: Taboo and the Censoring of Language* (Cambridge: Cambridge University
Press, 2006), 17.

23. Ibid., 31.

24. Ibid., 31–32.

25. Comedian Bill Cosby, whose "bread
and butter" was his clean comedy routines,
openly opposes the use of the word "nigger" in
comic routines. Cosby considers it "cheap linguistic pandering." Oprah Winfrey refuses to
allow rappers to be on her show if their song
lyrics include the N-Word. See, http://movin-
goutmovingon.bloghi.com/2007/05/21/the-n-
word.html (accessed August 12, 2008). Richard
Pryor had built quite a reputation for the use
of the N-Word, one that he would work to di-
minish at the end of his career (*International
Herald Tribune*, December 15, 2005). Chris
Rock's *Bring the Pain* (1996) show, called "Niggers vs. Blacks" brings the question of the N-
Word back into discussion. "I hate niggers,"
Rock says. "You can't have anything valuable in
your house. Niggers will break in and take it
all! Everything white people don't like about
black people, black people really don't like
about black people. It's like our own personal
civil war. On one side, there's black people. On
the other, you've got niggers. The niggers have
got to go. I love black people, but I hate niggers. I am tired of niggers. Tired, tired, tired."

26. See Murray Forman, "'Represent':
Race, Space and Place in Rap Music," *Popular
Music* 19, no. 1 (2000): 65–90.

27. For more information on Uncle Ruckus,
see http://en.wikipedia.org/wiki/Uncle_Ruckus.

28. John Limon, *Stand-up Comedy in Theory, or, Abjection in America* (Durham: Duke
University Press, 2000), 4. -

29. Ibid., 79.

30. Elizabeth Ludwig, *American Stand-up
and Sketch Comedy: Between Race and Gender:
The Works of Dave Chappelle and Margaret
Cho* (Thesis, University of Alberta, 2007),
10–11.

31. See "'Seinfeld' Star Richards Under Fire
For Racial Outburst," Newswire, Reuters, November 11, 2006, http://www.reuters.com/ar-
ticle/entertainmentNews/idUSN20413400200
61120 (accessed August 13, 2008). A clip of

Michael Richard's performance is available on YouTube.

32. John Strausbaugh, *Black Like You: Blackface, Whiteface, Insult & Imitation in American Popular Culture* (New York: Jeremy P. Tarcher/Penguin, 2006), 9–10.

33. Roger Cohen and Ryan Richards, "When the Truth Hurts, Tell a Joke: Why America Needs Its Comedians," *Humanity in Action USA* (2006): 1.

34. Clayton Bigsby is clearly alluding to Southern Rednecks, one of the stereotypes of this group being an incestuous nature.

35. Bakari Kitwana, *Why White Kids Love Hip-hop: Wanksta, Wiggers, Wannabes, and the New Reality of Race in America* (New York: Basic Civitas Books, 2005), 113.

36. Ibid.

37. When Clarence bursts back into the kitchen to yell out "Niggars," he breaks the fourth wall, as his utterance jumps from the stage to the audience. The fourth wall is the imaginary wall at the front of the stage in a proscenium theater, the window through which the audience watches a play. The fourth wall serves to create a separation between the audience and the stage which permits the audience to suspend its disbelief. The term "breaking the fourth wall" in theater (and in television) generally means that a character acknowledges awareness of the audience. The concept originated from Bertolt Brecht's theory of epic theater. For more on the concept of the fourth wall, see Brecht's *Brecht on Theatre: The Development of an Aesthetic*, trans. John Willett (New York: Hill and Wang, 1994).

38. For a similar argument regarding the humor in *Family Guy*, see Andrew Terjesen, "What Are You Laughing At (And Why?) Exploring the Humor of *Family Guy*" in *Family Guy and Philosophy: A Cure for the Petarded*, ed. Jeremy Wisnewski (Malden: Wiley-Blackwell, 2007), 128–138.

Chapter 2

1. Mel Watkins, *On the Real Side: Laughing, Lying, and Signifying — the Underground Tradition of African American Humor that Transformed American Culture, From Slavery to Richard Pryor* (New York: Simon and Schuster, 1994), 41.

2. Michael Eric Dyson, *Mike: Reflections on Race, Sex, Culture and Religion* (New York: Basic Civitas Books, 2003), 256–257.

3. Bambi Haggins, *Laughing Mad: The Black Comic Persona in Post-Soul America* (New Brunswick, NJ: Rutgers University Press, 2007), 179.

4. Ibid.
5. Ibid., 184.
6. Ibid.
7. Tricia Rose, *Black Noise: Rap Music and Black Culture in Contemporary America* (Hanover, NH: Wesleyan University Press, 1994), 21.

8. Angela Ards, "Organizing the Hip-hop Generation," in *That's the Joint: The Hip-Hop Studies Reader*, eds. Murray Forman and Mark Anthony Neal (New York: Routledge Press, 2004), 312.

9. Haggins, *Laughing Mad*, 178.
10. Dave Chappelle, interview by Terry Gross, *Fresh Air*, NPR, Sep. 2, 2004.
11. Haggins, *Laughing Mad*, 181–182.
12. Novotny Lawrence, *Blaxploitation Films of the 1970s: Blackness and Genre* (New York: Routledge Press, 2007), 18.
13. Ibid.
14. Melvin Donalson, *Masculinity in the Interracial Buddy Film* (Jefferson, NC: McFarland and Company, 2006), 9.
15. Christopher John Farley, "That Old Black Magic," *Time*, November 27, 2000, 14.
16. Heather J. Hicks, "Hoodoo Economics: White Men's Work and Black Men's Magic in Contemporary American Film," *Camera Obscura* 53, vol. 18, no. 2 (2003): 28.
17. Haggins, *Laughing Mad*, 181.
18. Donald Bogle, *Toms, Coons, Mulattoes, Mammies, and Bucks: An Interpretive History of Blacks in American Films*, 4th ed. (New York: Continuum, 2003), 259.
19. Gerald Martinez, Diana Martinez, and Andres Chaves, *What It Is ... What It Was!: The Black Film Explosion of the '70s in Words and Pictures* (New York: Hyperion Books, 1998), 207.
20. Dave *Chappelle's Block Party*, DVD, directed by Michel Gondry (Bob Yari Productions, 2005).
21. Ibid.
22. Ibid.
23. On July 9, 2008, JonBenet Ramsey's family members made headlines again when DNA evidence cleared them of having any involvement in the child's murder. Scott Michels, "Ramseys Cleared in JonBenet's Death: Prosecutors Clear Family in 6 year-old Beauty Queen's Death," ABC News, July 9, 2008, http://abcnews.go.com/TheLaw/story?id=5341559&page=1 (accessed July 22, 2008).
24. Kyra D. Gaunt, *The Games that Black Girls Play: Learning the Ropes from Double Dutch to Hip-Hop* (New York: New York University Press, 2006), 119.
25. In *Hip-Hop: Beyond Beats and Rhymes* (2006), Byron Hurt effectively demonstrates how American films, TV programs, commer-

cials, and other forms of popular entertainment also continue to perpetuate sexism. In short, hip-hop represents a small part of a larger cultural problem that has historically positioned women as inferior. *Hip-Hop: Beyond Beats and Rhymes*, Dir. Byron Hurt, Perf. Mos Def, Jadakiss, and Busta Rhymes, 61 min., PBS, 2006, DVD.

26. Septima Clark, *Ready from Within: Septima Clark and the Civil Rights Movement* (Navarro, CA: Wild Trees Press, 1986), 79.

27. Calvin Hernton, "The Sexual Mountain and Black Women Writers," *Black Scholar* 16, no. 2 (1985): 7.

28. Judy Klemesrud, "Tamara Dobson — Not Super Fly but Super Woman," *New York Times*, sec. 2, August 19, 1973, 11. It is important to note that Dobson's sentiments about the Women's Liberation Movement were common among black females in the 1970s. For example, In *Disfigured Images*, Patricia Morton explains how a segment of the black population viewed the movement: "Feminism has been very suspect from some Afro-American perspectives. Often seen as a white woman's movement, some have seen it as anti-black." Patricia Morton, *Disfigured Images: The Historical Assault on Afro-American Women* (New York: Greenwood Press, 1991), 11. For more, also see, Nathan Hare, "Revolution without a Revolution," Black Scholar 9 (1978): 16–18.

29. Haggins, *Laughing Mad*, 196.

30. *Shut Up and Sing* (2006) chronicles the backlash that ensued after the Dixie Chick's lead singer, Natalie Maines, made the remark in response to President Bush's decision to invade Iraq. *Shut Up and Sing*, DVD, directed by Barbara Kopple and Cecilia Peck (Cabin Creek Films, 2006).

31. Vito Russo, *The Celluloid Closet: Homosexuality in the Movies*, revised ed. (New York: Harper and Row, 1987).

32. Ibid., 4.

33. Ibid.

34. Hurt, *Beyond Beats and Rhymes*, 2006.

35. Ibid.

36. Stephen Tropiano, *Primetime Closet: A History of Gays and Lesbians on TV* (New York: Applause Theatre & Cinema Books, 2002), 189.

37. Randall Kennedy, *Nigger: The Strange Career of a Troublesome Word* (New York: Vintage Books, 2002), 4.

38. Ibid.

39. Qtd. in Kennedy, *Nigger*, 5.

40. Darryl Littleton, *Black Comedians on Black Comedy: How African Americans Taught Us to Laugh* (New York: Applause Theatre and Cinema Books, 2006), 10.

41. Kennedy, *Nigger*, 5.

42. Ibid.

43. Ibid., xvii.

44. It is important to point out an important irony. As the discussion of popular culture in the 1800s and 1900s illustrates, whites wrote songs that featured both "nigga" and "nigger" as a form of insult. While some blacks consider and use "nigga" to be an acceptable term of affection, hip-hop artists (and other members of the black community) use terms like "bitch ass nigga," and "punk ass nigga," as pejorative terms, transforming "nigga's" relevance as a friendly salutation into the slur associated with white racists.

45. Dave Chappelle, interview by Bob Simon, *60 Minutes*, CBS, Oct. 20, 2004.

46. Ibid.

47. Qtd. in Kennedy, *Nigger*, 29.

48. Haggins, *Laughing Mad*, 225.

49. Qtd. in Haggins, *Laughing Mad*, 226.

50. Farai Chideya, *The Color of Our Future: Race in the 21st Century* (New York: Harper Perennial, 2000), 9; *Monteiro v. Tempe Union High School District*, 158 F.3d 1022; Margaret M. Russell, "Representing Race: Beyond 'Sellouts' and 'Race Cards': Black Attorneys and the Straightjacket of Legal Practice," *Michigan Law Review* 95, (1997): 765.

51. Dave Chappelle, interview by Terry Gross, *Fresh Air*, 2004.

52. Haggins, *Laughing Mad*, 7.

Chapter 3

1. Laura Mulvey, "Visual Pleasure and Narrative Cinema," *Screen* 16, no. 3 (1975): 6–18.

2. Judith Butler, "Imitation and Gender Subordination," in *Inside/Out: Lesbian Theories, Gay Theories*, ed. Diana Fuss (New York: Routledge, 1991): 29.

3. Diane Elam, *Feminism and Deconstruction: Ms. en Abyme* (New York: Routledge, 1994):120.

4. Dave Chappelle and Maya Angelou, "Dave Chappelle + Maya Angelou," *Iconoclasts*, Season Two, directed by Joe Berlinger (Sundance Channel and Grey Goose Entertainment, 2006).

5. Dave Chappelle, "Hoes Uniform," *YouTube*, http://www.youtube.com/watch?v=_uscmRI9ZrE (accessed August 31, 2008). See, *Dave Chappelle: Killin' Them Softly*, DVD, directed by Stan Lathan (Sony Pictures, 2000).

6. I would be remiss here if I did not acknowledge that to a great extent — as contended in the works of Judith Butler and, par-

ticularly, in Sedgwick's *Touching Feeling*—all utterance, all speech, all action is in some way/s performative. Such is absolutely the case. My point here is only to contend that Chappelle is making his comedy explicitly and obviously performative, thus removing it from the very normalcy that it seems to profess. A further study of Chappelle's humor, and humor in general, as performative is certainly warranted, but such an exploration is not my intention in this essay. See Eve Kosofky Sedgwick, *Touching Feeling: Affect, Pedagogy, and Performativity* (Durham, NC: Duke University Press, 2003).

7. Thomas C. Veatch, "A Theory of Humor," *Humor, the International Journal of Humor Research* 11 (1998): 161–215. http://www.tomveatch.com/else/humor/paper/humor.html.

8. At another level, the viewer, as Mulvey posits, can both understand her/his role as subject and object of the joke specifically because of her/his ability to see herself/himself portrayed in the scene even while she/he laughs at the joke at her/his own expense. The viewer can relate not only to the scene but also to the role of observer that she/he is being asked to play because the act of joke telling, too, is commonplace.

9. Veatch, "A Theory of Humor."

10. Ibid.

11. It is important to note that in Veatch's theory the violation is to what he terms, "the subjective moral order." Such violations transgress on a "moral principle that the perceiver cares about. That is, it violates a principle about which the perceiver believes, 'This is the way things *should* be,' and which the perceiver backs up with some affective—that is to say, emotional commitment." See Veatch, "A Theory of Humor."

12. Mulvey, "Visual Pleasure and Narrative Cinema," 18.

13. Judith Butler, *Gender Trouble: Feminism and the Subversion of Identity* (New York: Routledge, 1990): 148.

14. Dave Chappelle, *Killin' Them Softly*.

15. Elam, *Feminism and Deconstruction*, 28.

16. Elam, *Feminism and Deconstruction*, 27.

17. Elam, *Feminism and Deconstruction*, 33.

18. Dave Chappelle, interview with Oprah Winfrey, *The Oprah Winfrey Show*, ABC, February 3, 2006.

Chapter 4

1. This lack of visibility has been noted in many different areas. In the case of gay pornography, Richard Fung argues, "[w]e are seen as too peripheral, not commercially visible — not the general audience." While Fung's concerns are limited to pornography, this sentiment can be applied to any number of fields whether they be sitcoms, dramatic television or popular music. David Palumbo-Liu and Richard Chang have each argued that the model minority notion is a myth which turns Asian Americans into stand-ins for Whites, at the same time that it denies the existence of discrimination against Asian Americans and legitimizes oppression of other minorities, especially African Americans. See David Palumbo-Liu, *Asian/American* (Stanford: Stanford University Press, 1999), 1; Richard Fung, "Looking for My Penis," in *Asian American Studies: A Reader*, eds. Jean Yu-wen Shen Wu and Min Song (New Brunswick: Rutgers University Press, 2000), 340; Richard Chang, "Why We Need a Critical Asian American Legal Studies," *Asian American Studies: A Reader*, eds. Jean Yu-wen Shen Wu and Min Song, (New Brunswick: Rutgers University Press, 2000), 363–378.

2. This list is not an exhaustive list but rather a sampling of the roles that Asian American actors have played on the show.

3. Gary Y. Okihiro, *Margins and Mainstreams* (Seattle: University of Washington Press, 1994), 34.

4. Arjun Appadurai, *Modernity at Large* (Minneapolis: University of Minnesota Press, 1996), 31.

5. Benedict Anderson, *Imagined Communities* (London: Verso, 1991), 1–8.

6. Vijay Prashad, *Everybody Was Kung Fu Fighting* (Boston: Beacon Press, 2001), 65–66.

7. Ibid., 66.

8. Leroi Jones, *Blues People* (New York: William Morrow, 1963), 46, 62.

9. Call-and-response form is an underlying pattern of much hip-hop music. Early groups like the Sugarhill Gang, the Furious Five and Run-DMC all employed it to some extent and that influence continues to this day, especially in live performance.

10. Paul Gilroy, *The Black Atlantic* (London: Verso, 1993), 78.

11. Ibid.

12. Ibid., 79.

13. Ibid., 110.

14. Ibid.

15. Ibid., 79. Emphasis, here, was added by the author.

16. Paul Gilroy, *Small Acts* (New York: Serpent's Tail, 1993), 181–182.

17. Nelson George, *Hip-hop America* (New York: Penguin, 1998), 113.

18. Kodwo Eshun, *More Brilliant than the Sun* (London: Quartet Books, 1998), 47–48.

19. The RZA with Chris Norris, *The Wu-Tang Manual* (New York: Penguin, 2005), 189–192.

20. Ibid., 58. For example, "Da Mystery of Chessboxing," from 1993's *Enter the Wu-Tang*, appropriates its title from *The Mystery of Chessboxing* (1979), while employing vocal samples at the song's beginning from *Shaolin and Wu-Tang* (1981) and *Five Deadly Venoms* (1978), which, respectively compare sword fighting to chess and declare the invincibility of "toad style."

21. Stephen Leckart, "Wu-Tang Clan's RZA Breaks Down His Kung Fu Samples by Film and Song." *Wired Online*, October 23, 2007, http://www.wired.com/entertainment/music/magazine/15–11/pl_music (accessed August 1, 2008).

22. Meaghan Morris, Introduction to *Hong Kong Connections*, eds. Meaghan Morris, Siu Leung Li and Stephen Chan Ching-kiu (Durham, NC: Duke University Press, 2005), 2.

23. Stephen Teo, "*Wuxia* Redux," *Hong Kong Connections*, ed. Meaghan Morris, Siu Leung Li and Stephen Chan Ching-kiu (Durham, NC: Duke University Press, 2005), 196.

24. David Palumbo-Liu suggests replacing the space in "Asian American" with a forwards-slash to mark the hybrid nature of Asian Americans and their experience of America. See, Palumbo-Liu, *Asian/American*, 1.

25. The Wu-Tang Clan, "Intro (Shaolin Finger Jab)/Chamber Music," *The W*, CD, (New York: LOUD Records, 2000).

26. Ibid.

27. Dave Chappelle and Neal Brennan, "Commentaries" Episode 7, Disc 1, *Chappelle's Show: Season 1*, DVD (New York: Comedy Central, 2004).

28. Christopher John Farley, "Dave Speaks," *Time*, May 14, 2005, http://www.time.com/time/arts/article/0,8599,1061418,00.html (accessed August 1, 2008).

29. One of the sites where Asian America and African America have been defined against each other has been gender and sexuality. Lisa Lowe argues that the historical construction of a "technology" of simultaneous racialization and gendering was central to Asian American immigration and citizenship. Critics such as Richard Fung and David L. Eng have traced the ultimate results of this "technology," which has tended towards a "feminization" of male Asian Americans. See, Lisa Lowe, *Immigrant Acts* (Durham, NC: Duke University Press, 1996), 11; David L. Eng, *Racial Castration* (Durham, NC: Duke University Press, 2001), 1–34; Fung, "Looking for My Penis," 340.

30. For a detailed look at these traumatic histories, Eric Lott's *Love and Theft* is a remarkably detailed and astute look at antebellum blackface minstrelsy. Eric Lott, *Love and Theft* (New York: Oxford University Press, 1993).

31. Frank Chin, "Confessions of a Chinatown Cowboy," in *Bulletproof Buddhists and Other Essays* (Honolulu: University of Hawaii Press, 1998), 74.

32. Ibid.

Chapter 5

1. Simon Dentith, *Parody* (New York: Routledge, 2000), 189.

2. Devin Gordon, "Fears of a Clown," *Newsweek*, May 16, 2005, 60.

3. Christopher John Farley, "Dave Speaks," *Time*, May 14, 2005, http://www.time.com/time/arts/article/0,8599,1061418,00.html (accessed June 12, 2008).

4. Ibid.

5. Mikhail Mikhailovich Bakhtin, *Rabelais and His World*, trans. Helene Iswolsky (Bloomington, Indiana University Press, 1984), 143; Farley, "Dave Speaks."

6. Farley, "Dave Speaks."

7. Ibid.

8. Danny Hooley, "What Was He Thinking? 'Lost Episodes' Explain," *News & Observer*, July 9, 2006.

9. Kevin Powell, "Heaven, Hell, Dave Chappelle," *Esquire*, May 2006, 96.

10. Gordon, "Fears of a Clown," 60.

11. Farley, "Dave Speaks."

12. Linda Hutcheon, *A Theory of Parody: The Teachings of Twentieth-Century Art Forms* (Chicago: University of Illinois Press, 1985), 56.

13. Farley, "Dave Speaks."

14. Hutcheon, *A Theory of Parody*, 60.

15. Hutcheon, *A Theory of Parody*, 18; Krista Ratcliffe, *Rhetorical Listening: Identification, Gender, Whiteness* (Carbondale: Southern Illinois University Press, 2005), 37. Hutcheon reminds us that "parody's 'target' text is always another work of art or, more generally, another form of coded discourse." Furthermore, Hutcheon "stresses this basic fact throughout [*A Theory of Parody*] because even the best works on parody tend to confuse it with satire." Hutcheon, *A Theory of Parody*, 16. Ratcliffe significantly builds upon the work of AnnLouise Keating, "Interrogating 'White-

ness,' (De)Constructing 'Race,'" *College English* 57, no. 8 (1995): 901–918, by adding a consideration of the coded nature of racial discourse to Keating's consideration of the conditional nature of racial discourse.

16. Hutcheon, *A Theory of Parody*, 37.
17. Hutcheon, *A Theory of Parody*, 69.
18. Judith Butler, *Gender Trouble: Feminism and the Subversion of Identity* (New York: Routledge, 1990), 189.
19. Mikhail Mikhailovich Bakhtin, *The Dialogic Imagination*, ed. Michael Holquist, trans. Caryl Emerson and Michael Holquist (Austin: University of Texas Press, 1981), 342.
20. Ibid.
21. Ibid., 343.
22. Ibid.
23. Butler, *Gender Trouble*, 189.
24. Ibid.
25. Farley, "Dave Speaks."
26. Mark de la Vina, "Chappelle: Lost and Found," *San Jose Mercury News*, July 31, 2006, http://find.galegroup.com.
27. Virginia Heffernan, "Two Sides of the Comic Missing in Action," *New York Times*, July 7, 2006, E18(L).
28. Hutcheon, *A Theory of Parody*, 93.
29. Bakhtin, *The Dialogic Imagination*, 342.
30. Hutcheon, *A Theory of Parody*, 92.
31. Here, I use "authoritative discourse" in much the same way Bakhtin describes authoritative discourse. See Bakhtin, *The Dialogic Imagination*, 342–344.
32. In particular, I'm thinking of the culture industry as described by Theodore Adorno and Max Horkheimer, "The Culture Industry: Enlightenment as Mass Deception," in *The Dialectic of Enlightenment*, trans. John Cumming (London: Verso, 1979), 120–167.
33. Ibid.
34. Michael Holquist, "Dialogism," in *The Dialogic Imagination*, 427.
35. Bakhtin, *The Dialogic Imagination*, 23.
36. Diane D. Davis, *Breaking Up [at] Totality: A Rhetoric of Laughter* (Carbondale: Southern Illinois University Press, 2000), 104. In *Breaking Up*, Davis describes a giving laughter. Although giving laughter "celebrates the play of the universe," giving laughter seems relegated to overflowing "binary structures." Davis, *Breaking Up [at] Totality*, 63. Racial discourse, I contend, shatters binaries and, therefore, leads to a laughter that flows more freely than the laughter Davis describes.
37. Ibid., 114.
38. Ratcliffe, *Rhetorical Listening*, 94.
39. Ibid., 95.
40. Ibid., 99.
41. Ibid., 98.

42. Valerie Babb, *Whiteness Visible: The Meaning of Whiteness in American Literature and Culture* (New York: New York University Press, 1998), 43.
43. Ruth Frankenburg, *White Women, Race Matters: The Social Construction of Whiteness* (Minneapolis: University of Minnesota Press, 1993), 1.
44. Babb, *Whiteness Visible*, 2.
45. Ibid., 42.
46. Ibid., 177.
47. Ibid., 168.
48. Ratcliffe, *Rhetorical Listening*, 97.
49. Babb, *Whiteness Visible*, 172.
50. Ibid.
51. For an explanation of this racial stereotype, see *The Lost Episodes'* bonus material entitled "The Fabulous Making of *Chappelle's Show*."
52. Margaret Cho, interview by Michele Norris, *All Things Considered*, NPR, December 9, 2002.
53. Roger Hailes, "My Whiteness," *Live at Gotham*, Comedy Central, 2008, http://www.comedycentral.com (accessed July 12, 2008).
54. Ibid.

Chapter 6

1. Charlie Murphy's True Hollywood Stories are a series of anecdotes based on the escapades of one of the show's writers and actors, Charlie Murphy (older brother to the actor Eddie Murphy). The first three were broadcast in Episode 4 of Season 2 of *Chappelle's Show* (2004) and recreate various encounters with the singer Rick James. Episode 5 featured a further story about a basketball game with the singer Prince. Two more unaired stories were also included as bonus material on the Uncensored Season 2 DVD.
2. Jim Carnes, "Rude Crowd not Funny to Comic," *Sacramento Bee*, June 18, 2004, http://sacbee.com (accessed August 15, 2008).
3. Stuart Hall, "The Question of Cultural Identity," in *Modernity and Its Futures*, eds. Stuart Hall, David Held, and Tony McGrew (Cambridge: Polity Press, 1993), 277.
4. Slavoj Žižek, *The Parallax View* (Cambridge, MA: Massachusetts Institute of Technology Press, 2006).
5. Žižek, *Parallax View*, 6.
6. Ibid, 7.
7. Ibid, 159.
8. Ibid, 281.
9. Chris Barker and Dariusz Galasiński, *Cultural Studies and Discourse Analysis* (London: SAGE Publications, 2001), 28.
10. Ibid, 21.

11. Ibid, 29.
12. On its release in 2004 the DVD of *Chappelle's Show Season One Uncensored!* sold over two million units, making it the best-selling DVD of a television show of all time (a title previously held by *The Simpsons Complete Season One* DVD).
13. Including Charlie Murphy's son, who plays Eddie Murphy.
14. Richard Dyer, *Stars* (London: British Film Institute, 1979), 22.
15. Addressing multiple audiences that include the interviewer, the studio audience, the broadcast audience, DVD audience and so forth.
16. Chappelle and others, "The Rick James Extended Interview," *Chappelle's Show Season 2.*
17. Chappelle and others, "Audio Commentary," *Chappelle's Show Season 2.*
18. Chappelle and others, "The Rick James Extended Interview," *Chappelle's Show Season 2.*
19. "About the Movie," *I'm Rick James*, Hiddendoor Documedia, 2007, http://www.rickjamesdocumentary.com/I_M_RICK_JAMES_HOME.php (accessed July 1, 2008).
20. Chappelle and others, "The Rick James Extended Interview," *Chappelle's Show Season 2.*
21. Chappelle and others, "Audio Commentary," *Chappelle's Show Season 2.*
22. Chappelle and others, "The Rick James Extended Interview," *Chappelle's Show Season 2.*
23. Ibid.
24. Ibid.
25. Barker and Galasiński, *Cultural Studies and Discourse Analysis*, 1.
26. Ibid, 42.
27. M.A.K. Halliday lists various examples of lexico-grammatical categories, which include material processes (concrete statements, referring to doing or happening), mental statements (feeling, thinking, seeing), relational (having an attribute), behavioural, verbal, and existential (existing and being). See Barker and Galasiński, *Cultural Studies and Discourse Analysis*, 70.
28. Neal Brennan and Dave Chappelle confirm this statement as improvised in the episode 4 commentary.
29. Chappelle and others, "Audio Commentary," *Chappelle's Show Season 2.*
30. Mark Currie, *Postmodern Narrative Theory*, 17.
31. Ibid, 127.
32. Prince Fans United Group, *Prince Fans United*, 2007, http://www.princefansunited.com (accessed August 12, 2008).

33. Sway Callaway, "Prince: Hoops-shooting Music Expert," MTV, 2007, http://www.mtv.com/bands/p/prince/news_feature_040428/
34. Jon Tevlin, "The Quiet One: A High School Classmate Recalls the Artist as a Young Man," *Star Tribune*, March 13, 2004, http://www.startribune.com/entertainment/11527586.html
35. Richard Dyer, *Only Entertainment*, 2nd ed. (London: Routledge, 2002), 177.
36. Richard Dyer, *Heavenly Bodies*, 2nd ed. (London: Routledge, 2004), 18.
37. Dyer, *Stars*, 69.
38. Ibid, 69–70.
39. Ibid, 22.
40. Ibid, 23.
41. P. David Marshall, *Celebrity and Power: Fame in Contemporary Culture* (Minneapolis, MN: University of Minnesota Press, 2006), xi.
42. Barker and Galasiński, *Cultural Studies and Discourse Analysis*, 30.
43. Roger Whitson, "Panelling Parallax: The Fearful Symmetry of William Blake and Alan Moore," *ImageTexT: Interdisciplinary Comics Studies* 3, no. 2 (2006), http://www.english.ufl.edu/imagetext/archives/v3_2/whitson/index.shtml?print (accessed August 12, 2008).
44. College Slackers, "Rick James Soundboard," *College Slackers*, http://www.collegeslackers.com/soundboard/rick_james (accessed August 12, 2008).

Chapter 7

1. Mel Stuart's *Wattstax* focuses on the 1972 Wattstax music festival, organized by Stax Records to commemorate the seventh anniversary of the Watts riots. Beginning on August 11, 1965, the riots in Watts, a suburb of Los Angeles, lasted for six days as a response to the injurious treatment by the LA police department; *Dave Chappelle's Block Party*, DVD, directed by Michel Gondry (Universal City, CA: Universal Studios, 2006).
2. Kevin Carr, "Dave Chappelle Block Party Review," 7(M) Pictures, http://www.7mpictures.com/inside/reviews/blockparty_review.htm (accessed July 12, 2008).
3. Harry F. Wolcott, *Ethnography: A Way of Seeing* (Lanham, MD: Rowman Altamira, 1999). Wolcott offers that more attention should be paid to the "ethnographicness" of ethnography or the conditions under which some studies seem more ethnographic than others (150). The question of ethnographicness is principally one of convention and intention. Ethnography is both a genre and a research

tool or practice. Using the term "semi-ethno-graphic" to describe *Block Party* highlights two aspects of production: 1) the major intent was to reach a wide audience and make profit, and 2) neither cast nor crew is trained as ethnog-rapher. While this is not to suggest that the genre of ethnographic film has escaped the trappings of commodification, far less fre-quently are they given wide release.

4. The term "native ethnography" was coined by anthropologist Russ Bernard to de-scribe his work with coauthor Jesús Salinas Pe-draza in producing their book, *Native Ethnog-raphy: A Mexican Indian Describes His Culture* (Newbury Park, CA: Sage Publications, 1989).

5. David Fetterman, *Ethnography: Step by Step* (Thousand Oaks, CA: Sage Publications, 1998), 22.

6. Ibid.

7. John L. Jackson, Jr., "An Ethnographic *Film*flam: Giving Gifts, Doing Research, and Videotaping the Native Subject/Object," *Amer-ican Anthropologist* 106, no. 1 (2008): 33–34.

8. Citing Ingraham, D. Soyini Madison defines politics as the "social materials prac-tices in which the distribution of power is at stake." *Block Party* also helps us to distinguish theories of difference through its investment in addressing the politics of culture and repre-sentation. As Madison explains, "theories of difference are concerned with the histories, consequences, and contexts of what it means to be unlike the norm, the majority, the compre-hended, or to be outside certain registers of power...[they] confront thte complexities of identity, belonging, and language by and within the realm of politics." *See*, D. Soyini Madison, *Critical Ethnography: Method, Ethics, and Performance* (Thousand Oaks, CA: Sage Publications, 2005), 70.

9. Paul Gilroy, *Small Acts: Thoughts on the Politics of Black Cultures* (London: Serpent's Tail, 1993), 135.

10. Michaela Di Leonardo, *Exotics at Home: Anthropologies, Others, American Modernity* (Chicago: University of Chicago Press, 1998), 27–28.

11. Ethnographic work on black folk cul-ture conducted by Zora Neale Hurston, a pio-neer in the field of anthropology, is a historic example of the kinds of strategies necessary to study black vernacularism. Hurston's work on the "dirty dozens" is particularly instructive for scholars who examine the role of humor in ethnographic practice. Boyd's biography, *Wrapped in Rainbows*, is meticulous in its de-scriptions of Hurston's fieldwork. See, Valerie Boyd, *Wrapped in Rainbows: The Life of Zora Neale Hurston* (New York: Scribner, 2003).

12. Erve Chambers, "Thalia's Revenge: Ethnography and Theory of Comedy," *Ameri-can Anthropologist* 91, no. 3 (1989): 596.

13. The line-up includes Kanye West, Mos Def, Erykah Badu, the Fugees, Talib Kweli, Common, Dead Prez, The Roots, Jill Scott, and others.

14. David Samuels, "The Rap on Rap: The 'Black Music' that Isn't Either," in *That's the Joint! The Hip-Hop Studies Reader*, eds. Mark Anthony Neal and Murray Forman (New York: Routledge, 2004), 147. 147–154

15. Bakari Kitwana, *Why White Kids Love Hip-hop: Wangstas, Wiggers, Wannabees, and the New Reality of Race in America* (New York: Basic Civitas Books, 2005), 82–83.

16. John L. Jackson, Jr., *Real Black: Adven-tures in Racial Sincerity* (Chicago: University of Chicago Press, 2005), 15.

17. Fred Moten, *In the Break: The Aesthetics of the Black Radical Tradition* (Minneapolis, MN: University of Minnesota Press, 2003), 1.

18. Ibid, 9.

19. Michael Eric Dyson, *Holler If You Hear Me: Searching for Tupac Shakur* (New York: Basic Civitas Books, 2003), 167.

20. Ibid, 15.

21. Craig S. Wilder, *A Covenant with Color: Race and Social Power in Brooklyn* (New York: Columbia University Press, 2000), 177–178.

22. Ibid.

23. Ibid, 194.

24. Ibid, 210.

25. Ibid, 214.

26. S. Craig Watkins, "A Nation of Mil-lions: Hip-hop Culture and the Legacy of Black Nationalism," *The Communication Review* 4 (2001): 381.

27. Charis Kubrin, "Gangstas, Thugs, and Hustlas: Identity and the Code of the Street in Rap Music," *Social Problems* 52, no. 3 (2005), 363.

28. Giuliana Bruno, *Public Intimacy: Archi-tecture and the Visual Arts* (Cambridge, MA: MIT Press, 2007).

29. Patricia Aufderheide, "Public Intimacy: The Development of First-person Documen-tary," *Afterimage* 25, no. 1 (1997): 16.

30. Ibid.

31. See, for example, Greg Dimitriadis, "'In the Clique': Popular Culture, Constructions of Place and the Everyday Lives of Urban Youth," *Anthropology & Education Quarterly* 32, no. 1 (2001), 29–51, and Oneka LaBennett, "Read-ing *Buffy* and 'Looking Proper': Race, Gender, and Consumption among West Indian Girls in Brooklyn," in *Globalization and Race: Trans-formations in the Cultural Production of Black-ness*, eds. Kamari Maxine Clark and Deborah A. Thomas (Durham, NC: Duke University Press, 2006), 279–298.

32. Victoria Johnson, "Polyphony and Cultural Expression: Interpreting Musical Traditions in 'Do the Right Thing,'" *Film Quarterly* 47, no. 2 (1993), 23.

33. Ibid.

34. Manohla Dargis, "A Comedian's Ultimate Goal: Rock the Block," *New York Times,* March 3, 2006, E1.

35. Ibid.

36. Mark A. Neal, *Soul Babies: Black Popular Culture and the Post-Soul Aesthetic* (New York: Routledge, 2002), 2–3.

37. Dead Prez, *Let's Get Free,* Loud Records, 2000.

38. Dick Hebdige, *Subculture: The Meaning of Style* (London: Methuen, 1979).

39. Lawrence Grossberg, "On Postmodernism and Articulation: An Interview with Stuart Hall," *Journal of Communication Inquiry* 10, no. 2 (1986): 47.

40. Edward Pavlic, "Rap, Soul, and the Vortex at 33.3 rpm: Hip-Hop's Implements and African American Modernisms," *Callaloo* 29, no. 3 (2006): 956.

41. Jean-Francois Lyotard, "Prescription," *L'Esprit Créateur* 31, no. 1 (1991): 15.

42. Simon Malpas, *Jean-Francois Lyotard* (New York: Routledge, 2002), 89.

43. Melissa Victoria Lacewell-Harris, *Barbershops, Bibles and BET: Everyday Talk and Black Political Thought* (Princeton: Princeton University Press, 2004).

44. See Douglas Brode, *The Films of Steven Spielberg* (New York: Citadel, 2000), 90–98; and Maria Puente, "Indiana Jones: He's Everyman, with Wit and a Whip," *USA Today,* May 22, 2008, 5E.

45. David Machin, *Ethnographic Research for Media Studies* (London: Arnold, 2002), 87–89.

46. Ibid.

Chapter 8

1. Dave Itzkoff, "Dave Chappelle is Alive and Well (And Playing Las Vegas)," *The New York Times,* November 27, 2005, Arts & Leisure, http://www.nytimes.com/2005/11/27/arts/television/27itzkoff.html (accessed June 11, 2008).

2. "Introduction," *The Chappelle Theory,* http://www.chappelletheory.com/introduction3.html (accessed June 11, 2008).

3. "The Theory, March 2004," *The Chappelle Theory,* http://www.chappelletheory.com/theory_mar_2004.html (accessed June 11, 2008).

4. See Helena Andrews, "Go to Chappelle Theory.com for T-Shirts, Not Conspiracy,"

New York Times, July 22, 2006, Television, http://www.nytimes.com/2006/07/22/arts/television/22chap.html (accessed June 11, 2008).

5. Randall Kennedy, *Sellout: The Politics of Racial Betrayal* (New York: Pantheon Books, 2008), 3.

6. Karl Marx, *Karl Marx: Selected Writings,* ed. D. McLellan (Oxford: Oxford University Press, 1977): 176.

7. Steve Jones, *Antonio Gramsci* (London: Routledge, 2006), 29.

8. Jones, *Antonio Gramsci,* 34.

9. Robert Bocock, *Hegemony* (Sussex: Ellis Horwood, 1986), 33–34.

10. Bocock, *Hegemony,* 35.

11. Ibid., 33.

12. Ibid., 35.

13. Gramsci's writings on hegemony are scattered, but see: Antonio Gramsci, *Selections from the Prison Notebooks,* ed. and trans. Quintin Hoare and Geoffrey Nowell Smith (New York: International Publishers, 1971), 206–276; Perry Anderson, "The Antinomies of Antonio Gramsci," *New Left Review* 100 (Nov-Dec 1976): 5–78; Derek Boothman, "The Sources of Gramsci's Concept of Hegemony," *Rethinking Marxism* 20, no. 2 (April 2008): 201–215; Thomas Bates, "Gramsci and the Theory of Hegemony," *Journal of the History of Ideas* 36, no. 2 (April-June 1975): 351–366.

14. Renate Holub, *Antonio Gramsci: Beyond Marxism and Postmodernism* (London: Routledge, 1992), 6.

15. Williams quoted in Holub, *Antonio Gramsci,* 104.

16. Antonio Gramsci, *Selections from the Prison Notebooks,* 324

17. Walter Adamson, *Hegemony and Revolution: A Study of Antonio Gramsci's Political and Cultural Theory* (Berkeley: University of California Press, 1980), 150.

18. Marcia Landy, *Film, Politics, and Gramsci* (Minneapolis: University of Minnesota Press, 1994), 25.

19. Giuseppe Vacca, "Intellectuals and the Marxist Theory of the State," in *Approaches to Gramsci,* ed. Anne Showstack Sassoon (London: Writers and Readers Publishing, 1982), 37–69. Also see, Jerome Karabel, "Revolutionary Contradictions: Antonio Gramsci and the Problem of Intellectuals," *Politics & Society* 6 (1976): 123–172. Gramsci's writings on the intellectual have also sparked much interdisciplinary interest. See, for example, Carole Elliot, "Representations of the Intellectual: Insights from Gramsci on Management Education," *Management Learning* 34, no. 4 (December 2003): 411–427; Iram Siraj-Blatchford, "Critical Social Research and the Academy: The Role of Organic Intellectuals in Educa-

tional Research," *British Journal of Sociology of Education* 16, no. 2 (1995): 205–220; Robert Fatton, Jr., "Gramsci and the Legitimization of the State: The Case of the Senegalese Passive Revolution," *Canadian Journal of Political Science* 19, no. 4 (December 1986): 729–750; Dani Filc, "Physicians as 'Organic Intellectuals,'" *Acta Sociologica* 49, no. 3 (September 2006): 273–285. For a good overview of the literature, see, Charles Kurzman and Lynn Owens, "The Sociology of Intellectuals," *Annual Review of Sociology* 28 (2002): 63–90.

20. See, Holub, *Antonio Gramsci*, 151–170.

21. Gramsci, *Selections from the Prison Notebooks*, 9.

22. Ibid.

23. Jones, *Antonio Gramsci*, 82.

24. Gramsci, *Selections from the Prison Notebooks*, 12.

25. Jones, *Antonio Gramsci*, 89.

26. Gramsci, *Selections from the Prison Notebooks*, 5.

27. Adamson, *Hegemony and Revolution*, 143.

28. Gramsci, *Selections from the Prison Notebooks*, 334.

29. Adamson, *Hegemony and Revolution*, 143.

30. For the significance of programs like *The Daily Show*, see, Julia Fox, Glory Koloen, and Volkan Sahin, "No Joke: A Comparison of Substance in *The Daily Show with Jon Stewart* and Broadcast Network Television Coverage of the 2004 Presidential Election Campaign," *Journal of Broadcasting & Electronic Media* 51, no. 2 (June 2007): 213–227; R. Lance R. Holbert, Jennifer Lambe, et al., "Primacy Effects of *The Daily Show* and National TV News Viewing: Young Viewers, Political Gratifications, and Internal Political Self-Efficacy," *Journal of Broadcasting & Electronic Media* 51, no. 1 (March 2007): 20–38; Aaron McKain, "Not Necessarily Not the News: Gatekeeping, Remediation, and *The Daily Show*," *Journal of American Culture* 28, no. 4 (December 2005): 415–430.

31. See Dannagal Young, "Late-Night Comedy in Election 2000: Its Influence on Candidate Trait Ratings and the Moderating Effects of Political Knowledge and Partisanship," *Journal of Broadcasting & Electronic Media* 48, no. 1 (March 2004): 1–22; Ji Hoon Park, Nadine Gabbadon and Ariel Chernin, "Naturalizing Racial Differences Through Comedy: Asian, Black, and White Views on Racial Stereotypes in *Rush Hour 2*," *Journal of Communication* 56 (2006): 157–177; Lawrence Mintz, "Standup Comedy as Social and Cultural Mediation," *American Quarterly* 37, no. 1 (Spring 1985): 71–80.

32. Lawrence Mintz, "Humor and Popular Culture," in *Handbook of Humor Research*, Volume II, ed. Paul McGhee and Jeffrey Goldstein (New York: Springer-Verlag, 1983), 132.

33. Don Nilsen, "The Social Functions of Political Humor," *The Journal of Popular Culture* 24, no. 3 (1990): 35. For more on the social role of comedians, see: Stephanie Koziski, "The Standup Comedian as Anthropologist: Intentional Culture Critic," *The Journal of Popular Culture* 18, no. 2 (Fall 1984): 57–76; Lawrence Mintz, "Standup Comedy as Social and Cultural Mediation," *American Quarterly* 37, no. 1 (Spring 1985): 71–80.

34. Majken Jul Sorensen, "Humor as a Serious Strategy of Nonviolent Resistance to Oppression," *Peace & Change* 33, no. 2 (April 2008): 167–190.

35. Holub, *Antonio Gramsci*, 104.

36. Respectively, black, brown, yellow on the outside, and white on the inside.

37. Kennedy, *Sellout*, 4, 5. For African American fears regarding intermarriage, see Kennedy, *Sellout*, 62; Audrey Edwards, "Bring Me Home a Black Girl," I, November 2002, 177; Michael Eric Dyson, "Another Saturday Night, or Have All the Brothers Gone to White Women," in *The Michael Eric Dyson Reader*, ed. Michael Eric Dyson (New York: Basic Civitas Books, 2004), 147–166.

38. Kennedy, *Sellout*, 34.

39. Thomas quoted in Kennedy, *Sellout*, 40.

40. Washington quoted in Kennedy, *Sellout*, 42.

41. King quoted in Kennedy, *Sellout*, 49–50.

42. Ron Walters, "Barack Obama and the Politics of Blackness," *Journal of Black Studies* 38, no. 1 (September 2007): 7–29.

43. Beinart quoted in Kennedy, *Sellout*, 7.

44. Bryant Keith Alexander, "Fading, Twisting, and Weaving: An Interpretive Ethnography of the Black Barbershop as Cultural Space," *Qualitative Inquiry* 9, no. 1 (2003): 120.

45. Grier and Cobbs quoted in Melissa Victoria Harris-Lacewell, *Barbershops, Bibles, and BET* (Princeton: Princeton University Press, 2004), 162.

46. Alexander, "Fading, Twisting, and Weaving," 107.

47. Christopher John Farley, "Dave Speaks," *Time*, May 14, 2005, http://www.time.com/time/arts/article/0,8599,1061418,00.html (accessed June 11, 2008).

48. Dave Chappelle, interview with Oprah Winfrey, *The Oprah Winfrey Show*, ABC, February 3, 2006.

49. Quoted in Farley, "Dave Speaks."

50. Chappelle, *The Oprah Winfrey Show.*

51. Ibid.

52. Ibid.

53. Kevin Powell, "Heaven Hell Dave Chappelle," *Esquire,* April 30, 2006, http://www.esquire.com/features/ESQ0506CHAPPELLE_92 (accessed June 11, 2008).

54. Dave Chappelle, "Chappelle: 'An Act of Freedom,'" interview by Bob Simon, *60 Minutes,* CBS, October 20, 2004, http://www.cbsnews.com/stories/2004/10/19/60II/main650149.shtml (accessed June 11, 2008).

55. Dave Chappelle, interview by James Lipton, *Inside the Actor's Studio,* Bravo, February 12, 2006.

56. Chappelle, *Inside the Actor's Studio.*

57. Powell, "Heaven Hell Dave Chappelle."

Chapter 9

1. Matt Feeney, "Black Comedy: Why is Dave Chappelle's Malice So Winning?," *Salon.com,* March 4, 2004, http://www.slate.com/id/2096599/ (accessed June 1, 2008).

2. Katrina Bell Jordan, "Speaking Fluent 'Joke': Pushing the Racial Envelope Through Comedic Performance on *Chappelle's Show,*" *Performance Research* 12, no. 3 (2007): 80.

3. Ibid.

4. Sander Gilman, *Difference and Pathology: Stereotypes of Sexuality, Race, and Madness* (Ithaca, NY: Cornell University Press, 1985), 18.

5. Cornel West, *Race Matters* (New York: Vintage, 1993), 43.

6. Judith Butler, *Gender Trouble* (New York: Routledge, 1990), 4; Homi Bhabha, "The Postcolonial and the Postmodern: the Question of Agency," *The Cultural Studies Reader,* 2nd ed., ed. Simon During (London: Routledge, 1999), 196.

7. Stuart Hall, "Cultural Studies and Its Theoretical Legacies," *The Cultural Studies Reader,* 2nd ed., ed. Simon During (London: Routledge, 1999), 105.

8. Stuart Hall, "Old and New Identities, Old and New Ethnicities," *Theories of Race and Racism,* ed. Les Back and John Solomos (London: Routledge, 2000), 146–7.

9. Gilman, *Difference and Pathology,* 17.

10. Ibid., 18.

11. Feeney, "Black Comedy."

12. Butler, *Gender Trouble* (New York: Routledge, 1990), 138.

13. Anne Anlin Cheng, *The Melancholy of Race: Psychoanalysis, Assimilation, and Hidden Grief* (New York: Oxford University Press, 2001), 55.

14. Toni Morrison, *Playing in the Dark:*

Whiteness and the Literary Imagination (Cambridge, MA: Harvard University Press, 1992), 17.

15. Slavoj Žižek, "Enjoy Your Nation as Yourself!" in *Theories of Race and Racism,* ed. Les Back and John Solomos (London: Routledge, 2000), 596.

16. Cheng, *Melancholy of Race,* 72.

Chapter 10

1. Mos Def, *Black On Both Sides,* Rawkus/Umgd, 1999.

2. Imani Perry, *Prophets of the Hood: Politics and Poetics in Hip-hop* (Durham, NC: Duke University Press, 2004), 10–11.

3. The album provides several examples to show that the specific referent of the "we" is Black people beyond even the title and the excerpt provided at the opening of the paper; for example, Track 8, "Umi Says," reads, "I want Black people to be free, to be free, to be free. I want my people to be free, to be free, to be free," alternating the chorus between "my people" and "Black people." Similarly, Track 10, "Rock N Roll," declares, "I am, yes I am, the descendant of those folks whose backs got broke, who fell down inside the Black smoke (*background vocal:* Black people). Dreams on their ankles and feet. I am descendents of the builders of your streets (Black people). Tenders to your cotton money. I am hip-hop. I am rock n roll." Mos Def, *Black On Both Sides.*

4. Ronald Walters, "Book Launch — *Waiting 'til the Midnight Hour: A Narrative History of Black Power in America* by Joseph Peniel" The Woodrow Wilson International Center for Scholars. October 19, 2006, Washington, D.C.

5. Richard Pryor, *Pryor Convictions and Other Life Sentences* (New York: Pantheon Books, 1995), 117.

6. *Merchants of Cool,* Frontline Documentary, PBS, February 27, 2001.

7. For example, in the wake of Don Imus' remark about the Rutgers women's basketball team as "nappy headed hoes," there was significant popular discussion about the negative impact of hip-hop highlighted on such shows as Oprah with visceral critics like Stanley Crouch.

8. William Jelani Cobb, *To the Break of Dawn: A Freestyle on the Hip-hop Aesthetic* (New York: New York University Press, 2007), 6. Emphasis added.

9. Robin D. G. Kelley, "Looking for the 'Real' Nigga: Social Scientists Construct the Ghetto," in *That's the Joint! The Hip-Hop*

Studies Reader, eds. Murray Foreman and Mark Anthony Neal (New York: Routledge, 2004), 119.

10. Cobb, *To the Break of Dawn*, 6.

11. Harold Cruse, *The Crisis of the Negro Intellectual* (New York: New York Review Books, 1967), 564.

12. Ibid., 548.

13. Ibid., 560.

14. Ibid.

15. Indeed, point #7 explicitly references the "Second Amendment to the Constitution of the United States" which "gives a right to bear arms. We therefore believe that all Black people should arm themselves for self-defense." Point #9 also specifically references the Constitution and the right to be tried by a jury of peers. Indeed the closing paragraphs of the platform are passages from the Declaration of Independence. "Black Panther Party Platform and Program," *The Sixties Project* (1993), http://www2.iath.viginia.edu/sixties/HTML_d ocs/Resources/Primary/Manifestos/Panther_pl atform.html (accessed August 4, 2008).

16. Rod Bush, *We Are Not What We Seem: Black Nationalism in the American Century* (New York: New York University Press, 1999), 35.

17. For further discussion of a Black mainstream with interests, needs, and perspectives distinctly different from a White hegemony, See Ronald Walters, *White Nationalism, Black Interests: Conservative Public Policy and the Black Community* (Detroit, MI: Wayne State University Press, 2003).

18. Toni Morrison, *Playing in the Dark: Whiteness and the Literary Imagination* (Cambridge, MA: Harvard University Press, 1992), 38.

19. Amiri Baraka (LeRoi Jones), "The Revolutionary Theatre," *Liberator* (1965): 4.

20. Larry Neal, *Visions of a Liberated Future: Black Arts Movement Writings* (New York: Thunder's Mouth Press, 1989), 62.

21. "Pryor, Richard," Museum of Broadcast Communications, http://www.museum.tv/archives/etv/P/htmlP/pryorrichar/pryorrichar.htm (accessed August 4, 2008).

22. Robin R. Means Coleman, *African American Viewers and the Black Situation Comedy: Situating Racial Humor* (New York: Garland Publishing, 1998), 4.

23. Lawrence E. Mintz, "Standup Comedy as Social and Cultural Mediation," *American Quarterly* 37, no. 1 (1985): 72.

24. Ibid., 78.

25. Dave Chappelle, interview by James Lipton, *Inside the Actor's Studio*, February 12, 2006. Also in the interview, it is discussed that Chappelle is the son of two professors, and his mother was hired by Patrice Lumumba to work with him directly and also established in 1974 one of the first Ph.D. programs in Black Studies. Chappelle's link to Black Power and the tenets of the Black Arts Movement then is tangible.

26. Ibid.

27. This is in contrast to his comic predecessors and contemporaries, many of whom, despite their race, developed a particular image that would define their comic persona so that the clothing became inseparable from the comic—Moms Mabley with house coat and slippers, Phyllis Diller in her wacky outfits, Mort Sahl with his sweaters, Dick Gregory and Bill Cosby in suits.

28. Michael Eric Dyson, *Is Bill Cosby Right? Or Has the Black Middle Class Lost Its Mind?* (New York: Basic Civitas Books, 2005), 31.

29. Jeffrey O. G. Ogbar, *Hip-Hop Revolution: The Culture and Politics of Rap* (Lawrence: University Press of Kansas, 2007), 14.

30. Chappelle's critique of race is noticeably sharper than that on class, which is not particularly evident in his work, harkening Cruse's characterization of the young nationalists as economically naïve with bourgeois aspirations. In fact, in his stand-up DVD, *For What It's Worth*, Chappelle's defense of Bill Cosby—people forgetting that "he's just a nigga from Philly who might say some real shit from time to time"—references Cosby's lambasting the public behavior of a sector of Blacks, which is the subject of Dyson's critique of Cosby. This is just one example of Chappelle speaking uncritically from a particularly middle-class perspective. But, being the product of a middle-class home, his lack of critique is consistent with my argument that he speaks specifically and unapologetically from his viewpoint. Prohibited by length, there is not space here to go into Chappelle's representations of class, but his depersonalized, stereotyped sketches of Tyrone Biggums indicate a significantly less sophisticated analysis of class as a structure that is at least worth mentioning. *Dave Chappelle: For What It's Worth. Live! At the Fillmore*, DVD, directed by Stan Lathan (Sony Pictures, 2004).

31. Dyson, 32.

32. Ibid., 33.

33. Pryor, *Pryor Convictions*, 143.

34. Ibid., 125.

35. Joanne Gilbert, *Performing Marginality: Humor, Gender and Cultural Critique* (Detroit, MI: Wayne State University Press, 2004), 178.

36. Tricia Rose, *Black Noise: Rap Music*

and Black Culture in Contemporary America (Hanover, NH: Wesleyan University Press, 1994), 39.

37. Ibid., 61.

38. Ogbar, *Hip-Hop Revolution*, 7.

39. Paul Gilroy, *The Black Atlantic: Modernity and Double Consciousness* (Cambridge, MA: Harvard University Press, 1993), 33.

40. Dead Prez, "It's Bigger than Hip-hop," *Let's Get Free*, Relativity, 2000.

41. Bambi Haggins, *Laughing Mad: The Black Comic Persona in Post-Soul America* (New Brunswick, NJ: Rutgers University Press, 2007), 181–182.

42. Cobb, 8.

43. Aaron McGruder, "Behind-the-Scenes Featurette," *The Boondocks: The Complete First Season*, DVD (Sony Pictures, 2006).

44. Chappelle, *Inside the Actor's Studio.*

45. Nick A. Zaino III, "Ask a Black Dude," *The Progressive* 67, no. 11 (2003): 36.

46. Ibid.

47. See Perry, *Prophets of the Hood*; and Bakari Kitwana, *Why White Kids Love Hip-hop: Wanksters, Wiggers, Wannabes, and the New Reality of Race in America* (New York: Basic Civitas Books, 2005), xii.

48. KRS-One, "Hip-hop Lives," H*ip-hop Lives*, Koch Records, 2007.

49. Bakari Kitwana, *Why White Kids Love Hip-hop*, 150.

50. Ibid., 97.

51. Ibid., 96. Italics added for emphasis.

52. "September in Brooklyn: The Making of *Block Party*," *Block Party*, DVD.

53. James Smethurst, *The Black Arts Movement: Literary Nationalism in the 1960s and 1970s* (Chapel Hill: University of North Carolina Press, 2005), 9–10.

54. Kitwana, *Why White Kids Love Hiphop*, 49.

55. Chappelle, *Inside the Actor's Studio.*

Chapter 11

1. On the nature of the racial humor on *Chappelle's Show*, see Bambi Haggins, *Laughing Mad: The Black Comic Persona in Post-Soul America* (New Brunswick, NJ: Rutgers University Press, 2007), 207.

2. On folk humor as the origin of carnival, see Dominick LaCapra, "From 'Bakhtin, Marxism, and the Carnivalesque,'" rpt. in *Critical Essays on Mikhail Bakhtin*, ed. Caryl Emerson (New York: G.K. Hall and Company, 1999), 240.

3. James C. Scott, *Domination and the Arts of Resistance: Hidden Transcripts* (New Haven, CT: Yale University Press, 1990), 172–

173; Stephen Nissenbaum, *The Battle for Christmas* (New York: Knopf, 1996), 266–270; Natalie Zemon Davis, "The Reasons of Misrule: Youth Groups and Charivaris in Sixteenth-Century France," *Past and Present*, no. 50 (1971): 42; Davis, "Women on Top," rpt. in *Feminism and Renaissance Studies*, ed. Lorna Hutson (New York: Oxford University Press, 2005), 156–177.

4. Sandra L. Richards, "Horned Ancestral Masks, Shakespearean Actor Boys, and Scotch-Inspired Set Girls: Social Relations in Nineteenth-Century Jamaican Jonkonnu," in *The African Diaspora: African Origins and New World Identities*, eds. Isidore Okpewho, Carole Boyce Davies, and Ali A. Mazrui (Bloomington: Indiana University Press, 1999), 254–271; Robert Dirks, *The Black Saturnalia: Conflict and Its Ritual Expression on British West Indian Slave Plantations* (Gainesville: University of Florida Press, 1987); Nissenbaum, *Battle for Christmas*, 285–291; Elizabeth A. Fenn, "'A Perfect Equality Seemed to Reign': Slave Society and Jonkonnu," *North Carolina Historical Review* 65, no. 2 (1988): 127–153; Ira De A. Reid, "The John Canoe Festival: A New World Africanism," *Phylon* 3, no. 4 (1942): 349–370.

5. Nissenbaum, *Battle for Christmas*, 264–282.

6. Claire Sponsler, *Ritual Imports: Performing Medieval Drama in America* (Ithaca: Cornell University Press, 2004), 42–44, 53–61; A.J. Williams-Myers, *Long Hammering: Essays on the Forging of an African American Presence in the Hudson River Valley to the Early Twentieth Century* (Trenton: Africa World Press, Inc., 1994), 85–98; Shane White, "Pinkster: Afro-Dutch Syncretization in New York City and the Hudson Valley," *Journal of American Folklore* 102, no. 403 (1989): 68–75; White, "'It Was a Proud Day': African Americans, Festivals, and Parades in the North, 1741–1834," *Journal of American History* 81, no. 1 (1994): 24–25.

7. White, "'It Was a Proud Day,'" 17.

8. Ibid., 31–48; Williams-Myers, 96. White also attributes the decline of the Northern festivals to opposition by African Americans who increasingly stressed proper comportment as key to racial equality.

9. Nissenbaum, *Battle for Christmas*, 291–300; Steven Hahn, "'Extravagant Expectations' of Freedom: Rumour, Political Struggle, and the Christmas Insurrection Scare of 1865 in the American South," *Past and Present*, no. 159 (1997): 122–158.

10. Mikhail Bakhtin, *Rabelais and His World*, trans. Helene Iswolsky (Cambridge, MA: M.I.T. Press, 1968), 255, 269; Scott, *Dom-*

ination and the Arts of Resistance, 177–182; Peter Stallybrass and Allon White, "From *The Politics and Poetics of Transgression*," rpt. in Emerson, ed., 246–251. Also see Davis, "Women on Top," 160–162; and LaCapra, "From 'Bakhtin, Marxism, and the Carnivalesque,'" 242–243.

11. Absalom Aimwell, *A Pinkster Ode for the Year 1803. Most Respectfully Dedicated to Carolus Africanus, Rex.; Thus Rendered in English: King Charles, Captain-General and Commander in Chief of the Pinkster Boys* (Albany: n.p., 1803).

12. Scott, *Domination and the Arts of Resistance*, 176.

13. Nissenbaum, *Battle for Christmas*, 273–279.

14. Scott, *Domination and the Arts of Resistance*, 15.

15. George Schuyler, *Black No More: Being an Account of the Strange and Wonderful Workings of Science in the Land of the Free, A.D. 1933–1940* (New York: Macaulay, 1931; reprint, Boston: Northeastern University Press, 1989), 194–218. Also see Oscar R. Williams, *George S. Schuyler: Portrait of a Black Conservative* (Knoxville: University of Tennessee Press, 2007), 48–54; and Jeffrey B. Ferguson, *The Sage of Sugar Hill: George S. Schuyler and the Harlem Renaissance* (New Haven, CT: Yale University Press, 2005), 212–244.

16. Christine Acham, *Revolution Televised: Prime Time and the Struggle for Black Power* (Minneapolis: University of Minnesota Press, 2004), 143, 161–162.

17. It should be noted that the incident in MTV's *Real World* that led to the black roommate's eviction involved a complaint by a black female housemate.

Chapter 12

1. Glenda R. Carpio, *Laughing Fit to Kill: Black Humor in the Fictions of Slavery* (New York: Oxford University Press, 2008), 110.

2. Ibid., 114.

3. Bambi Haggins, *Laughing Mad: The Black Comic Persona in Post-Soul America* (New Brunswick, NJ: Rutgers University Press, 2007), 179.

4. John L. Jackson discusses Dave Chappelle's departure from his show as an example of "racial paranoia." Jackson conceives of "racial paranoia" as the way the subtleties of persistent racism, especially couched within systems of "political correctness," render experiences and claims of racism as manifestations of psychological pathology, such as paranoia. He explains, "What I am calling racial

paranoia delineates something essential about how all Americans confront social differences in their lives, a racial paranoia constituted by extremist thinking, general social distrust, the nonfalsifiable embrace of intuition, and an unflinching commitment to contradictory thinking." Even though paranoia connotes having obsessive suspicions of things that may or may not be there, Jackson uses this terminology to describe how people develop well-founded suspicions based on their experiences of ubiquitous racial animus. John L. Jackson, Jr., *Racial Paranoia: The Unintended Consequences of Political Correctness* (New York: Basic Civitas Books, 2008), 7.

5. Haggins, *Laughing Mad*, 236.

6. Ibid., 231; Other individuals include Glenda Carpio, William Jelani Cobb, and John L. Jackson. William Jelani Cobb, *The Devil and Dave Chappelle and Other Essays* (New York: Thunder's Mouth Press, 2007).

7. Jackson, *Racial Paranoia*, xiii.

8. Avery F. Gordon, *Ghostly Matters: Haunting and the Sociological Imagination* (Minneapolis, MN: University of Minnesota Press, 2008), 190.

9. Ibid., 19.

10. So-called social progress includes the racial desegregation of black humor in the late 1960s; see Carpio, *Laughing Fit to Kill*, 110. However, as Watkins contends, the convergence of "discrepant comic faces" brought along unique problems where representations of black humor differed depending on the context. A divide grew between the "distorted *outside* presentation in mainstream media (initially by non-blacks) and the authentic *inside* development of humor in black communities (from slave shanties and street corners to cabarets) as well as in folklore and black literature, films, and race records." To an extent, Dave Chappelle's comedy follows along this exact trajectory of bifurcated and polarized mis/representations. Mel Watkins, *On the Real Side: Laughing, Lying, and Signifying—The Underground Tradition of African American Humor that Transformed American Culture, from Slavery to Richard Pryor* (New York: Simon & Schuster, 1994), 41.

11. Gordon, *Ghostly Matters*, xvi.

12. For helpful analyses of current ideologies of colorblindness, please see Eduardo Bonilla-Silva's *Racism without Racists: Color-Blind Racism and the Persistence of Racial Inequality in the United States* (New York: Rowman and Littlefield 2003) and Michael K. Brown, Martin Carnoy, Elliott Currie, Troy Duster, David B. Oppenheimer, Marjorie M. Shultz, and David Wellman's *Whitewashing Race: The Myth of a Color-Blind Society*

(Berkeley: University of California Press, 2003).

13. Saidiya Hartman, *Scenes of Subjection: Terror, Slavery, and Self-Making in Nineteenth-Century America* (New York: Oxford University Press, 1997).

14. Ibid., 4.

15. Ibid.

16. Ibid., 22.

17. Carpio, *Laughing Fit to Kill*, 115.

18. Hartman, *Scenes of Subjection*, 23.

19. This discussion of blackness does not refer to racial identity, but to the phenotypic racial ascriptions used for instating power dynamics in social relations. I draw upon Saidiya Hartman's usage of blackness where she describes how "blackness is defined here in terms of social relationality rather than identity; thus blackness incorporates subjects normatively defined as black, the relations among blacks, whites, and others, and the practices that produce racial difference. Blackness marks a social relationship of dominance and abjection and potentially one of redress and emancipation; it is a contested figure at the very center of social struggle." Hartman, *Scenes of Subjection*, 56–57.

20. Frantz Fanon, *Black Skin, White Masks* (New York: Grove Press, 1967), 112.

21. Hartman, *Scenes of Subjection*, 7.

22. Ibid., 57.

23. Fanon, *Black Skin, White Masks*, 112.

24. Karen Sotiropoulos, *Staging Race: Black Performers in Turn of the Century America* (Cambridge, MA: Harvard University Press, 2006).

25. Ibid., 222.

26. Haggins, *Laughing Mad*, 231.

27. Hartman, *Scenes of Subjection*, 32.

28. Gordon, *Ghostly Matters*, 22.

29. This is especially with regards to gender and sexuality. (See note 37.)

30. Derrick Bell, *Faces at the Bottom of the Well: The Permanence of Racism* (New York: Basic Books, 1992), ix.

31. Carpio, *Laughing Fit to Kill*, 4.

32. Hartman, *Scenes of Subjection*, 32.

33. Ibid., 207.

34. Ibid., 13.

35. Haggins, *Laughing Mad*, 220.

36. Hartman, *Scenes of Subjection*, 22.

37. One lingering specter that Dave Chappelle did not grapple with and probably helped reinforce concerned sexuality. Throughout *Chappelle's Show*, jokes about sex catered solely to and reflected the perspectives of heterosexual men. From the first episode when Chappelle shares his delight in a female actor's breast accidentally falling out of her shirt to the sketch on "What Men Want," an abundance of "titty"

jokes peppered the sketch comedy and fed the dominance of the standpoint of straight male sexuality. Additionally, Chappelle explores supposed sexual fantasies of straight men when he offers aroused descriptions of lesbian sex, such as in the skit on "Black Bush" (Season 2; Episode 13), even while expressing disgust over sex between men. (During "Black Bush," Chappelle discusses gay sex in the context of being critical of how the Bush administration would divert attention away from important issues like the war by stoking the fires of widespread homophobia. While he is partially mocking homophobia, he nonetheless reveals his own disgust with gay sex between men in a moment between episodes.) His "titty" humor leaves open the possibility of being read not as sexist but as a manifestation of his sincere appreciation of the female form, frankness about his own sexuality, and actually mockery of straight men's crassness in objectifying women. However, these titillating jokes lent themselves to attracting an audience that could simply eat the "yellow titty jokes" cereal and take pleasure in the surface-level sexism and homophobia of his comedy. Moreover, Chappelle's uncomplicated expression of straight male sexuality, especially as embodied by him and refracted through his epidermal blackness, could play into a racist imagination of hypersexualized black men. For instance, in "Blackzilla," Dave Chappelle's sexual desires (shown through his masturbating via a volcano) could be understood through the interpretive lens of sexual agency, yet they are likely seen through a historical and haunted lens of racialized sexuality. Chappelle then turns into just another reincarnation of the stereotypical hypersexual black man with an insatiable and threatening sexual appetite. Therefore, since he didn't wrestle with this specter of sexuality to narrate a countermemory, his work falls into a trap of promoting a historical and persistent haunting of intersecting racism, sexism and homophobia. Moreover, his perhaps unintended complicity with this specter facilitated a crossover audience's co-optation of him and his work for their experience of "bawdy pleasures."

38. Cobb, *The Devil and Dave Chappelle*, 248.

39. Ibid., 251.

40. This is similar to Watkins' comment about how black humor could be distorted when moving from inside the community to outside. (See note 10.)

41. Carpio, *Laughing Fit to Kill*, 26.

42. Cobb, *The Devil and Dave Chappelle*, 249.

43. In this way, *Chappelle's Show* displayed

all of the symptoms of what Paul Gilroy describes as the "Beavis and Butthead" syndrome which is "a condition of mass popularity in which any original satirical intentions are misrecognized as an affirmation of the object or process they try to subvert or ridicule." Paul Gilroy, *Postcolonial Melancholia* (New York: Columbia University Press, 2005), 134.

44. Gordon, *Ghostly Matters*, 8.
45. Ibid., xvi.
46. Sotiropoulos, *Staging Race*, 238.
47. Hartman, *Scenes of Subjection*, 26.
48. Ibid., 29.
49. Gordon, *Ghostly Matters*, 28.
50. Carpio, *Laughing Fit to Kill*, 103. Chappelle is quoted here originally from Tom Nawrocki, "Repeat Offender," *Rolling Stone*, February 5, 2004, 27.

Conclusion

1. For more of the auction, see, Michael Janofsky, "Mock Auction of Slaves: Education or Outrage?," *New York Times*, October 8, 1994, sec. 1, 7; Clarence Waldron, "Staged Slave Auction Sparks Debate on Slavery and Racism," *Jet*, October 31, 1994, 12. Also of interest might be the history of the evolution of Colonial Williamsburg as a living museum: Richard Handler and Eric Gable, *The New History in an Old Museum: Creating the Past at Colonial Williamsburg* (Durham: Duke University Press, 1997). Another key text on memory and race is David W. Blight, *Race and Reunion: The Civil War in American Memory* (Cambridge: Belknap Press of Harvard University Press, 2001).

2. Pierre Nora, "Between Memory and History: Les Lieux de Mémoire," trans. Marc Roudebush, *Representations* 26 (1989): 13.

3. Michel-Rolph Trouillot, *Silencing the Past: Power and the Production of History* (Boston: Beacon Press, 1995).

4. Anne C. Bailey, *African Voices of the Atlantic Slave Trade* (Boston: Beacon Press, 2005), 61.

5. Richard Klein, *Cigarettes are Sublime* (Durham: Duke University Press, 1993), 26–27.

6. Michel Foucault, *Discipline and Punish: The Birth of the Prison*, trans. Alan Sheridan (New York: Random House, 1977), 199. Also see Foucault, *The Order of Things*, trans. Alan Sheridan (New York: Random House, 1970).

7. Mary Douglas, *Purity and Danger: An Analysis of Concept of Pollution and Taboo* (London: Routledge, 2005), 160–172.

8. Julia Kristeva, *Powers of Horror*, trans.

Leon Roudiez (New York: Columbia University Press, 1984), 77.

9. The idea of comic contagion is also found in Jerry Aline Flieger, *The Purloined Punch Line: Freud's Comic Theory and the Postmodern Text* (Baltimore: Johns Hopkins University Press, 1991), 14.

10. Lawrence E. Mintz, "Standup Comedy as Social and Cultural Mediation," *American Quarterly* 37, no. 1 (Spring 1985): 73–74. It's important to note here that throughout *Chappelle's Show*, Chappelle himself reminds us, "It's a celebration!" This eerily parallels the theories of the anthropologists cited here by Mintz.

11. See Homi K. Bhabha, "Of Mimicry and Man: The Ambivalence of Colonial Discourse," in Bhabha, *The Location of Culture* (New York: Routledge, 1994), 88–91; Edward Said, *Culture and Imperialism* (London: Vintage, 1993).

12. Mary Louise Pratt, *Imperial Eyes: Travel Writing and Transculturation* (London: Routledge, 1992), 6–7.

13. A quick overview of the Declaration of Independence may be found in Joseph J. Ellis, ed., *What Did the Declaration Declare?* (Boston: Bedford/St. Martin's, 1999); histories of Jefferson's and Washington's connections to slavery may be found in the following: Joseph J. Ellis, *American Sphinx: The Character of Thomas Jefferson* (New York: Knopf, 1997); Thomas Jefferson Memorial Foundation Research Committee, *Report on Thomas Jefferson and Sally Hemings* (Charlottesville, VA: Thomas Jefferson Memorial Foundation, 2000); Nicholas Wade, "After Jefferson, a Question About Washington and a Young Slave," *New York Times*, July 7, 1999, A12; Henry Wiencek, *An Imperfect God: George Washington, His Slaves, and the Creation of America* (New York: Farrar, Straus, and Giroux, 2003).

14. Richard Sennett, *The Fall of Public Man* (New York: Norton, 1992), 259–268.

15. Ibid., 300.

16. Jean Baudrillard, *The Illusion of the End*, trans. Chris Turner (Cambridge: Polity Press, 1994), 122. Also see, Francis Fukuyama, *The End of History and the Last Man* (London: Hamish Hamilton, 1992).

17. William Gibson, "The [Inter]Net is a Waste of Time and that's Exactly What's Right about it." *New York Times Magazine*, July 14, 1996, 31.

18. Raymond Williams, *Keywords: A Vocabulary of Culture and Society* (London: Fontana, 1976), 87.

19. Dave Chappelle, interview with James Lipton, *Inside the Actors Studio*, Bravo. February 12, 2006.

20. Dave Chappelle, interview with James Lipton, *Inside the Actors Studio*, Bravo, November 10, 2008.

21. *Dave Chappelle: For What It's Worth. Live! At the Fillmore*. DVD. Directed by Stan Lathan. Sony Pictures, 2004.

22. Lisa M. Heldke, "Food Politics, Political Food," in *Cooking, Eating, Thinking: Transformative Philosophies of Food*, ed. Deane W. Curtin and Lisa M. Heldke (Bloomington: Indiana University Press, 1992), 310.

Bibliography

Abrahams, Roger D., and John F. Szwed, ed. *After Africa.* New Haven: Yale University Press, 1983.

Acham, Christine. *Revolution Televised: Prime Time and the Struggle for Black Power.* Minneapolis: University Of Minnesota Press, 2005.

Adamson, Walter. *Hegemony and Revolution: A Study of Antonio Gramsci's Political and Cultural Theory.* Berkeley: University of California Press, 1980.

Adorno, Theodore, and Max Horkheimer. "The Culture Industry: Enlightenment as Mass Deception." *The Dialectic of Enlightenment.* Translated by John Cumming. London: Verso, 1979.

Aimwell, Absalom. *A Pinkster Ode for the Year 1803. Most Respectfully Dedicated to Carolus Africanus, Rex.; Thus Rendered in English: King Charles, Captain-General and Commander in Chief of the Pinkster Boys.* Albany, 1803.

Allan, Keith, and Kate Burridge. *Forbidden Words: Taboo and the Censoring of Language.* Cambridge: Cambridge University Press, 2006.

Alexander, Bryant Keith. "Fading, Twisting, and Weaving: An Interpretive Ethnography of the Black Barbershop as Cultural Space." *Qualitative Inquiry* 9, no. 1 (2003): 105–128.

Anderson, Benedict. *Imagined Communities: Reflections on the Origin and Spread of Nationalism.* London: Verso, 1983.

Anderson, Perry. "The Antinomies of Antonio Gramsci." *New Left Review* 100 (Nov-Dec 1976): 5–78.

Andrews, Helena. "Go to ChappelleTheory. com for T-Shirts, Not Conspiracy." *The New York Times,* July 22, 2006, Television. http://www.nytimes.com/2006/07/22/arts/television/22chap.html (accessed June 11, 2008).

Appadurai, Arjun. *Modernity at Large: Cultural Dimensions of Globalization.* Minneapolis: University of Minnesota Press, 1996.

Ards, Angela. "Organizing the Hip Hop Generation." In *That's the Joint: The Hip-Hop Studies Reader.* Edited by Murray Forman and Mark Anthony Neal, 311–324. New York: Routledge Press, 2004.

Babb, Valerie. *Whiteness Visible: The Meaning of Whiteness in American Literature and Culture.* New York: New York University Press, 1998.

Bailey, Anne C. *African Voices of the Atlantic Slave Trade.* Boston: Beacon Press, 2005.

Bakhtin, Mikhail Mikhailovich. *The Dialogic Imagination: Four Essays.* Edited by Michael Holquist, translated by Caryl Emerson and Michael Holquist. Austin: University of Texas Press, 1981.

Bakhtin, Mikhail. *Rabelais and His World.* Translated by Helene Iswolsky. Cambridge: MIT Press, 1968.

Baraka, Amiri (LeRoi Jones). "The Revolutionary Theatre." *National Humanities Center.* http://nationalhumanitiescenter.org/pds/maai3/protest/text12/barakatheatre.pdf (accessed October 1, 2008).

Barth, Fredrik, ed. *Ethnic Groups and Boundaries.* Boston: Little, Brown, 1969.

Barker, Chris, and Dariusz Galasinski. *Cultural Studies and Discourse Analysis.* London: Sage, 2001.

Bates, Thomas. "Gramsci and the Theory of Hegemony." *Journal of the History of Ideas* 36, no. 2 (April-June 1975): 351–366.

Baudrillard, Jean. "Ecstasy of Communication." Translated by John Johnston. In *The Anti-Aesthetic: Essays on Postmodern Culture.* Edited by Hal Foster, 126–134. Seattle: Bay Press, 1983.

_____. *The Illusion of the End.* Translated by Chris Turner. Cambridge: Polity Press, 1994.

_____. *Simulacra and Simulation.* Translated by Sheila Faria Glaser. Ann Arbor:University of Michigan Press, 2004.

_____. *The Spirit of Terrorism.* Translated by Chris Turner. London: Verso, 2003.

Bell, Derrick. *Faces at the Bottom of the Well: The Permanence of Racism.* New York: Basic Books, 1992.

Bell Jordan, Katrina. "Speaking Fluent 'Joke': Pushing the Racial Envelope Through Comedic Performance on Chappelle's Show." *Performance Research* 12, no. 3 (2007): 80.

Benjamin, Walter. *Illuminations.* Translated by Harry Zohn. New York: Schocken Books, 1969.

———. "The Work of Art in the Age of Mechanical Reproduction." In *Visual Culture: The Reader.* Edited by Jessica Evans and Stuart Hall, 72–79. London: Sage, 2004.

Bennet, Andy. "Subcultures or Neo-Tribes?: Rethinking the Relationship Between Youth, Style, and Musical Taste," *Sociology* 3, no. 3 (1999): 599–617.

Berger, Phil. *The Last Laugh: The World of Stand-Up Comics.* New York: Ballantine, 1976.

Bergson, Henri. *Le Rire: Essai sur la Signification du Comique.* Paris: Presses Universitaires de France, 1964.

Bernard, Russ, and Jesús Salinas Pedraza. *Native Ethnography: A Mexican Indian Describes His Culture.* Newbury Park, CA: Sage Publications, 1989.

Best, Steven. "The Commodification of Reality and the Reality of Commodification: Jean Baudrillard and Postmodernism." *Current Perspectives in Social Theory* 9 (1989): 23–51.

Bhabha, Homi K. *The Location of Culture.* New York: Routledge, 1994.

———. "The Postcolonial and the Postmodern: the Question of Agency." In *The Cultural Studies Reader,* 2nd ed. Edited by Simon During, 189–208. London: Routledge, 1999.

"Black Panther Party Platform and Program." *The Sixties Project.* 1993, http://www2.iath. viginia.edu/sixties/HTML_docs/Resources/P rimary/Manifestos/Panther_platform.html (accessed August, 24, 2008).

Blake, Casey. "The Usable Past, the Comfortable Past, and the Civic Past: Memory in Contemporary America." *Cultural Anthropology* 14 (1999): 423–435.

Blight, David W. *Race and Reunion: The Civil War in American Memory.* Cambridge, MA: Belknap Press of Harvard University Press, 2001.

Bocock, Robert. *Hegemony.* Sussex: Ellis Horwood, 1986.

Bodnar, John. *Remaking America: Public Memory, Commemoration, and Patriotism in the Twentieth Century.* Princeton: Princeton University Press, 1992.

Bogle, Donald. *Toms, Coons, Mulattoes, Mammies, and Bucks: An Interpretive History of Blacks in American Films.* 4th ed. New York: Continuum, 2003.

Bonilla-Silva, Eduardo. *Racism Without Racists: Color-Blind Racism and the Persistence of Racial Inequality in the United States.* New York: Rowman and Littlefield, 2003.

Boothman, Derek. "The Sources of Gramsci's Concept of Hegemony." *Rethinking Marxism* 20, no. 2 (April 2008): 201–215.

Borsook, Paulina. *Cyberselfish: A Critical Romp Through the Terribly Libertarian Culture of High Tech.* New York: Public Affairs, 2000.

Boskin, Joseph. "American Political Humor: Touchables and Taboos." *International Political Science Review* 11, no. 4 (1990): 473–482.

———. *Sambo: The Rise and Demise of an American Jester.* New York: Oxford University Press, 1986.

Bovard, James. *Freedom in Chains: The Rise of the State and the Demise of the Citizen.* New York: St. Martin's Press, 1999.

Boyd, Todd. *Am I Black Enough for You? Popular Culture from the 'Hood and Beyond.* Bloomington: Indiana University Press, 1997.

Boyd, Valerie. *Wrapped in Rainbows: The Life of Zora Neale Hurston.* New York: Scribner, 2003.

Brooks, David. *Bobos in Paradise: The New Upper Class and How They Got There.* New York: Simon & Schuster, 2001.

Brown, Michael K., et al. *Whitewashing Race: The Myth of a Color-Blind Society.* Berkeley: University of California Press, 2003.

Burns, Elizabeth. *Theatricality: a Study of Convention in the Theatre and in Social Life.* Harlow: Longman, 1972.

Bush, Rod. *We Are Not What We Seem: Black Nationalism in the American Century.* New York: New York University Press, 1999.

Butler, Judith. *Gender Trouble: Feminism and the Subversion of Identity.* New York: Routledge, 1990.

———. "Imitation and Gender Subordination." In *Inside/Out: Lesbian Theories, Gay Theories.* Edited by Diana Fuss, 13–31. New York: Routledge, 1991.

Callaway, Sway. "Prince: Hoops-Shooting Music Expert." MTV. 2007. http://www. mtv.com/bands/p/prince/news_feature_ 040428/ (accessed 14 June 14, 2008).

Carnes, Jim. "Dave Chappelle Lets Rude Crowd Have It, Sticks Up for Cosby's Comment." *Sacramento Bee,* June 17, 2004, http://www. freerepublic.com/focus/f-news/1156342/ posts (accessed September 8, 2008).

_____. "Rude Crowd not Funny to Comic." *Sacramento Bee*, June 28, 2004. http://www.sacbee.com (accessed September 8, 2008).

Carpio, Glenda R. *Laughing Fit to Kill: Black Humor in the Fictions of Slavery*. New York: Oxford University Press, 2008.

Carr, Kevin. Dave Chappelle's Block Party Movie Review. 7(M) Pictures. 2006. http://www.7mpictures.com/inside/reviews/blockparty_review.htm (accessed January 23, 2007).

Carroll, Noel. "Horror and Humor." *Journal of Aesthetics and Art Criticism* 57, no. 2 (1999): 145–160.

Carter, Bill. "The Laughter is Fading in Sitcomland." *New York Times*, 24 May 2004, E1, E5.

Casey, Bernadette, et al., eds. *Television Studies: The Key Concepts*. London: Routledge, 2002.

Chambers, Erve. "Thalia's Revenge: Ethnography and Theory of Comedy." *American Anthropologist* 91, no. 3 (1989): 589–598.

Chang, Richard. "Why We Need a Critical Asian American Legal Studies." In *Asian American Studies: A Reader*. Edited by Jean Yu-wen Shen Wu and Min Song, 363–378. New Brunswick, NJ: Rutgers University Press, 2000.

The Chappelle Theory. 2005. http://www.chappelletheory.com/ (accessed July 6, 2008).

Charney, Maurice. *Comedy High and Low*. New York: Oxford University Press, 1978.

Cheng, Anne Anlin. *The Melancholy of Race: Psychoanalysis, Assimilation, and Hidden Grief*. New York: Oxford University Press, 2001.

Chideya, Farai. *The Color of Our Future: Race in the 21st Century*. New York: Harper Perennial, 2000.

Chin, Elizabeth. *Purchasing Power: Black Kids and American Consumer Culture*. Minneapolis: University of Minnesota Press, 2001.

Chin, Frank. "Confessions of a Chinatown Cowboy." In *Bulletproof Buddhists and Other Essays*, 63–109. Honolulu: University of Hawaii Press, 1998.

Cho, Margaret, interview by Michele Norris. "All Things Considered: Comedy and Race in America." NPR. December 9, 2002. http://www.npr.org/programs/atc/features/2002/dec/comedians/ (accessed September 8, 2008).

Clark, Septima. *Ready from Within: Septima Clark and the Civil Rights Movement*. Navarro, CA: Wild Trees Press, 1986.

Cobb, William Jelani. "The Devil & Dave Chappelle." In *The Devil & Dave Chappelle & Other Essays*, 247–254. New York: Thunder's Mouth Press, 2007.

Cobb, Jelani William. *To the Break of Dawn: A Freestyle on the Hip Hop Aesthetic*. New York: New York University Press, 2007.

Coleman, Robin. *Say It Loud!: African American Audiences, Media and Identity*. London: Routledge, 2002.

Cooper, Evan. "Is It Something He Said: The Mass Consumption of Richard Pryor's Culturally Intimate Humor." *The Communication Review* 10, no.3 (1997): 223–247.

Corrigan, Robert W., ed. *Comedy: Meaning and Form*. 2nd ed. New York: Harper & Row, 1981.

Cox, Samuel S. *Why We Laugh*. New York: Benjamin Blom, 1969.

Cruse, Harold. *The Crisis of the Negro Intellectual*. New York: New York Review Books, 1967.

Cumbo, Andrea, and Kevin A. Wisniewski. "Crossing the Line: Using Comedy to Discuss Culture in the Classroom." In *From Hip Hop to Hypertext: Practical Approaches for Teaching Culture in the Composition Classroom*. Edited by Joanna Paul, 112–135. Newcastle-upon-Tyne: Cambridge Scholars, 2008.

Currie, Mark. *Postmodern Narrative Theory*. Basingstoke, Hampshire: Macmillan, 1998.

Dargis, Manohla. "A Comedian's Ultimate Goal: Rock the Block." *New York Times*, Movie Review. March 3, 2006. http://movies.nytimes.com/2006/03/03/movies/03chap.html (accessed January 23, 2007).

Davis, D. Diane. *Breaking Up [at] Totality: A Rhetoric of Laughter*. Carbondale: Southern Illinois University Press, 2000.

Davis, Natalie Zemon. "The Reasons of Misrule: Youth Groups and Charivaris in Sixteenth-Century France." *Past and Present*, no. 50 (1971): 41–75.

_____. "Women on Top." In *Feminism and Renaissance Studies*. Edited by Lorna Hutson, 156–185. New York: Oxford University Press, 2005.

De la Vina, Mark. "Chappelle: Lost and Found." *San Jose Mercury News*, July 31, 2006. http://find.galegroup.com (accessed September 8, 2008).

Deleuze, Gilles, and Felix Guattari. *Anti-Oedipus*. Translated by Robert Hurley, et al. Minneapolis: University of Minnesota Press, 1983.

_____ and _____. *A Thousand Plateaus*. Translated by Brian Massumi. Minneapolis: University of Minnesota Press, 2002.

Dentith, Simon. *Parody*. The New Critical Idiom Series. New York: Routledge, 2000.

Dery, Mark. *Escape Velocity: Cyberculture at the*

End of the Century. New York: Grove Press, 1996.

Diawara, Manthia. "Black Spectatorship: Problems of Identification and Resistance." In *Film Theory and Criticism.* Edited by Leo Braudy and Marshall Cohen, 845–853. New York: Oxford University Press, 1999.

Di Leonardo, Michaela. *Exotics at Home: Anthropologies, Others, American Modernity.* Chicago: University of Chicago Press, 1998.

Dimitriadis, Greg. "In the Clique": Popular Culture, Constructions of Place and the Everyday Lives of Urban Youth. *Anthropology & Education Quarterly* 32, no.1 (2001): 29–51.

Dirks, Robert. *The Black Saturnalia: Conflict and Its Ritual Expression on British West Indian Slave Plantations.* Gainesville: University of Florida Press, 1987.

Donalson, Melvin. *Masculinity in the Interracial Buddy Film.* Jefferson, N.C.: McFarland, 2006.

Douglas, Mary. *Implicit Meanings.* London: Routledge & Kegan Paul, 1993.

_____. *Purity and Danger: An Analysis of Concept of Pollution and Taboo.* London: Routledge & Kegan Paul, 2005.

Dudden, Arthur Power. "American Humor." *American Quarterly* 37, no. 1 (1985): 7–12.

_____. "The Record of Political Humor." *American Quarterly* 37, no. 1 (1985): 50–70.

Dyer, Richard. *Heavenly Bodies.* 2nd ed. London: Routledge, 2004.

_____. *Only Entertainment.* 2nd ed. London: Routledge, 2002.

_____. *Stars.* London: British Film Institute, 1979.

_____. *White.* London: Routledge, 1997.

Dyson, Michael Eric. "Another Saturday Night, or Have All the Brothers Gone to White Women." In *The Michael Eric Dyson Reader.* Edited by Michael Eric Dyson, 147–166. New York: Basic Civitas Books, 2004.

_____. *Holler If You Hear Me: Searching for Tupac Shakur.* New York: Basic Civitas Books, 2003.

_____. *Is Bill Cosby Right? (Or Has the Black Middle Class Lost Its Mind?).* New York: Basic Civitas Books, 2005.

_____. *Open Mike: Reflections on Philosophy, Race, Sex, Culture, and Religion.* New York: Basic Civitas Books, 2003.

Edwards, Audrey. "Bring Me Home a Black Girl." *Essence* (November 2002): 176–179.

Ehrenzweig, Anton. *The Psychoanalysis of Artistic Vision and Hearing: A Theory of Unconscious Perception.* London: Routledge & Kegan Paul, 1953.

Elam, Diane. *Feminism and Deconstruction: Ms. en Abyme.* New York: Routledge, 1994.

Elliot, Carole. "Representations of the Intellectual: Insights from Gramsci on Management Education." *Management Learning* 34, no. 4 (December 2003): 411–427.

Ellis, Joseph J. *American Sphinx: The Character of Thomas Jefferson.* New York: Knopf, 1997.

Ellis, Joseph J., ed. *What Did the Declaration Declare?* Boston: Bedford/St. Martin's, 1999.

Eng, David L. *Racial Castration: Managing Masculinity in Asian America.* Durham: Duke University Press, 2001.

Entman, Robert M., and Andrew Rojecki. *The Black Image in the White Mind: Media and Race in America.* Chicago: University of Chicago Press, 2001.

Eshun, Kodwo. *More Brilliant than the Sun: Adventures in Sonic Fiction.* London: Quartet Books, 1998.

Fanon, Frantz. *Black Skin, White Masks.* New York: Grove Press, 1967.

Farley, Christopher John. "Dave Speaks." *Time,* May 14, 2005. http://www.time.com/time/arts/article/0,8599,1061418,00.html (accessed September 8, 2008).

_____. "That Old Black Magic." *Time,* November 27, 2000, 14.

Feeney, Matt. "Why is Dave Chappelle's Malice So Winning?" *Salon.com,* March 4, 2004. http://www.slate.com/id/2096599/ (accessed September 8, 2008).

Fatton, Robert, Jr. "Gramsci and the Legitimization of the State: The Case of the Senegalese Passive Revolution." *Canadian Journal of Political Science* 19, no. 4 (December 1986): 729–750.

Fenn, Elizabeth A. "'A Perfect Equality Seemed to Reign': Slave Society and Jonkonnu." *North Carolina Historical Review* 65, no. 2 (1988): 127–153.

Ferguson, Jeffrey B. *The Sage of Sugar Hill: George S. Schuyler and the Harlem Renaissance.* New Haven, CT: Yale University Press, 2005.

Fetterman, David. *Ethnography: Step by Step.* Thousand Oaks, CA: Sage, 1998.

Filc, Dani. "Physicians as 'Organic Intellectuals.'" *Acta Sociologica* 49, no. 3 (September 2006): 273–285.

Flieger, Jerry Aline. *The Purloined Punch Line: Freud's Comic Theory and the Postmodern Text.* Baltimore: Johns Hopkins University Press, 1991.

Ford, Thomas E. "Effects of Stereotypical Television Portrayals of African Americans on Person Perception." *Social Psychology Quarterly* 60, no. 3 (1997): 266–275.

Forman, Murray, and Mark Anthony Neal, eds. *That's the Joint! The Hip-Hop Studies Reader*. New York: Routledge, 2004.

Foucault, Michel. *Discipline and Punish: The Birth of the Prison*. Translated by Alan Sheridan. New York: Random House, 1977.

_____. *The Order of Things*. Translated by Alan Sheridan New York: Random House, 1970.

Fox, Julia, Glory Koloen, and Volkan Sahin. "No Joke: A Comparison of Substance in *The Daily Show with Jon Stewart* and Broadcast Network Television Coverage of the 2004 Presidential Election Campain." *Journal of Broadcasting & Electronic Media* 51, no. 2 (June 2007): 213–227.

Frankenburg, Ruth. *White Women, Race Matters: The Social Construction of Whiteness*. Minneapolis: University of Minnesota Press, 1993.

Freud, Sigmund. *The Joke and Its Relation to the Unconscious*. New York: Penguin, 2003.

Fuchs, Lawrence H. *The American Kaleidoscope: Race, Ethnicity, and the Civic Culture*. Hanover, NH: Wesleyan University Press, 1990.

Fukuyama, Francis. "The End of History?" In *Globalization and the Challenges of a New Century: A Reader*. Edited by Patrick O'Meara, Howard D. Mehlinger, and Matthew Krain, 161–180. Bloomington, IN: Indiana University Press, 2000.

_____. *The End of History and the Last Man*. London: Hamish Hamilton, 1992.

Fung, Richard. "Looking for My Penis: The Eroticized Asian in Gay Video Porn." In *Asian American Studies: A Reader*. Edited by Jean Yu-wen Shen Wu and Min Song, 338–353. New Brunswick: Rutgers University Press, 2000.

Gates, Henry Louis, Jr. *The Signifying Monkey: A Theory of African American Literary Criticism*. New York: Oxford University Press, 1989.

Gaunt, Kyra D. *The Games that Black Girls Play: Learning the Ropes from Double Dutch to Hip-Hop*. New York: New York University Press, 2006.

George, Nelson. *Hip Hop America*. New York: Penguin, 1998.

_____. *Post-soul Nation: The Explosive, Contradictory, Triumphant, and Tragic 1980s as Experienced by African Americans (Previously known as Blacks and before that Negroes)*. New York: Viking, 2004.

Gibson, William. "The [Inter]Net is a Waste of Time and that's Exactly What's Right about it." *New York Times Magazine*, July 14, 1996, 31.

Gilbert, Joanne. *Performing Marginality: Humor, Gender, and Cultural Critique*. De-

troit, MI: Wayne State University Press, 2004.

Gill, R.B. "Why Comedy Laughs: The Shape of Laughter and Comedy," *Literary Imagination* 8, no. 2 (2006): 233–250.

Gilman, Sander. *Difference and Pathology: Stereotypes of Sexuality, Race, and Madness*. Ithaca: Cornell University Press, 1985.

Gilroy, Paul. *The Black Atlantic: Modernity and Double Consciousness*. London: Verso, 1993.

_____. *Postcolonial Melancholia*. New York: Columbia University Press, 2005.

_____. *Small Acts: Thoughts on the Politics of Black Cultures*. New York: Serpent's Tail, 1993.

Gordon, Avery F. *Ghostly Matters: Haunting and the Sociological Imagination*. Minneapolis: University of Minnesota Press, 2008.

Gordon, Devin. "Fears of a Clown." *Newsweek*, May 16, 2005: 60.

Gordon, Dexter B. "Humor in African American Discourse: Speaking of Oppression." *Journal of Black Studies* 29, no. 2 (1998): 254–276.

Gramsci, Antonio. *Selections from the Prison Notebooks*, edited and translated by Quintin Hoare and Geoffrey Nowell Smith. New York: International Publishers, 1971.

Gregory, Dick. *Nigger: An Autobiography*. New York: Pocket Books, 1964.

Guerrero, Ed. *Framing Blackness: The African American Image in Film*. Philadelphia: Temple University Press, 1993.

Gurewitch, Morton. *Comedy: The Irrational Vision*. Ithaca, NY: Cornell University Press, 1975.

Haggins, Bambi. *Laughing Mad: The Black Comic Persona in Post-Soul America*. New Brunswick, NJ: Rutgers University Press, 2007.

Hahn, Steven. "'Extravagant Expectations' of Freedom: Rumour, Political Struggle, and the Christmas Insurrection Scare of 1865 in the American South." *Past and Present* 159 (1997): 122–158.

Hailes, Roger. "My Whiteness." *Live at Gotham*. Comedy Central, 2008. http://www.comedycentral.com/videos/index.jhtml?videoId=173794&title=roger-hailes-my-whiteness.

Halbwachs, Maurice. *On Collective Memory*. Chicago: University of Chicago Press, 1992.

Hall, Stuart. "Cultural Studies and Its Theoretical Legacies," In *The Cultural Studies Reader*, 2nd ed. Edited by Simon During, 97–109. London: Routledge, 1999.

_____. "Old and New Identities, Old and New

Ethnicities," In *Theories of Race and Racism*. Edited by Les Back and John Solomos, 144–153. London: Routledge, 2000.

Handler, Richard, and Eric Gable, *The New History in an Old Museum: Creating the Past at Colonial Williamsburg*. Durham: Duke University Press, 1997.

Hare, Nathan. "Revolution Without a Revolution." *Black Scholar* 9 (1978): 16–18.

Harris-Lacewell, Melissa Victoria. *Barbershops, Bibles, and BET*. Princeton: Princeton University Press, 2004.

Hartman, Saidiya. *Scenes of Subjection: Terror, Slavery, and Self-Making in Nineteenth-Century America*. New York: Oxford University Press, 1997.

Haygood, Wil. "Why Negro Humor Is So Black," *American Prospect* 11, no. 26 (2000): 26.

Hebdige, Dick. *Subculture: The Meaning of Style*. London: Methuen, 1979.

Heffernan, Virginia. "Two Sides of the Comic Missing in Action." *The New York Times*, July 7, 2006: E18(L). http://find.galegroup.com.

Heldke, Lisa M. "Food Politics, Political Food." In *Cooking, Eating, Thinking: Transformative Philosophies of Food*. Edited by Deane W. Curtin and Lisa M. Heldke, 301–327. Bloomington: Indiana University Press, 1992.

Hernton, Calvin. "The Sexual Mountain and Black Women Writers." *Black Scholar* 16, no. 2 (1985): 2–11.

Hicks, Heather J. "Hoodoo Economics: White Men's Work and Black Men's Magic in Contemporary American Film." *Camera Obscura* 53, vol. 18, no. 2 (2003): 27–55.

Hiddendoor Documedia. "I'm Rick James." *I'm Rick James*, 2007. http://www.rickjamesdocumentary.com/I_M_RICK_JAMES_HOME.php (accessed April 22, 2008).

Hirschberg, Lynn. "How Black Comedy Got the Last Laugh." *New York Times*, September 3, 2000, SM34.

Holbert, R. Lance, Jennifer Lambe, et al. "Primacy Effects of *The Daily Show* and National TV News Viewing: Young Viewers, Political Gratifications, and Internal Political Self-Efficacy." *Journal of Broadcasting & Electronic Media* 51, no. 1 (March 2007): 20–38.

Holland, Norman N. *Laughing: Psychology of Humor*. Ithaca, NY: Cornell University Press, 1982.

Holub, Renate. *Antonio Gramsci: Beyond Marxism and Postmodernism*. London: Routledge, 1992.

Hooley, Danny. "What Was He Thinking?" *News & Observer*, July 9, 2006.

Hunt, Darnell M., ed. *Channeling Blackness: Studies on Television and Race in America*. New York: Oxford University Press, 2004.

Itzkoff, Dave. "Dave Chappelle is Alive and Well (And Playing Las Vegas)." *The New York Times*, November 27, 2005, Arts & Leisure. http://www.nytimes.com/2005/11/27/arts/television/27itzkoff.html (accessed June 11, 2008).

Jackson, John L., Jr. "An Ethnographic Film*flam*: Giving Gifts, Doing Research, and Videotaping the Native Subject/Object." *American Anthropologist* 106, no.1 (2008): 32 – 42.

_____. *Racial Paranoia: The Unintended Consequences of Political Correctness*. New York: Basic Civitas Books, 2008.

_____. *Real Black: Adventures in Racial Sincerity*. Chicago: University of Chicago Press, 2005.

Jacobs-Huey, Lanita. "The Natives are Gazing and Talking Back: Reviewing the Problematics of Positionality, Voice, and Accountability among 'Native' Anthropologists." *American Anthropologist* 104, no. 3 (2002): 791–804.

Jaffe, Aaron. *Modernism and the Culture of Celebrity*, Cambridge: Cambridge University Press, 2005.

Jameson, Frederic. *Postmodernism: Or, the Cultural Logic of Late Capitalism*. Durham, NC: Duke University Press, 1991.

Janofsky, Michael. "Mock Auction of Slaves: Education or Outrage?" *New York Times*, October 8, 1994, sec. 1, p. 7.

Jhally, Sut, and Justin Lewis. *Enlightened Racism: The Cosby Show, Audiences, and the Myth of the American Dream*. Boulder: West-view Press, 1992.

Johnson, Victoria. "Polyphony and Cultural Expression: Interpreting Musical Traditions in *Do the Right Thing*." *Film Quarterly* 47, no. 2 (1994): 18–29.

Jones, Leroi (Amiri Baraka). *Blues People: Negro Music in White America*. New York: William Morrow, 1963.

Jones, Steve. *Antonio Gramsci*. London: Routledge, 2006.

Judy, R.A.T. "On the Question of Nigga Authenticity." In *That's the Joint: The Hip-Hop Studies Reader*. Edited by Murray Forman and Mark Anthony Neal, 105–117. New York: Routledge, 2004.

Kahlenberg, Richard D. *The Remedy: Class, Race, and Affirmative Action*. New York: Basic Books, 1996.

Kammen, Michael. *American Culture/American Tastes: Social Change and the 20th Century*. New York: Basic Books, 1999.

_____. *Mystic Chords of Memory: The Trans-*

formation of Tradition in American Culture. New York: Knopf, 1991.

Karabel, Jerome. "Revolutionary Contradictions: Antonio Gramsci and the Problem of Intellectuals." *Politics & Society* 6 (1976): 123–172.

Kelley, Robin D. G. *Race Rebels: Culture, Politics, and the Black Working Class.* New York: Free Press, 1996.

Kennedy, Randall. "Allen and the N-Word. White Lie." *The New Republic*, October 16, 2006, 9–10.

_____. *Nigger: The Strange Career of a Troublesome Word.* New York: Vintage, 2002.

_____. *Sellout: The Politics of Racial Betrayal.* New York: Pantheon Books, 2008.

Kitwana, Bakari. *Why White Kids Love Hip Hop: Wankstas, Wiggers, Wannabes, and the New Reality of Race in America.* New York: Basic Civitas Books, 2005.

Klein, Richard. *Cigarettes are Sublime.* Durham, NC: Duke University Press, 1993.

Klemesrud, Judy. "Tamara Dobson — Not Super Fly but Super Woman." *New York Times*, sec. 2, August 19, 1973, 11.

Koziski, Stephanie. "The Standup Comedian as Anthropologist: Intentional Culture Critic." *Journal of Popular Culture* 18, no. 2 (Fall 1984): 57–76.

Kristeva, Julia. *Powers of Horror: An Essay on Abjection.* Translated by Leon S. Roudiez. New York: Columbia University Press, 1982.

Kubrin, Charis. "Gangstas, Thugs, and Hustlas: Identity and the Code of the Street in Rap Music." *Social Problems* 52, no. 3 (2005): 360–378.

Kurzman, Charles and Lynn Owens. "The Sociology of Intellectuals." *Annual Review of Sociology* 28 (2002): 63–90.

LaBennett, Oneka. "Reading *Buffy* and 'Looking Proper': Race, Gender, and Consumption among West Indian Girls in Brooklyn." In *Globalization and Race: Transformations in the Cultural Production of Blackness*, eds. Kamari Maxine Clark, Deborah A. Thomas, 279–298. Durham, NC: Duke University Press, 2006.

LaCapra, Dominick. "From 'Bakhtin, Marxism, and the Carnivalesque.'" In *Critical Essays on Mikhail Bakhtin.* Edited by Caryl Emerson, 239–245. New York: G.K. Hall, 1999.

Lacewell-Harris. *Barbershops, Bibles and BET: Everyday Talk and Black Political Thought.* Princeton, NJ: Princeton University Press, 2004.

Landy, Marcia. *Film, Politics, and Gramsci.* Minneapolis: University of Minnesota Press, 1994.

Lane, Lupino. *How to Become a Comedian*, 3rd ed, London: Frederick Muller, 1946.

Langdon, Harry. *The Comedian as Metteur-en-scène*, London: Joyce Rheuban Associated University Presses Inc, 1983.

Lawrence, Novotny. *Blaxploitation Films of the 1970s: Blackness and Genre.* New York: Routledge Press, 2007.

Leckart, Stephen. "Wu-Tang Clan's RZA Breaks Down His Kung Fu Samples by Film and Song." *Wired Online*, October 23, 2007, http://www.wired.com/entertainment/music/magazine/15–11/pl_music

Lhamon, W.T., Jr. *Raising Cain: Blackface Performance from Jim Crow to Hip Hop.* Cambridge, MA: Harvard University Press, 1998.

Limon, John. *Stand-Up Comedy in Theory, or Abjection in America.* Durham, NC: Duke University Press, 2000.

Lind, Michael. *The Next American Nation: The New Nationalism and the Fourth American Revolution.* New York: Free Press, 1995.

Littleton, Darryl. *Black Comedians on Black Comedy: How African Americans Taught Us to Laugh.* New York: Applause Theatre and Cinema Books, 2006.

Lott, Eric. *Love and Theft: Blackface Minstrelsy and the American Working Class.* New York: Oxford University Press, 1993.

Lowe, John. "Theories of Ethnic Humor: How to Enter, Laughing." *American Quarterly* 38, no. 3 (1986): 439–460.

Ludwig, Elizabeth, "American Stand-up and Sketch Comedy: Between Race and Gender: The Works of Dave Chappelle and Margaret Cho." Thesis, University of Alberta, 2007.

Lyotard, Jean-Francois. *The Postmodern Condition: A Report on Knowledge.* Translated by Geoff Bennington and Brian Massumi. Minneapolis: University of Minnesota Press, 1999.

_____. "Prescription." *L'Esprit Créateur* 31, no.1 (1991): 15–32.

MacDonald, J. Fred. *Blacks and White TV: African Americans in Television Since 1948.* 2nd ed. Chicago: Nelson-Hall, 1992.

Machin, David. *Ethnographic Research for Media Studies.* London: Arnold, 2002.

Madison, D. Soyini. *Critical Ethnography: Method, Ethics, and Performance.* Thousand Oaks, CA: Sage Publications, 2005.

Malpas, Simon. *Jean-Francois Lyotard.* New York: Routledge, 2002.

Marc, David. *Comic Visions: Television Comedy and American Culture.* Boston: Unwin Hyman, 1989.

Marshall, P. David. *Celebrity and Power: Fame*

in Contemporary Culture. Minneapolis: University of Minnesota Press, 2006.

Martinez, Gerald, Diana Martinez, and Andres Chaves. *What It Is ... What It Was!: The Black Film Explosion of the '70s in Words and Pictures.* New York: Hyperion Books, 1998.

Marx, Karl. *Capital: A Critique of Political Economy.* Translated by Samuel Moore and Edward Aveling. London: Lawrence and Wishart, 1996.

_____. *Karl Marx: Selected Writings.* Edited by David McLellan. Oxford: Oxford University Press, 1977.

Marx, Leo. *The Pilot and the Passenger: Essays on Literature, Technology and Culture in the United States.* New York: Oxford University Press, 1988

McKain, Aaron. "Not Necessarily Not the News: Gatekeeping, Remediation, and *The Daily Show.*" *Journal of American Culture* 28, no. 4 (December 2005): 415–430.

McNeil, William. *Polyethnicity and National Unity in World History.* Toronto: University of Toronto Press, 1986.

Merrit, Bishetta D. "Pryor, Richard." Museum of Broadcast Communications. 2006. http://www.museum.tv/archives/etv/P/htmlP/pryorrichar/pryorrichar.htm (accessed April 22, 2008).

Michels, Scott. "Ramseys Cleared in JonBenet's Death: Prosecutors Clear Family in 6 year-old Beauty Queen's Death." *ABC News,* July 9, 2008, http://abcnews.go.com/The Law/story?id=5341559&page=1 (accessed July 22, 2008).

Miller, John J. *The Unmaking of Americans: How Multiculturalism has Undermined the Assimilation Ethic.* New York: Free Press, 1998.

Miller, Mark C. *Boxed In: The Culture of TV.* Evanston, IL: Northwestern University, 1998.

Mintz, Lawrence. "Humor and Popular Culture." In *Handbook of Humor Research, Volume II,* ed. Paul McGhee and Jeffrey Goldstein, 129–142. New York: Springer-Verlag, 1983.

Mintz, Lawrence E. "Standup Comedy as Social and Cultural Mediation." *American Quarterly* 37, no. 1 (1985): 71–80.

Mitchell, Elvis. "Chappelle's 'Show': A Successor to 'In Living Color'?" *New York Times,* March 23, 2003, C24.

Moffat, Charles. *The Work of Art in the Age of Digital Reproduction.* 2005. http://www.arthistoryarchive.com/arthistory/contemporary/The-Work-of-Art-in-the-Age-of-Digital-Reproduction.html (accessed January 23, 2007).

Monteiro v. Tempe Union High School District, 158 F.3d 1022.

Morgan, Edmund S. *American Slavery, American Freedom: The Ordeal of Colonial Virginia.* New York: Norton, 1975.

Morris, Meaghan. "Introduction: Hong Kong Connections." In *Hong Kong Connections: Transnational Imagination in Action Cinema.* Edited by Meaghan Morris, Siu Leung Li and Stephen Chan Ching-kiu, 1–18. Durham, NC: Duke University Press, 2005.

Morrison, Toni. *Playing in the Dark: Whiteness and the Literary Imagination.* Cambridge: Harvard University Press, 1992.

Morton, Patricia. *Disfigured Images: The Historical Assault on Afro-American Women.* New York: Greenwood Press, 1991.

Moten, Fred. *In the Break: The Aesthetics of the Black Radical Tradition.* Minneapolis: University of Minnesota Press, 2003.

Mulvey, Laura. "Visual Pleasure and Narrative Cinema." *Screen* 16, no.3 (1975): 6–18.

Nadel, Alan. *Television in Black-and-White America: Race and National Identity.* Lawrence: University Press of Kansas, 2005.

Neal, Larry. *Visions of a Liberated Future: Black Arts Movement Writings.* New York: Thunder's Mouth Press, 1989.

Neal, Mark Anthony. *Soul Babies: Black Popular Culture and the Post-Soul Aesthetic.* New York: Routledge, 2002.

"Niggerdom." Urban Dictionary. 2008. http://www.urbandictionary.com/ (accessed August 4, 2008).

Nilsen, Don. "The Social Functions of Political Humor." *The Journal of Popular Culture* 24, no. 3 (1990): 35–47.

Nissenbaum, Stephen. *The Battle for Christmas.* New York: Knopf, 1996.

Nora, Pierre. "Between Memory and History: Les Lieux de Mémoire." Translated by Marc Roudebush, *Representations* 26 (1989): 7–25.

Ogbar, Jeffrey O. G. *Hip-Hop Revolution: The Culture and Politics of Rap.* Lawrence: University Press of Kansas, 2007.

Ogunnaike, Lola. "A Comic Who Won't Hold Back." *New York Times,* February 18, 2004, E1, E5.

Okihiro, Gary Y. *Margins and Mainstreams: Asians in American History and Culture.* Seattle: University of Washington Press, 1994.

Paletz, David L. "Political Humor and Authority: From Support to Subversion." *International Political Science Review* 11, no. 4 (1990): 483–493.

Palumbo-Liu, David. *Asian/American: Historical Crossings of a Racial Frontier.* Stanford: Stanford University Press, 1999.

Park, Ji Hoon, Nadine Gabbadon and Ariel Chernin. "Naturalizing Racial Differences Through Comedy: Asian, Black, and White Views on Racial Stereotypes in *Rush Hour 2*." *Journal of Communication* 56 (2006): 157–177.

Pavlic, Edward. "Rap, Soul, and the Vortex at 33.3 rpm: Hip-Hop's Implements and African American Modernisms." *Callaloo* 29, no. 3 (2006): 956–968.

Perry, Imani. *Prophets of the Hood: Politics and Poetics in Hip Hop*. Durham, NC: Duke University Press, 2004.

Poniewozik, James. "Who Can Say What?" *Time*, April 23, 2007, 32–37.

Pope, Kyle. "How Dave Spent his Summer (and Fall, Winter and Spring) Vacation." *Blender* 5, no. 3 (2006): 70–8.

Powell, Kevin. "Heaven, Hell, Dave Chappelle." *Esquire*, May, 2006: 92–9, 147–8.

Prashad, Vijay. *Everybody Was Kung Fu Fighting: Afro-Asian Connections and the Myth of Cultural Purity*. Boston: Beacon Press, 2001.

Pratt, Mary Louise. *Imperial Eyes: Travel Writing and Transculturation*. London: Routledge, 1992.

Prince Fans United Group. "Prince Fans United." 2007. *http://www.princefansunited.com* (accessed April 22, 2008).

Protherough, Robert. "Is Culture an Industry?" *Kenyon Review* 21, no. 3–4 (1999): 135–147.

Pryor, Richard. *Pryor Convictions: and Other Life Sentences*. New York: Pantheon Books, 1995.

Purdie, Susan. *Comedy: The Mastery of Discourse*. Toronto: University of Toronto Press, 1993.

Ranum, Orest, ed. *National Consciousness, History, and Political Culture*. Baltimore: Johns Hopkins University Press, 1975.

Ratcliffe, Krista. *Rhetorical Listening: Identification, Gender, Whiteness*. Carbondale: Southern Illinois University Press, 2005.

Reid, Ira De A. "The John Canoe Festival: A New World Africanism." *Phylon* 3, no. 4 (1942): 349–370.

Richards, Sandra L. "Horned Ancestral Masks, Shakespearean Actor Boys, and Scotch-Inspired Set Girls: Social Relations in Nineteenth-Century Jamaican Jonkonnu." In *The African Diaspora: African Origins and New World Identities*. Edited by Isidore Okpewho, Carole Boyce Davies, and Ali A. Mazrui, 254–271. Bloomington: Indiana University Press, 1999.

Roberts, Fletcher. "Explosive, Realistic, but Most of All Funny." *New York Times*, February 3, 2002, L4.

Rose, Tricia. *Black Noise: Rap Music and Black Culture in Contemporary America*. Hanover, NH: Wesleyan University Press, 1994.

Russell, Margaret M. "Representing Race: Beyond 'Sellouts' and 'Race Cards': Black Attorneys and the Straightjacket of Legal Practice." *Michigan Law Review* 95 (1997): 765.

Russo, Vito. *The Celluloid Closet: Homosexuality in the Movies*, revised ed. New York: Harper and Row, Publishers, 1987.

The RZA, with Chris Norris. *The Wu-Tang Manual*. New York: Penguin, 2005.

Said, Edward. *Culture and Imperialism*. London: Vintage, 1993.

Samuel, David. "The Rap on Rap: The 'Black Music' That Isn't Either." In *That's the Joint! The Hip-Hop Studies Reader*. Edited by Mark Anthony Neal, 147–154. New York: Routledge, 2004.

Schutz, Charles E. *Political Humor: From Aristophanes to Sam Ervin*. Cranberry, NJ: Farleigh Dickinson University Press, 1977.

Schuyler, George. *Black No More: Being an Account of the Strange and Wonderful Workings of Science in the Land of the Free, A.D. 1933–1940*. New York: Macaulay Co., 1931. Reprint, Boston: Northeastern University Press, 1989.

Scott, James C. *Domination and the Arts of Resistance: Hidden Transcripts*. New Haven: Yale University Press, 1990.

Sedgwick, Eve Kosofsky. *Touching Feeling: Affect, Pedagogy, Performativity*. Durham, NC: Duke University Press, 2003.

Sennett, Richard. *The Fall of Public Man*. New York: Norton, 1992.

Siraj-Blatchford, Iram. "Critical Social Research and the Academy: The Role of Organic Intellectuals in Educational Research." *British Journal of Sociology of Education* 16, no. 2 (1995): 205–220.

Skelton, Tracey and Gill Valentine, eds. *Cool Places: Geographies of Youth Cultures*. London: Routledge, 1998.

Slocum, Karla. "Negotiating Identity and Black Feminist Politics in Caribbean Research." In *Black Feminist Anthropology: Theory, Praxis, Poetics, and Politics*. Edited by Irma McClaurin, 126–149. Camden, NJ: Rutgers University Press, 2001.

Smethurst, James Edward. *The Black Arts Movement: Literary Nationalism in the 1960s and 1970s*. Chapel Hill: University of North Carolina Press, 2005.

Smith, Anthony D. *National Identity*. Reno: University of Nevada Press, 1991.

_____. "Towards a Global Culture?" *Theory, Culture, and Society* 7 (1990): 171–191.

Smith-Shomade, Beretta E. *Pimpin' Ain't Easy:*

Selling Black Entertainment Television. London: Routledge, 2007.

_____. Shaded Lives: African American Women and Television. New Brunswick, NJ: Rutgers University Press, 2002.

Sohigian, Diran John. "Contagion of Laughter: The Rise of the Humor Phenomenon in Shanghai in the 1930s." Positions: East Asia Cultures Critique 15, no. 1 (2007): 137–163.

Sorensen, Majken Jul. "Humor as a Serious Strategy of Nonviolent Resistance to Oppression." Peace & Change 33, no. 2 (April 2008): 167–190.

Sotiropoulos, Karen. Staging Race: Black Performers in Turn of the Century America. Cambridge, MA: Harvard University Press, 2006.

Sponsler, Claire. Ritual Imports: Performing Medieval Drama in America. Ithaca: Cornell University Press, 2004.

Stallybrass, Peter, and Allon White. "The Politics and Poetics of Transgression." In Critical Essays on Mikhail Bakhtin. Edited by Caryl Emerson, 246–251. New York: G.K. Hall, 1999.

Strausbaugh, John. Black Like You: Blackface, Whiteface, Insult & Imitation in American Popular Culture. New York: Jeremy P. Tarcher/Penguin, 2006.

Tate, Greg, ed. Everything But the Burden: What White People Are Taking from Black Culture. New York: Broadway Books, 2003.

Tevlin, Jon. "The Quiet One: A High School Classmate Recalls the Artist as a Young Man." Star Tribune, March 13, 2004. http://www.startribune.com/entertainme nt/11527586.html (accessed April 22, 2008).

Teo, Stephen. "Wuxia Redux: Crouching Tiger, Hidden Dragon as a Model of Late Transnational Production." In Hong Kong Connections: Transnational Imagination in Action Cinema, edited by Meaghan Morris, Siu Leung Li and Stephen Chan Ching-kiu, 191–204. Durham: Duke University Press, 2005.

Trend, David, ed. Reading Digital Culture. Malden, MA: Blackwell, 2004.

Thomas Jefferson Memorial Foundation Research Committee. "Report on Thomas Jefferson and Sally Hemings." Charlottesville, VA: Thomas Jefferson Memorial Foundation, 2000.

Tropiano, Stephen. Primetime Closet: A History of Gays and Lesbians on TV. New York: Applause Theatre & Cinema Books, 2002.

Trouillot, Michel-Rolph. Silencing the Past: Power and the Production of History. Boston: Beacon Press, 1995.

Turkle, Sherry. Life on the Screen: Identity in the Age of the Internet. New York: Simon & Schuster, 1995.

Vacca, Giuseppe. "Intellectuals and the Marxist Theory of the State." In Approaches to Gramsci. Edited by Anne Showstack Sassoon, 37–69. London: Writers and Readers Publishing, 1982.

Veatch, Thomas C. "A Theory of Humor." Humor, the International Journal of Humor Research 11 (1998): 161–215. http://www. tomveatch.com/else/humor/paper/humor.ht ml (accessed April 22, 2008).

Wade, Nicholas. "After Jefferson, a Question About Washington and a Young Slave." New York Times, July 7, 1999, A12.

Waldron, Clarence. "Staged Slave Auction Sparks Debate on Slavery and Racism." Jet, October 31, 1994, 12.

Walters, Ron. "Barack Obama and the Politics of Blackness." Journal of Black Studies 38, no. 1 (September 2007): 7–29.

Walters, Ronald. White Nationalism, Black Interests: Conservative Public Policy and the Black Community. Detroit, MI: Wayne State University Press, 2003.

Watkins, Mel. On the Real Side: Laughing, Lying and Signifying, The Underground Tradition of African American Humor that Transformed American Culture, from Slavery to Richard Pryor. New York: Touchstone, 1995.

Watkins, S. Craig. "A Nation of Millions: Hip Hop Culture and the Legacy of Black Nationalism." The Communication Review 4 (2001): 373–398.

West, Cornel. Race Matters. Boston: Beacon Press, 1993.

White, Shane. "'It Was a Proud Day': African Americans, Festivals, and Parades in the North, 1741–1834." Journal of American History 81, no. 1 (1994): 13–50.

_____. "Pinkster: Afro-Dutch Syncretization in New York City and the Hudson Valley." Journal of American Folklore 102, no. 403 (1989): 68–75.

Whitson, Roger. "Panelling Parallax: the Fearful Symmetry of William Blake and Alan Moore." ImageTexT: Interdisciplinary Comics Studies 3, no. 2 (2006), http://www. english.ufl.edu/imagetext/archives/v3_2/w hitson/index.shtml?print (accessed April 1, 2008).

Wiencek, Henry. An Imperfect God: George Washington, His Slaves, and the Creation of America. New York: Farrar, Straus, and Giroux, 2003.

Wilder, Craig S. A Covenant with Color: Race and Social Power in Brooklyn. New York: Columbia University Press, 2000.

Williams, Oscar R. George S. Schuyler: Portrait

of a Black Conservative. Knoxville: University of Tennessee Press, 2007.

Williams, Raymond. *Keywords: A Vocabulary of Culture and Society.* London: Fontana, 1976.

Williams-Myers, A.J. *Long Hammering: Essays on the Forging of an African American Presence in the Hudson River Valley to the Early Twentieth Century.* Trenton: Africa World Press, Inc., 1994.

Wilson, Christopher P. *Jokes: Form, Content, Use and Function.* London: Academic Press, 1979.

Wolcott, Harry. *Ethnography: A Way of Seeing.* Lanham, MD: Rowman Altamira, 1999.

Wynter, Leon E. *American Skin: Popular Culture, Big Business, & the End of White America.* New York: Crown, 2002.

Young, Dannagal. "Late-Night Comedy in Election 2000: Its Influence on Candidate Trait Ratings and the Moderating Effects of Political Knowledge and Partisanship." *Journal of Broadcasting & Electronic Media* 48, no.1 (March 2004): 1–22.

Zaino, Nick A, III. "Ask a Black Dude." *The Progressive.* 67, no. 11 (Nov 2003): 36.

Žižek, Slavoj. *The Parallax View.* Cambridge: MIT Press, 2006.

_____. *Welcome to the Desert of the Real!* London: Verso, 2002.

About the Contributors

Amarnath Amarasingam is a doctoral student in the Laurier-Waterloo Ph.D. in religious studies program in Waterloo, Ontario. His areas of research are the sociology of religion, religion and science as well as religion and modernity. He has published in the *Journal of Contemporary Religion, Mental Health, Religion and Culture*, and *The Journal of Religion & Film*, and is currently editing a book on new atheism and religion.

Chiwen Bao is completing a Ph.D. in sociology at Boston College. Her research focuses on high stakes testing and the perpetuation of racial disparities in education. Her other research and teaching passions include interrogating representations of race in popular media and exploring the history and psychology of racial politics. She received her B.A. magna cum laude in psychology from Harvard College in 2001.

Andrea Cumbo is an assistant professor of English at Cecil College where she teaches creative writing, developmental writing, and composition. Her academic interests span from gender theory, to the ideas of light, to Lizzie Borden, and to the lyric essay.

Francesca Gamber is a doctoral candidate in history at Southern Illinois University at Carbondale and received a B.A. in Afro-American studies from Harvard University in 2003. Her writing has appeared in *Slavery and Abolition; Souls: A Critical Journal of Black Politics, Culture, and Society; Women's Review of Books; Journal of African American History; Southern Studies: An Interdisciplinary Journal of the South; Bitch* magazine; and the edited collection *Teen Television: Essays on Programming and Fandom*.

Brian Gogan is a Ph.D. student in rhetoric and writing at Virginia Tech, where he serves as a research assistant in the Center for the Study of Rhetoric in Society. His current research examines the public discourse surrounding digital accessibility issues.

Richard J. Gray II is an assistant professor of French at Carson-Newman College. He is a diachronist in French theater (18th–20th centuries) with a theoretical focus in comic theory. He has published previously with Greenwood.

Novotny Lawrence is an assistant professor of race, media, and popular culture in the radio-television department at Southern Illinois University–Carbondale where he teaches courses such as "Media and Society" and "Documenting the Black Experience." His book *Blaxploitation Films of the 1970s: Blackness and Genre* was published by Routledge Press in 2007.

Katherine Lee is an assistant professor of English and women's studies at Indiana State University. Her research interests include gender theory, race studies, and American popular culture. She has published works on *Sex and the City*, *The Sopranos*, and Asian American women's literature.

Graham Preston is currently working on a Ph.D. at the University of Melbourne. He holds a B.A. (honours) in English from the University of British Columbia and an M.A. in English from the University of Toronto. He as published on the lyrics of Nas and the technology of writing in the *Journal of Popular Music Studies*.

Michael Putnam is an assistant professor of German and linguistics at Carson-Newman College. His research and teaching interests include syntactic theory, sociolinguistics, psycholinguistics and ethnomusicology. He has published previous work with John Benjamins Publishing Company, Unterrichtspraxis and *Popular Music and Society*.

Julia Round is a lecturer in communication (literature and linguistics) at Bournemouth University, UK. She holds a Ph.D. in English literature from Bristol University and M.A. in creative writing from Cardiff University. Her research focuses on contemporary British-American comic books, and she has published and presented work internationally on cross-media adaptation, the "graphic novel" redefinition, the application of literary terminology to comics, and the presence of gothic and fantastic motifs and themes in this medium. (See www.juliaround.com.)

C. Riley Snorton is a Ph.D. candidate at the Annenberg School for Communication, University of Pennsylvania. His academic interests include media ethnography, feminist and queer theory, independent media, and media reform. His research explores the relationships between and among black sexuality, urban space, and popular culture in an examination of discourses, which surround the cultural phenomenon of the "down low."

K. A. Wisniewski lectures on literature and political science at Cecil College in North East, Maryland. He has studied creative writing at the University of Baltimore and is completing additional graduate work at the University of Pennsylvania. His critical essays, reviews, and poetry have appeared in a variety of publications. While he is interested in both film and youth culture, his current research project centers on early America and eco-criticism.

Kimberley A. Yates is a Ph.D. candidate in dissertation phase in the American Studies Department at George Washington University in Washington, D.C. Her research is on four black, male comedians/humorists and their television shows, asking the question of how they secured television shows and fared on television given the Black nationalist bent of their comedy and their interaction with the Black nationalist artistic movements of their time. Dave Chappelle is among the four. She recently taught a course entitled "Post World War II U.S. Race and Comedy."

Index

231